# FROM POWER SHARING TO DEMOCRACY

STUDIES IN NATIONALISM AND ETHNIC CONFLICT
General Editors: Sid Noel, Richard Vernon

Studies in Nationalism and Ethnic Conflict examines the political dimensions of nationality in the contemporary world. The series includes both scholarly monographs and edited volumes that consider the varied sources and political expressions of national identities, the politics of multiple loyalty, the domestic and international effects of competing identities within a single state, and the causes of – and political responses to – conflict between ethnic and religious groups. The books are designed for use by university students, scholars, and interested general readers.

The editors welcome inquiries from authors. If you are in the process of completing a manuscript that you think might fit into the series, you are invited to contact them.

1  Nationalism and Minority Identities in Islamic Societies
   *Edited by Maya Shatzmiller*

2  From Power Sharing to Democracy
   Post-conflict Institutions in Ethnically Divided Societies
   *Edited by Sid Noel*

# From Power Sharing to Democracy

*Post-conflict Institutions*
*in Ethnically Divided Societies*

EDITED BY SID NOEL

McGill-Queen's University Press
Montreal & Kingston · London · Ithaca

© McGill-Queen's University Press 2005
ISBN 0-7735-2947-0 (cloth)
ISBN 0-7735-2948-9 (paper)

Legal deposit third quarter 2005
Bibliothèque nationale du Québec

Printed in Canada on acid-free paper that is 100% ancient forest
free (100% post-consumer recycled), processed chlorine free.

McGill-Queen's University Press acknowledges the support of the
Canada Council for the Arts for our publishing program. We also
acknowledge the financial support of the Government of Canada
through the Book Publishing Industry Development Program (BPIDP)
for our publishing activities.

**Library and Archives Canada Cataloguing in Publication**

From power sharing to democracy: post-conflict institutions
in ethnically divided societies/edited by Sid Noel.

Includes bibliographical references and index.
ISBN 0-7735-2947-0 (cloth)
ISBN 0-7735-2948-9 (pbk)

1. Ethnic conflict – Political aspects. 2. Political stability.
3. Democratization. I. Noel, S. J. R. (Sidney John Roderick), 1938–

JC423.F768 2005        320'.089        C2005-901975-1

Typeset in Sabon 10.5/13.5
by Infoscan Collette, Quebec City

*For Arend Lijphart*

# Contents

# Introduction

## SID NOEL

Finding a basis for sustainable peace in countries that have been torn by violent ethnic conflict[1] is an enterprise fraught with difficulty and haunted by past failures. Again and again, hopefully brokered ceasefires collapse before meaningful negotiations between the warring parties can take place, or negotiations lead nowhere, or the outcome is an armed stalemate while the combatants replenish their supplies of money, arms, and recruits to their militias. Even a painstakingly crafted peace accord that is made under United Nations auspices and with the aid of a battery of facilitators, mediators, and expert advisers means little by itself if the terms of the accord are subsequently ignored or subverted, if promises are not kept, and if changes that are necessary to sustain peace over the long term are not implemented. In the most notorious of failures, the genocide in Rwanda occurred *after* the Arusha Peace Agreement of 1993.

It came to be widely understood in the latter part of the twentieth century that the implementation of peace accords is in many respects the most difficult part. Peace accords of that era and since have therefore tended to give elaborate and specific instructions on matters of implementation – including precisely detailed blueprints for the engineering (or re-engineering) of governmental and political structures. Typically, power-sharing mechanisms are intended to serve the dual purpose of promoting post-conflict peace building and serving as a foundation for the future growth of democratic institutions. In nearly every case, therefore, the planned structures are designed with a view to ensuring that political power will be shared equitably among the groups in conflict. The guiding principle, explicit or implicit, is that power sharing is essential for the building of sustainable peace and democratic governance in ethnically divided societies. While theoretically power may be shared under certain conditions through non-democratic means if peace is the only goal (and historically it has been so shared in a number of societies), the modern reality is that, to be legitimate, it must be shared through functioning democratic institutions. Moreover, in some countries there are compelling demographic or other practical reasons why ethnic power sharing must be combined with territorial power sharing. Hence, two political conceptions have loomed large in the making of modern peace accords. The first is consociationalism,[2] as practised in a number of ethnically divided, mainly smaller democracies in Europe and elsewhere and as influentially theorized in the works of Arend Lijphart and the ever-growing body of literature that Lijphart has inspired. The second is federalism,[3] as variously practised in numerous countries worldwide, from great to small, from multi-ethnic to ethnically homogeneous, and as theorized in a vast literature descending from the American *Federalist Papers* of 1787–88.

The value of each of these conceptions in the amelioration of ethnic conflict and as guideposts for the workings of democracy in divided societies is much disputed, both in general and with reference to specific cases. It could hardly be otherwise, since the issues they address are among the most critical and consequential ones in contemporary political discourse.

The essays assembled in this volume address in particular the problems and prospects of making the transition from power-sharing accord to functioning democratic institutions in divided societies. Included are wide-ranging essays on consociationalism and federalism by two of the most distinguished and best-known scholars of political power sharing, John McGarry and Brendan O'Leary. These lively and lucid essays survey concepts and bodies of literature that are vital to a proper understanding of power sharing in its various theoretical conceptions and institutional manifestations. Their purpose, in other words, is to illuminate important aspects of the subject (and not, it should be made clear, to set forth a research agenda or methodology for the volume as a whole). The other contributions include case studies by authors whose aim is to assess and draw lessons from the experience to date of efforts to implement post-conflict power-sharing accords in specific countries or groups of countries. The cases were selected because they illustrate fundamental issues in the implementation of peace accords and the operation of power-sharing institutions, rather than on the basis of their degree of "seriousness"(as measured, for example, by the number of people killed to date) or their "representativeness" (either geographically or otherwise). The aim is to provide analysis in depth of a limited number of cases; hence, several of the cases are the subject of two quite different but complementary essays by different authors. Other essays develop important new themes, such as the role of regional international bodies and trade blocs in making the implementation of power sharing a condition of membership.

In chapter 1, Brendan O'Leary opens with an essay that is at once a reflection on the consociational idea, a comparative analysis of its many applications, a comprehensive review of the controversies, moral as well as political, that it has engendered – and a robust rebuttal of its many critics. This is an essay that tackles key issues head on with verve and passion.

In chapters 2 and 3, Stefan Wolff and Landon H. Hancock launch the cases studies with essays based on new research on aspects of the much-troubled peace process in Northern Ireland. In chapters 4, 5, and 6, Florian Bieber, Patrick J. O'Halloran, and Gordon Peake respectively bring their different areas of expertise and experience of Balkan peace processes to bear on problems of reconstruction and institution building in post-war Bosnia and Herzegovina, Kosovo, and the Former Yugoslav Republic of Macedonia.

In chapter 7, Kristin Henrard takes up the case of South Africa's transition to democracy, which is in many respects exceptional in that power sharing was employed as an interim measure and followed by a permanent constitution based not on power sharing but on unequivocal majority rule supplemented by legal guarantees of human rights. In the following essay, chapter 8, Matthijs Bogaards asks whether non-constitutional power-sharing arrangements have developed within South Africa's dominant political party, the African National Congress, as has happened in some other countries under similar circumstances. In chapter 9, Ian S. Spears looks beyond South Africa to survey the wreckage of the many futile attempts to bring lasting peace through power sharing in African countries where conditions of anarchy prevail.

Chapters 10 and 11 turn to prospective cases. In chapter 10, Reeta Chowdhari Tremblay examines the prospects for the introduction of power-sharing institutions in Afghanistan, where – under the United Nations-sponsored Bonn Agreement of 2002 – the projected goal is the rebuilding of Afghanistan as a multicultural democracy. In chapter 11, Tozun Bahcheli and I examine the prospects of reunifying the long-divided island of Cyprus, with reflections on the failed United Nations-sponsored Annan Plan of 2002–03 and the influence on the issue of the European Union (EU). In chapter 12, Steven I. Wilkinson brings new research to bear on the question of conditionality, focusing on the role of the EU in making the accession of prospective new member states whose populations contain significant ethnic minorities conditional on their adopting institutional reforms that reflect the norms of consociational power sharing. Finally, in chapter 13, John McGarry and Brendan O'Leary provide a thoroughgoing theoretical and historical consideration of federalism as a method for the regulation of ethnic conflict. Like chapter 1, on consociationism, it does not steer clear of controversial issues.

It will be obvious to readers that the authors represented in this volume are by no means of one mind. In fact, their assessments of actual working (or non-working) consociational and federal power-sharing institutions in cases such as Northern Ireland or Kosovo, and of the prospects for successful implementation in cases such as Afghanistan or Cyprus – let alone Burundi or Sierra Leone – range across a full spectrum from ardent endorsement to outright dismissal. The aim of the book is not to offer uniformity of view or approach but rather to bring together a collection of recent writings that will both provoke and inform.

It will also be obvious to readers that all who write on power sharing owe an intellectual debt to one scholar, Arend Lijphart, whose influence and inspiration, whether as a source of essential concepts or as a foil for counter-arguments, is central and inescapable. This book is gratefully dedicated to him.

NOTES

1 The term "ethnic conflict" is used here in a broad sense to denote conflicts in which at least one of the parties to the conflict is united by a common

identity (based on such factors as language, religion, culture, or sense of nationality, or some combination of these) and believes that its core ethnic interests or aspirations are at stake. In other words, it is based on the way the conflict is interpreted and pursued rather than on what caused (or may have caused) it. For a useful brief discussion of this and other related concepts by one of the authors represented in this volume, see Stefan Wolff, "Conceptualizing Conflict Management and Settlement," in Ulrich Schneckener and Stefan Wolff, ed., *Managing and Settling Ethnic Conflicts* (London: C. Hurst 2004), 1–17.

2 Consociationalism is defined by four basic characteristics: (1) *grand coalition* (the political leaders of all significant ethnic communities or "segments" of society are included in the executive); (2) *mutual veto* (the constitution guarantees that no segment will be subject to majority rule in matters where its vital interests are at stake); (3) *proportionality* (positions in the government and state resources generally are allocated to each segment according to its proportion of the population); and (4) *segmental autonomy* (each segment is internally self-governing in matters that are exclusively of concern to it). The classic exposition is found in Arend Lijphart, *Democracy in Plural Societies: A Comparative Exploration* (New Haven, Conn., and London: Yale University Press 1977), 25–44. For a discussion of the extensive literature, supportive and critical, that has grown up around the consociational idea, see chapter 1.

3 For a discussion of federal principles and practices, see chapter 13.

FROM POWER SHARING TO DEMOCRACY

# Debating Consociational Politics: Normative and Explanatory Arguments[1]

## BRENDAN O'LEARY

Consociational thinking has a long pedigree. Its lineages may be traced to the sixteenth-century Protestant philosopher Johannes Althusius (1557–1638), the early-twentieth-century Austro-Marxists Karl Renner and Otto Bauer, and, more recently, the Nobel laureate Sir Arthur Lewis. It is, however, inescapably associated in our times with Arend Lijphart, its contemporary creator and sculptor, the doyen of comparative politics, and a distinguished past president of the American Political Science Association.[2] Over the past thirty years, consociational theory has become one of the most influential theories of comparative politics, resulting in a vast and broadly applied literature.

Consociational thinking, moreover, has not been restricted to the academy. Politicians have refined, innovated, and reinvented consociational institutions and practices in Belgium, Canada, the Netherlands, Switzerland, Northern Ireland, Lebanon, and Macedonia. On occasions, in the guise of "power sharing,"[3] consociation has become the prescribed method of conflict regulation of the "international community" (i.e., the United States when it has the support of the European Union [EU] and the United Nations [UN]). This has been evident in the internationally supported, implemented, and maintained power-sharing agreements in Afghanistan, Macedonia, Bosnia-Herzegovina, and Northern Ireland, as well as in prospective power-sharing agreements in Cyprus and Sri Lanka. It may become evident in occupied Iraq. There is, however, no consensus over consociational theory, to

put it mildly. Here, two axes of disagreement are considered: consociationalists and their critics differ, sometimes radically, over the normative merits of consociation; and consociationalists disagree with
their critics, and often with each other, over how consociations are
established, maintained, or break down. This chapter reviews and
evaluates these arguments.[4]

## MORAL, NORMATIVE, AND POLITICAL ARGUMENTS OVER CONSOCIATION

Anyone who has followed the debates over consociation will be familiar
with how widespread and heated is the abuse that often displaces
argument in this field. Proponents of consociation are regularly accused
of racism, anti-Enlightenment thought, institutionalizing fallacious ethnicity, promoting apartheid, and even condoning ethnic cleansing. What
follows endeavours to provide a dispassionate account of the arguments
– and the passions that underlie them.

### The Counsels for the Prosecution:
### Futility, Perversity, Jeopardy, and Denial

Consociational prescription and explanation are attacked by conservatives, liberals, socialists, and feminists. Conservatives detect a hint of
utopianism in consociational thinking. They are right to detect "ratio-
nalism," meaning the belief that it is at least sometimes possible to
engage our reason in benign political engineering. Conservatives tend
to condemn consociational ideas as futile: such ideas will have no (or
no long-run) impact on deeply rooted, zero-sum identity based conflicts.
This, we may say, is the archetypal conservative anti-consociational
argument: consociations make no difference. They do not work; therefore, they are not a remedy. A more sophisticated variation of this
position holds that consociations are likely to work well only where
they are not needed or are redundant (that is, in moderately rather than
deeply divided societies). Donald Horowitz maintains that consociations "are more likely the product of resolved struggles or of relatively
moderate cleavages," and that they are "inapt to mitigate conflict in
severely divided societies."[5]

Critics of consociational ideas are especially prominent in the liberal,
socialist, and feminist traditions. They pride themselves on their

universalism and their democratic dispositions. They often argue that consociations are perverse, achieving the opposite of their ostensible purposes. Their standard objection that consociation is perverse follows a proverbial piece of advice: "When holes have been dug, don't entrench them." Consociation, such critics reason, reinforces the presumed sources of conflict. It freezes and institutionally privileges (undesirable) collective identities at the expense of more "emancipated" or more "progressive" identities, such as those focused on class or gender.[6] Consociation, in this perspective, does not resolve conflict: at best, it organizes and regulates a stalemate around the relevant collective identities. It encourages a politics of immobilism and gridlock. Paul Brass is typical of critics who think in this mode: he argues that the elites whose prudence is hailed by consociationalists are the very ones with vested interests in maintaining collective antagonisms. Consociation, he claims, reinforces their respective dominance within their own communities. Brass believes that consociation's proponents operate with the "mistaken assumption that cultural differences among ethnic groups are 'objective' factors." He thinks that consociationalists exaggerate the problems associated with strong collective identities and questions their core premise that "ethnic divisions are more inflammatory than other types."[7]

Liberal, socialist, and feminist critics of consociation unite in suggesting that the political and social opportunities for transforming identities are more extensive than is suggested by what they deem to be the primordial pessimism of consociational thinkers. Interestingly, they see consociationalists as conservatives, who take people as they are (or have been made to be) and not as they might be (and long to be). Ethnicity, according to Rupert Taylor, is seen by consociationalists as a social fact rather than a choice made by people: "The point that consociationalism has not grasped, but that has been central to both liberalism and Marxism, is that human freedom is a power, a Promethean force."[8] Political integration, the creation of a common citizenship and public sphere, and the non-recognition of cultural differences in the public domain, from this perspective, are much preferred over consociation. As Brass puts it, it is best to "keep some possibility for change, internal division [of communities], and secularization open, for the sake of the ultimate integration of the people in a common political order and to preserve individual rights and the future prospects of individual autonomy."[9]

Another standard objection to consociational arrangements, usually made by liberals, socialists, and feminists but also sometimes by conservatives, is that they jeopardize important values, principles, and institutions. Encouraging proportional representation (PR), they say, will lead to the likely irreversible formation of ethnic, communal, or sectarian parties, thereby breaking with the possibilities afforded by a politics of programs and interests and entrenching a more intractable politics based on identities. The use of quotas and proportionality in affirmative action programs or preferential policies will lead to the weakening of the merit principle – thereby creating new injustices as well as inefficiencies in resource allocation.[10] Recognition of difference in the public domain will progressively lead to respect for (unjustified) inequalities, the unequal treatment of similarly situated individuals and groups. Brass speaks for many of these critics when he asserts that "consociational democracy *inevitably* violates the rights of some groups and the rights of some individuals."[11]

The biggest stick with which consociationalists are beaten is the suggestion that they are not democrats. Consociational politics, it is said, is undemocratic; it excludes opposition; it is a loser-takes-all system. "A fully-developed consociational system is inherently undemocratic"; it is elitist and postpones rather than facilitates the "democratization of multi-ethnic societies."[12] It permits "the same combinations of elites to entrench themselves at the peaks of spoils and patronage hierarchies more or less continuously." It emphasizes "participation and representation to the virtual exclusion of opposition." The "democratic benefits that can accrue from 'tossing the rascals out' are unavailable." Consociational systems, it is further charged, "do not give powerful parliamentary players incentives to keep government honest by shining light in dark corners," and "mutual vetoes can be expected to lead to mutual logrolling, rather than to political confrontations among elites, and to promote insider clubism." The price of consociation is "abandoning a viable opposition politics." Consociational systems do not meet Samuel Huntington's definitional test of a democracy: two peaceful turnovers of power following elections.[13] The allegation that it is undemocratic is perhaps the strongest normative objection to consociation. Originally posed by Brian Barry, it is now endlessly recycled.[14]

Observing that Lijphart accepts Robert Dahl's definition of polyarchy, one critic maintains that Dahl's emphasis on competitive politics implies that consociational democracy is a contradiction in terms.[15] Arguments in this vein usually celebrate the merits of oppositional politics. Consociation's opposition to adversarial democratic politics is just wrongheaded, maintains Brass. Adversarial politics, he insists, "have in fact worked to an extent in non-homogeneous societies such as Great Britain ... and in the US."[16] Lijphart's claim that, where there is extensive segmental organization and a history of antagonism, the political choice is between consociational democracy and no democracy at all, Brass regards as empirically unwarranted. Adversarial politics in Canada, India, and Sri Lanka, he maintains, are no worse than the allegedly consociational experiences of Malaysia, Lebanon, Cyprus, and Algeria.[17]

A last argument sometimes deployed against consociations is one of outright denial of their existence. The tactic here is to define consociationalism so rigidly that no society, or almost none, fits the criteria. If atheism is the response to theism, we may call this "aconsociationalism" – the denial that consociations exist or have ever existed. Sometimes this argument rests on the alleged incoherence of consociational ideas. Roughly, the argument is that an incoherent concept explains nothing of what happens in the world.[18] A Marxist variation on the illusory quality of consociation is to suggest that it is a mirage with consequences: it divides and disorganizes the working class around false identities.[19]

The foregoing summation of anti-consociational arguments is not a caricature, nor is it based on a selection of the worst rhetorical excesses. Suspicious readers are counselled to inspect specimens of these arguments over the last thirty years through reading the citations at the end of this chapter. These normative responses to consociation are common to distinguished scholars representing a variety of disciplines and ideological perspectives, including liberal political philosophers such as Brian Barry and Ian Shapiro, liberal political scientists such as Ian S. Lustick[20] and Paul Brass, and conservative political scientists such as Donald L. Horowitz. It is of interest that it is possible to classify three of the standard political and ethical arguments against consociation according to the tropes of Albert Hirschman's The Rhetoric of Reaction: Perversity, Futility, Jeopardy.[21] As Hirschman observes in his delightful book, in any particular case of proposals for new institutions, the three rhetorical reactionary objections cannot be simultaneously true, even if they highlight different possible difficulties. Likewise, while one may freely concede that critics of consociation have frequently pointed to difficulties in Lijphart's formulations and expositions (to which he has made appropriately measured and reasoned responses),[22] it is also plainly the case that consociation cannot simultaneously be perverse – i.e., reinforce and re-entrench ethnic antagonisms and jeopardize key liberal, democratic, and international values – *and* futile, i.e., make no difference.

The futility thesis, which is plainly the weakest of the three rhetorical tropes, can hardly account for the many passionate criticisms of consociational theory that have been mounted over the last three decades. It is fair to say that the weight of the critics' normative briefs and their most compelling rhetoric rest on the perversity and jeopardy arguments, i.e., the claims that consociation reinforces what it is supposed to remedy and endangers democracy, liberty, individual rights (including women's rights), and more desirable forms of party organization and competition based on class, interest, or ideology.

### The Consociational Rebuttal:
### Realism, Necessity, and Accommodation

How do consociationalists understand themselves? As realists; as counsellors of necessary triage; and as democrats fully aware that consociations need not (and should not) be applied in every country or every possible policy sector where identity politics may manifest itself. They are just as concerned about justice as their critics. And, they submit, consociational settlements are "naturally" recurrent phenomena – generated through negotiations by politicians and not necessarily engineered into existence by political scientists.

Consociationalists present themselves as realists, but not in some caricatured Hobbesian or Machiavellian stereotype. They believe that certain collective identities, especially those based on nationality, ethnicity, language, and religion, are generally fairly durable once formed. To say that they are durable, or are likely to be durable, however, is not to say that they are either primordial or immutable. Nor is it to imply that they necessarily generate intense throat-cutting antagonisms, nor that they are generally desirable. But consociationalists insist that durable identities – as opposed to shallow, malleable, and short-run identifications – can be, and often are, mobilized in a politics of antagonism, perhaps especially during the democratization of political systems. Politicians, parties, and communities interpret their histories and futures through powerful narratives, myths, and symbols, as well as through realistic rather than merely prejudiced appraisals of past group antagonisms. These narratives, myths, and symbols may have significant resonance and truth content. Without those traits, politicians might be less successful in their manipulative endeavours.[23]

Consociationalists' self-styled realism is evident in how they demur and bristle at the suggestion that they are utopian. In their view, it is the "social constructionists" (those who believe that identities are constructed for specific purposes) and certain liberals and socialists who are too facile and too optimistic about the capacities of political regimes to dissolve, transform, or transcend inherited collective identities who are utopian. Consociationalists observe that many liberals and socialists eventually work within and embrace consociational arrangements – but only after they have imbibed a strong dose of realism.

Academic consociationalists have a sharp eye for the biases of the analyst: having studied national, ethnic, religious, and communal conflicts, they are aware of the dangers of imposing their own wishful readings on the attitudes and behaviours of others. They question the cosmopolitan or emancipatory protestations of many anti-consociationalists. These protestations, they think, too often cloak a partisan endorsement of one community's identity and interests (into which others are to be encouraged to integrate or assimilate, supposedly in their own best interests). The protestations may, however, be made in good faith; in which case, consociationalists think that they show a distressing lack of self-consciousness on the part of the relevant persons about their own cultural baggage and how it might be read by others.

Consociationalists argue from a standpoint of moral and political necessity: they do not embrace pluralism for its own sake, or because they want a romantic celebration of a thousand different flowers (or weeds). They maintain that a hard confrontation with reality forces certain options on decision makers in deeply divided territories. In some tough cases, their claim is that the only real choice is between consociational arrangements and worse alternatives. These worse alternatives may take the form of sustained armed conflict, genocide, ethnic expulsion, imposed partition, or imposed control (i.e., the coercive control by one community or coalition of communities of another). The consociationalists' claim is that dispassionate analysis sometimes shows that the choice is between consociational democracy and no (worthwhile) democracy at all. Their view is that it is best not to have to build

democracy after filling graveyards. A negotiated consociational settlement, they insist, is better than a winner-takes-all outcome – especially
where taking all implies killing, expelling, or assimilating the losers.

Consociationalists reply to liberals and socialists not by repudiating
their politics, since they themselves are usually either liberals or socialists, but by arguing that democratic versions of liberalism and socialism
may sometimes be feasible only within consociational structures (either
temporary or of more durable construction). They invoke necessity and
realism to challenge the confidence of liberals in majoritarian and
adversarial democracy. J.S. Mill famously warned of the dangers of a
tyranny of the majority, but in his most illustrious texts he interestingly
failed to emphasize that a national or ethnic tyranny is feasible within
democratic institutions.[24]

Consociationalists are mostly liberals, but they are cautiously sceptical
about the current celebration of civil society as *the* (or even *a*) vehicle
of transformation, peace making, and peace building. In divided territories there is more than one society and their relations may be far
from civil. Consociationalists caution that a well-designed state or
system of governance is necessary to enable effective civil societies to
flourish. They think that those who embrace a politics of deliberative
democracy as the prescription for conflict need reminding that deliber-
ation takes place in languages, dialects, accents, and ethnically toned
voices and that it is not possible to create "ideal speech situations."

Consociationalists respond to socialists in two ways: one, by showing
that consociational ideas have been present in the best of the socialist
and the Marxist tradition;[25] and two, by observing just how regularly
and pervasively working-class and popular unity has historically been
rendered hopeless by national, ethnic, religious, and communal divisions
that might have been amenable to at least temporary consociational
treatment. Within consociational arrangements, had they been tried,
trust might have developed that would have fostered wider working-
class or popular unity – for example, behind the welfare state or other
forms of progressive distributive politics.

Consociationalists are friends of democracy as well as critics of its
palpably inappropriate versions. Consociationalists want majorities –
rather than *the* majority or *the* plurality – to control or influence
government. Lijphart modestly credited the contemporary invention
(though not the naming) of consociational democracy to Sir Arthur
Lewis.[26] In his *Politics of West Africa* (1965), Lewis argued that the

post-colonial, multi-ethnic states of West Africa suffered from the inheritance of British and French majoritarian or winner-takes-all democratic systems. He reasoned that what they required were wide and inclusive coalition governments, electoral systems based on PR, and federations that would give ethnic communities territorial autonomy. Lewis's argument is all the more remarkable and prescient in that it was made by deduction, since he did not have an extensive empirical comparative politics of democratic types to draw upon.[27]

Majoritarian democracy – especially when it is based on a single-party government rooted in one community – is, consociationalists say, likely to provoke serious communal conflict in territories with two or more significantly sized communities with durable identities differentiated by nationality, ethnicity, language, and religion. Elite bargaining and adjustment in such territories should be designed to achieve widespread consensus – to prevent the possibility that democracy will degenerate into a war of communities. Realists should therefore, in their view, endorse a politics of accommodation, of leaving each group to their own affairs where that is possible and widely sought – "good fences make good neighbours."[28]

Consociationalists argue positively for consociation, rather than just by pointing to the horrors of the alternatives. Consociation, they maintain, provides autonomy for communities and facilitates sensible inter-community cooperation. Michael Walzer, thinking of regions once under the Ottoman Empire, suggests that consociation is a heroic and imaginative political enterprise: "Consociationalism is a heroic program because it aims to maintain imperial coexistence without the imperial bureaucrats and without the distance that made those bureaucrats more or less impartial rulers ... the different groups have to tolerate one another and work out among themselves the terms of their coexistence."[29]

Consociationalists generally claim that they have a better and more inclusive model of democracy than majoritarians. In a consociation, many more of the people than a plurality or a majority may influence or control the executive. Many more than a majority get effective "voice." Consociation does not eliminate democratic opposition within communities, but it does enable such divisions and oppositions as exist to flourish in conditions of generalized security. Nothing precludes intra-bloc democratic competition, or the turnover of political elites, or shifts of support between parties; and, in a liberal consociation, nothing necessarily blocks the dissolution of historic identities if that is what people want. Consociationalists do not say that achieving accountability over political leaders and parties is not a problem in consociational democracy: they merely claim that there is no insuperable problem. Consociationalists also point out that it is a fallacy to suppose that consociation mandates that all governments be wholly encompassing grand coalitions. Since this fallacy is so widespread, it is important that it be carefully rebutted.

## Complete, Concurrent, and Weak Consociations

The stipulation that Lijphart has sometimes made that consociation requires a grand coalition of all the political leaders of all significant ethnic segments in a region or state creates difficulties. As we have seen, it has led many to question whether democratic consociations have ever existed, or, alternatively, to maintain that the concept of consociation is disordered: "Grand coalition [is] a catch-all concept, describing any joint governmental or quasi-governmental activity pursued by segmental elites whether they undertake that activity as bloc representatives or not, or engage at all in 'summit diplomacy.'"[30] These difficulties may be addressed by distinguishing between complete, concurrent, and weak democratic consociational executives (which, in either parliamentary or separation of powers systems, creates a range of variation in oppositional possibilities).[31]

In a *complete* consociational executive, the leaders of all significant segments of an ethnically differentiated territory are represented. Imagine, for example, that there are two ethnic groups, $N_A$ and $N_B$, and that all voters in both groups split their votes between two political parties respectively, giving rise to a four-party political system: $A_1$, $A_2$, supported by segment $N_A$, and $B_1$, $B_2$, supported by segment $N_B$. In a complete consociation, these four parties would all be represented in the executive. This hypothetical scenario unambiguously corresponds to Lijphart's idea of "grand coalition." But Lijphart and others also want to count as consociational those executives in which not all political leaders of all significant segments are included. This is entirely reasonable, since it is the word "grand" – implying "total" and "all-encompassing" – that causes difficulties. What matters is meaningful, cross-community, joint decision making within the executive. And that may take place not only in complete consociational executives but in the following types as well.

In a *concurrent* consociational executive, each significant ethnic segment has representation in the executive and that executive has at least majority support in each significant segment. Unlike a complete consociational executive, a concurrent consociational executive is one in which each significant segment has over half of its voters supporting parties in the government. Thus, using the above example, a concurrent executive would comprise parties $A_I$ and $B_I$, and both of these parties would have majority support within their respective segments, $N_A$ and $N_B$.

In a *weak* consociational executive, each significant segment has competitively elected political leaders in the executive, but, in at least one segment, the relevant leadership has only plurality (rather than majority) support among voters. In other words, an executive is weakly consociational if one or more segment merely gives its plurality assent while other segments give majority or higher levels of support to the government. Thus, a weak executive would comprise parties $A_I$ and $B_I$, each of which is the largest party in its segment (though at least one is not a majority party), and each of which is opposed by a range of smaller parties.

The above classification is intended to help resolve a recurrent and widespread misunderstanding. It bears repeating that a democratic consociation does not require a complete, total, or all-encompassing grand coalition in the executive. What it must have is meaningful cross-community executive power sharing in which each significant segment is represented in the government with at least plurality levels of support within its segment.[32] This clarification is crucial rather than pedantic because it effectively rebuts the insistence by some that all consociational practices are inherently undemocratic because they preclude opposition.[33] This distinction between complete, concurrent, and weak consociational executives need not be applied just to executives. It may be applied equally fruitfully to legislative procedures and especially to constitutional-amendment procedures – not least because these will normally have a bearing upon the capacities of executives.

Having established that consociational executives need not be all-inclusive grand coalitions, we will now turn more briefly to other controversies concerning the democratic character of consociational executives. Consociations may exist which do not include all segments in government. This situation arises trivially in any large and complex state or region in which there are numerous small ethnic minorities and categories of persons (especially as a result of recent immigration) that are not sufficiently significant – demographically, electorally, or politically – to be organized into any consociational settlement. Thus, the non-representation in political arrangements of Polish immigrants to Lebanon, or of Indian immigrants to Northern Ireland, does not disprove the existence of a consociation. Moreover, consociational practices may also prevail without the participation of one or more ethnic segment that *is* demographically, electorally, or politically significant. Such consociations are of two types.

In the first type, a dominant coalition deliberately excludes another segment. This can be seen as a combination of consociation and control – consociation for the dominant group who in turn exercise control over the dominated. The logical extension of Lijphart's discussions[34] would be to regard Israel as an illustration of this scenario: concurrent executive consociation among Israeli Jews, under Labour or Likud coalitions, and control by the Israeli government over Palestinians in Israel and in the areas nominally governed by the Palestinian Authority.

In the second type, a whole segment, or a significant majority of a segment, deliberately refuses to participate in consociational arrangements, even though they have been offered places. This is voluntary self-exclusion. A majority of Northern Irish nationalists between 1976 and 1998, for example, refused to accept any solely internal cross-community executive power-sharing arrangement. They demanded, among other things, an Irish dimension: significant inter-governmental and cross-border institutions involving the government of Ireland.[35]

Another way in which a segment, or a party from a segment, may be excluded from representation in an executive is through threshold effects. Every electoral system automatically has some logical or formal threshold that candidates or parties have to achieve in order to win representation.[36] Likewise, consociational executives may have formal rules that produce thresholds of electoral support and legislative representation that parties must achieve before winning control over executive portfolios. In South Africa's transitional consociational arrangements – which were agreed upon in negotiations between the National Party and the African National Congress (ANC) in 1992–93 – political parties had to obtain 5 per cent of the vote before they could be guaranteed places in the cabinet, and 20 per cent of the vote if they wanted to be guaranteed one of the two executive vice-presidential posts. In Northern Ireland, after its 1998 settlement, ten cabinet positions were available to political parties in proportion to their voting shares. Allocation took place according to a specific algorithm, the d'Hondt formula, which effectively excludes parties that fail to achieve significant levels of electoral and legislative support. Four parties, with 22, 21, 20, and 18 per cent of the first-preference vote respectively, took all of the ten cabinet positions, leaving a fifth of the electorate without a cabinet member representing their first-preference vote.[37] These South African and Northern Irish examples illustrate how proportional-allocation rules and threshold effects may lead to the democratic exclusion of smaller segments, or some parties of smaller segments, from access to the executive.

Another issue here is the question of exclusion and inclusion of segments over time.[38] If a pivotal or dominant party alternates in its choice of segmental parties in sharing executive power (as occurred in the Netherlands before the 1970s), how may such a case be classified? One simple answer is that the executive is consociational with respect to the included segments (and variable in degree: i.e., the executive may enjoy complete, concurrent, or weak support from within the included segments). But it is not consociational with respect to the excluded segment(s).[39]

### Inter-ethnic, Non-ethnic, and Consociational Parties

It is necessary to insist further on the potentially democratic calibre of consociational arrangements, both with respect to representation and inclusiveness and with respect to oppositional politics. It is rare, even in an extremely ethnically, religiously, or culturally divided territory, for nearly all voters to vote cleanly for ethnic parties or candidates representing "their" segments. Some members of some minorities may vote for non-ethnic parties or candidates of other segments as proof of their integrationist or assimilationist intent. Where a political system deliberately obliges voters to vote only within their own segment for their own ethnic parties, then the system should be called *corporately* consociational. Separate electoral rolls for each ethnic community, with a requirement that everyone register on one and only one roll, illustrates this phenomenon – the British Raj's organization of separate electoral rolls before Indian independence is a well-known example of such a device. Another example is Cyprus (under the 1960 constitution), where citizens had to opt to be on Greek Cypriot or Turkish Cypriot rolls. By contrast, in a *liberal* consociation, all voters are on a common electoral register, and, though they may vote for their own ethnic parties, they are not required to do so. The distinction between corporate and liberal consociational practice corresponds to Lijphart's distinction between "pre-determined" and "self-determined" group identity.

In liberal consociational democracies, as in other democracies, there will, of course, be voters who vote for non-ethnic, inter-ethnic, and cross-ethnic parties. Where they are a minority in each significant segment, and a minority overall, they may oppose – but cannot successfully challenge – a consociational regime. In some cases, such voters create a new segment, a segment of "others" who reject the available ethnic and party identifications. This new segment may oppose consociational arrangements and support a new, transcendent, hybrid, or non-ethnic identity, or, alternatively, they may start to bargain for a proportionate stake in the system. In other cases, voters who back non-ethnic, inter-ethnic, and cross-ethnic parties are signalling integrationist or assimilationist dispositions. If such voters become majorities in each segment, it is likely that consociational arrangements will dissolve.

The informal "descriptive" representation of segments within otherwise formally non-ethnic parties may lead to the creation of weakly consociational executives, for example, when a large catch-all governing party enjoys plurality support from each segment. Large catch-all (or ideological or even confessional) parties that deliberately ensure that they have proportional quotas of candidates for parliamentary or ministerial office from all significant ethnic groups have clear intentions. They are trying both to appeal to voters as ethnic voters, by using consociational devices within their own organizations (for example, proportionality), and to ensure the party against possible withdrawals of support on ethnic criteria. Where such parties are successful and go on to form single-party governments, they are unlikely to resemble complete or concurrent consociational executives, but they may well enjoy plurality support within each significant segment. The Canadian Liberal Party may be seen as a descriptively consociational governing party because it alternates its party leadership between French and English speakers, allots informal quotas of cabinet seats to anglophones and francophones, and generally enjoys plurality support among both anglophones and francophones.[40] Similar interpretations have been advanced about the Indian National Congress in its heyday and are beginning to be suggested about the ANC in South Africa.[41] In summary,

governing parties may be classified as consociational by four criteria:
(1) the extent to which they draw support from each major segment
of voters at plurality levels or above; (2) the extent to which they are
descriptively representative in the legislature and the cabinet of the state
or region that they govern; (3) their internal party organizational
characteristics (i.e., the extent to which their internal governance follows
consociational traits of executive power sharing, autonomy, proportionality, and veto rights); and (4) the extent to which they follow
consociational practices to manage crises that have national, ethnic,
linguistic, or religious roots.[42]

### A Last Word on the Democratic Calibre
### of Consociational Arrangements

Elsewhere I have shown that presidencies, especially collective presidencies, have ranked at least as prominently as variants of parliamentary
premier-cabinet executives in "actual functioning consociational systems."[43] That suggests an interesting riposte to critics of consociation:
separation-of-power systems create formal mechanisms for accountability and checks and balances of a different nature to those in parliamentary systems, and the critics have an overly strong and unexamined bias
in favour of parliamentary systems (though in this respect they share
much in common with Lijphart). There is no reason why separation of
powers systems with collective presidencies need preclude either opposition or accountability. But what matters from the perspective of consociational theory is not whether a democratic regime is parliamentary
or presidential but whether it has cross-community power sharing over
executive functions and legislative agenda setting (and to what degree:
complete, concurrent, or weak). To the degree that it is complete, opposition will indeed be weak; to the degree that it is either concurrent or
weak, opposition will be more vigorously evident.

This analysis has qualified certain of Lijphart's views. First, rather
than requiring a grand coalition government, a democratic consociation
necessarily has an executive in which there is significant cross-segmental
representation, though the forms of representation may range from
complete to concurrent to weak. Consociations vary, in short, in the
extent to which segments are included and in the degree of opposition
to the governing coalition in the executive. Second, the degree to which
they are liberal or corporate in their popular and assembly voting

systems should distinguish democratic consociations. Third, consociational arrangements may co-exist with non-ethnic and inter-ethnic parties. Fourth, consociational executives are as likely to be presidential as parliamentary, and consociational advocates need have no necessary bias against collective as opposed to single-person presidencies.

Consociational arrangements, it bears saying again, need not be comprehensive: they may be confined to distinct constitutional and policy sectors (in the domain of the politics of identity, recognition, and constitutional change); or they may be applied piecemeal where they are deemed necessary. They need not be mechanically applied throughout the entirety of politics. Nor are consociationalists peddlers of a panacea: the practices they commend are not everywhere likely to be either feasible or desirable.

Consociational arrangements allow for and facilitate greater justice, both procedural and social, say its advocates. Groups govern themselves in agreed domains of autonomy. Distributions that follow proportional allocations may be seen as fair: to each according to their numbers. Within a democratizing world, this idea of fairness has an underlying moral appeal. There is also a correlation between numbers and potential power that makes such a mode of justice likely to be stable and legitimate.

Consociationalists argue that they are realistic, democratic, and interested in just and stable accommodations of differences between communities. They observe, however, that consociations may and do occur without their urgings. Politicians who are without explicit schooling in consociational theory continually invent (and reinvent) consociational rules and institutions. These inventions are "natural" creative political responses to a politics of antagonism: the outcomes of negotiated deals. Politicians, Lijphart observes, invented consociational rules and institutions in the Netherlands in 1917, in Lebanon in 1943, in Malaysia in 1958, and in Northern Ireland in 1972.[44] Consociations were reinvented by American diplomats to end the war in Bosnia-Herzegovina in 1995; by Lebanese and Northern Irish politicians with external prompting in 1989 and 1998 respectively; and by EU diplomats in promoting the Ohrid Agreement between Macedonian Slavs and Macedonian Albanians. The UN and the EU between them have been trying to mediate a consociational and federal settlement in Cyprus, and the United States may end up overseeing something similar in Iraq. Nor is it just politicians who reinvent consociational ideas. Jurists, constitutional designers, and political theorists constantly do so. As do so-called ordinary people. Jurists in the Holy Roman Empire proposed consociational ideas; and consociational propositions were freshly minted by the Austro-Marxists, especially by Karl Renner. Within academic political theory, without a full appreciation of the history of their ideas, many contemporary multiculturalists advance consociational agendas: inclusivity (cross-community power sharing), quotas (proportionality), and group rights (autonomy) are usually advanced as a package for remedying the participatory defects of contemporary democracies.[45]

To sum up the rebuttal: in response to the charge of futility, consociationalists respond with some modest but important success stories; to the accusation of perversity, they reply, first, that it is often more perverse to deny the existence and salience of ethnic identities (and provoke conflict thereby) than it is to build upon them, and second, that the dissolution of (undesirable) collective identities and antagonisms may be more likely to occur *after* a period of consociational governance. Lastly, to the charge of jeopardy, they emphatically plead "not guilty."

## EXPLANATORY THEORIES OF CONSOCIATION

The ethical and political controversy surrounding consociations and normative consociational theory should be evident. Debates are no less heated over the explanations of why consociations are established, maintained, and break down. The academic literature on this matter is surprisingly *ad hominem* and disputatious, perhaps because the normative, ethical, and political issues just discussed underpin it. The authors are not impartial in these matters. What is presented here is an attempt at a constructive synthesis with Lijphart's work: it seeks to build on Lijphart's achievements while avoiding *ad hominem* counterattacks on his critics.

Our focus is on genesis. It is on why consociations are formed, although what allows a consociation to be formed will often help to maintain it. There are two general means by which we might seek to explain the formation of consociations: the inductive and the deductive. The inductive approach seeks to identify all past and present consociations and the antecedent conditions they had in common before they were created, especially those conditions that differentiated these cases from cases where consociations were not formed. Whatever all these regime creations had in common might reasonably be presumed to facilitate (or, more weakly, not obstruct) consociations. The inductive approach thus seeks to identify different configurations or pathways that lead to the creation of consociations. The deductive approach, by contrast, seeks to identify the necessary conditions for consociations to be created through logical inspection of the definitional and operational indicators of consociation, and then to test for their existence (or non-existence) in explaining the formation or otherwise of consociations. In its most ambitious version, the deductive approach attempts to identify the necessary and sufficient causes of consociations.

As is often the case when philosophical contrasts are highlighted, evidence of both approaches may be found in the literature explaining consociations, sometimes within the work of the same author. No necessary confusion need result from this fact of life. Lijphart himself has been mostly inductivist while Adriano Pappalardo and Eric Nordlinger have been formal exponents of a deductive approach.[46] The following critical survey does not attempt to trace the historical order in which the factors conducive to consociationalism were identified and debated.[47] Instead, it focuses analytically on (a) the divisions between groups (the demography and historical sociology of group relations); (b) the domestic political regime (and the relations of its elites and citizens); and (c) the external relations of the state or region.

### (a) Divisions between Groups

Numbers surely matter in all aspects of inter-ethnic relations. But how do they matter in promoting consociations (or in disposing them to breakdown)? That requires a consideration of the numbers of groups and their inter-relationships, and their respective numerical shares of the state or region's population.

Is there a dominant segment? Lijphart himself identifies the absence of a majority segment in a given state or region as one of the two most important conditions facilitating the formation of a consociational democracy.[48] Earlier he saw "a multiple balance of power" as being more conducive to consociational democracy than either a "dual balance of power" or hegemony by a majority segment.[49] The latter intuition, regarding the presence or absence of a majority segment, seems sound. A hegemonic segment, with a demographic and electoral majority, has no obvious democratic incentive to be disposed towards consociational arrangements with segmental minorities.

Even so, Lijphart's thesis needs partial qualification. A dominant descriptively consociational party may exist in such an environment, rooted in the demographically and electorally hegemonic segment. Some suggest that this is true of the ANC in contemporary South Africa and was true of the Congress Party in India. Such a party need not be strongly disposed towards the full array of consociational institutions and practices, but the relevant minorities may have some credible bargaining power that induces consociational behaviour in the otherwise dominant party. A minority comprised of the co-religionists, co-ethnics, co-linguals, or co-nationals of a neighbouring and significant power may have such credible bargaining power (the Muslims of India were partly conceived of in this way in the early history of independent India). An economically vital minority, with high levels of human capital and the means to emigrate (the whites of South Africa may be an example), may be another candidate for consociational generosity by the leaders of the majority segment. In short, such minorities' resources, and their bargaining (or blackmail) potential, may constrain the hegemonic potential of a demographic and electoral majority segment.

A majority segment might also be inclined to appease with consociational practices a minority that is expanding demographically and thus on the verge of altering the segmental balance of power in the electoral arena. This will be especially so if the expanding minority cannot be easily assimilated, integrated, controlled, or expelled. The steady demographic expansion of cultural Catholics in Northern Ireland, and the concomitant rise in support for Irish nationalists, was a background variable in encouraging some members of the diminished cultural Protestant and Unionist segment to consider a new concurrent and comprehensive regional consociational experiment in 1998. The rapid demographic growth of the Albanian population in Macedonia, and recent international constraints on ethnic expulsion in the region, likewise persuaded some Slavic Macedonians to support the consociational Ohrid Agreement in 2000. The argument for consociation within the respective majority segments in Northern Ireland and Macedonia takes the form of saying, "It is better to make a generous deal now than face having a full reversal of status dictated to us in the future." For this to be plausible, the dominant group's political class needs to be persuaded that the growing minority, if treated well, will not behave as an oppressor when it becomes a majority.

Lastly, demographically, electorally, and fully hegemonic majority segments may adopt some consociational practices as acts of generosity. They may do so in response to the demands of indigenous peoples. The latter may appeal to the consciences of the descendants of the settlers who overran (and sometimes exterminated) the prior holders of the land. Such minorities may be treated generously in compensation for historic maltreatment, and because they lack any credible demographic or electoral capacity to overturn their historic conquest. Likewise, dominant majorities may tolerate consociational claims from isolated, small, and religiously or linguistically intense minorities that pose no threat to their dominance.

The pathways just considered are logically reversible, in the manner of good explanations. That is to say, where demographically and electorally hegemonic majorities have no strategic reasons to accommodate potentially subversive or credibly threatening minorities, they are likely to be anti-consociational. Or, analogously, if minorities lose their bargaining power through the loss of population or economic power, or through the weakening of their external supporters in neighbouring regimes or great powers, then the dominant segment will be correspondingly more disposed against consociation. Likewise, if the dominant experience no guilt, or are intolerant of religious and linguistic minorities, they will be deaf to consociational recipes for accommodating unthreatening communities. In addition, we may safely predict that, within hegemonic groups, there will be those who warn that making a consociational settlement with an ascendant minority will be the prelude to a full reversal in power relations. They will be correspondingly tempted by the options of control, expulsion, or territorial downsizing.

These considerations indicate that even the most plausible condition favouring the formation of a democratic consociation is not an invariable law: a demographically and electorally dominant segment may produce parties and politicians who may embrace some consociational practices and settlements. But the intuition that the demographic and electoral balance of power is critical in assessing the likelihood of consociational settlements is nevertheless politically and sociologically plausible. Secure and sovereign hegemonic groups are likely to be ill-disposed towards consociation. There are, however, many possible balances of power other than one in which there is a hegemonic group.

Two others are worth distinguishing: a dual balance of power, and a balance between what Lijphart terms "multiple equal but few segments."

Lijphart regards a dual balance of power as unlikely to promote consociation because each segment's leaders may hope to win a decisive majority and thus have insufficient incentives to create a stable consociation.[50] The intuition seems sound but requires careful qualification.

If demographic transformations convert the relations between groups from a situation of dominance towards one of dualism, then, other things being equal, the segment that is losing dominance has incentives to consider consociation. On the other side, the ascendant segment may have a clear present interest in preferring a share in power to the uncertainty of winning majority status in the future. The dynamics of demographic and electoral transformation are plainly critical to the respective calculations. We may hypothesize that a fast reversal in demographic shares is less likely to promote and stabilize a consociational settlement. A slow equalization of demographic shares, by contrast, may be more likely to generate a consociational equilibrium. Indeed, such a situation may lead to a "Nash equilibrium" in which each segment's best response to other segments' best response is to endorse a consociational settlement.[51]

There have been consociational settlements made in conditions approaching segmental dualism, such as in post-war Austria between Catholics ("Blacks") and Socialists ("Reds"), in Northern Ireland in 1998 between Irish nationalists and British unionists, and in 2000 in Macedonia between Slavs and Macedonians – though in all cases there was not pure dualism, and in the latter two cases each of the major segments had internal party divisions. What may have been decisive in each case was the respective calculation by sufficient leaders and parties in each segment that they could not decisively and immediately shift the balance of power in their favour to obtain or retain or recover hegemony. As Adriano Pappalardo puts it, "consociational democracy is not so much a pact among minorities in equilibrium or minorities *tout court*, as a pact among minorities who do not want and are not in a position to change the existing distribution of power."[52] These considerations suggest that the equalization of the demographic, electoral, and bargaining resources of the segments may help create and maintain consociations. They also suggest, however, that once equalization is achieved, or approached, it is critical that the balance of power remain; otherwise, the appreciations that produced a settlement will be undermined. The segmental leaders and their followers need to believe that holding their own share of power and autonomy is more prudent than moving towards dominance.

The existence of "multiple equal but few segments" may produce a different balance of power. This odd-sounding configuration of numbers of segments and their relations is one Lijphart has suggested as being the most conducive towards consociational settlements and their maintenance. To some extent, this argument has been confused with others about the merits of multi-party as opposed to two-party dynamics. It is a matter of logical deduction from the definition of consociational democracy that a multi-party environment is more likely when PR systems operate, which in turn makes the formation of coalition governments more likely. But no one should assume a one-to-one mapping between segments and parties, especially when there is PR.

Several considerations should make us question Lijphart's assumption that multiple, few, and equally sized segments are necessarily the optimal environment for generating consociations. One is practical. If there are multiple segments, there may also be multiple parties within each segment – a situation that may complicate the making of stable consociational pacts that enjoy pluralitarian or concurrent majority support across all segments. The number of potential negotiating partners, after all, multiplies as the number of equally significant parties expands. Another is political. Where there are three to five major segments, a dominant coalition may be possible, depending on the size of the respective groups. Two or more segments may coalesce – possibly as consociational partners – and then seek to dominate others. Bosnia-Herzegovina tragically illustrates this point. There, the presence of three substantial ethnic segments produced not an accommodating grand coalition but instead an unstable dominant coalition that sought to exercise control over the excluded segment.[53]

History matters, or does it? There is a simple path-dependency argument associated with Hans Daalder; namely, prior elite traditions of accommodation and "pillarization" – prior, that is, to democratization – make the forging and maintenance of a consociational settlement easier. He had the Netherlands and Switzerland in mind.[54] In one respect, this thesis seems trivially true: a history of inter-segmental accommodation makes its continuation more likely. However, it has a logical explanatory corollary. A prior history of elite antagonism – again, prior to democratization – must make a consociational settlement less likely. That, of course, means that recommending consociation where it is needed is likely to be akin to sowing seed in infertile soil, which is an anti-consociationalist argument. Lijphart, Gerhard Lehmbruch,[55] and Eric Nordlinger[56] all independently invoke the idea that elites may learn from history. Elites, they conclude, may engage in a self-denying prophecy and make a peaceful accommodation to avoid the costs of actual or possible protracted civil war, as did the Swiss in the nineteenth and the Lebanese in the twentieth century, and as the communities of Northern Ireland, Bosnia, and Macedonia may be doing now. That, too, seems obviously true, in which case, strikingly different histories have the same potential: histories of accommodation and histories of antagonism may both promote consociational settlements.

One can write the case histories of successful and failed consociations in two ways: showing how they had benign accommodative pasts, or showing how malign pasts contributed positively to the present. Non-colonial relationships between the segments are more likely to dispose communities towards accommodation.[57] By contrast, contestation over the identity of the authentic natives, over who are the homeland people, is likely to make consociational settlements more problematic,[58] as will a recent history of attempted genocide or of expulsion. That history can be used both as portent and as salutary prophecy is not, of course, unique to the politics of consociation. Neither facile determinism nor facile voluntarism makes social-scientific sense. We may conclude that elites who want to make a consociational settlement, or who want to maintain one, may draw upon traditions of accommodation – if they exist; or they may argue for accommodation to counteract a negative history and an appalling future – if that is what is required. That in turn implies that the conjunction of current motivations and beliefs of elites and their publics, current resources and sociology of group relations, and current institutional and external environments may be more important than received histories in accounting for consociational settlements. Persons, of course, make history, but not just as they please.

The nature of the cleavages in divided societies, and the relationship between cleavages, are clearly important factors. Lijphart writes as if all possible cleavages that give rise to enduring segmental antagonisms are equally amenable to consociational treatment. That does not seem to be so. Consociation alone may not be enough to overcome some types of divisions. There are good grounds for supposing that, where communities are already mobilized as nations or parts of nations, they

will not be content with consociational settlements that simply leave
the existing definitions of state sovereignty intact. Such groups may be
outright secessionists and refuse power sharing, or regard it as cooption. Hence, they may be willing to accept consociational arrangements only if other arrangements dilute the sovereignty or unitary
nature of the existing state. For example, they may require recognition
of their national identity in new political institutions and co-sovereign
or confederal relationships.[59] Consociational arrangements *alone* are
not enough to pacify a nationalist community with authentic and
feasible irredentist or secessionist ambitions, as in Northern Ireland, Sri
Lanka, or Cyprus, but they may, nonetheless, constitute a fundamental
*part* of a stable settlement. It follows that a shared national identity
among potentially rival communities, however weak, facilitates *simple*
consociational arrangements, i.e., ones that do not address the territorial
definition or sovereignty of the state.

But what of other cleavages? Brian Barry has suggested that consociation works better for religious and class cleavages than it does for
ethnic cleavages because "religious and class conflict is a conflict of
organizations. Ethnic conflict is a conflict of solidary groups [that] do
not need organization to work up a riot or pogrom as long as they
have some way of recognising who belongs to which group."[60] Ethnic
divisions are, he thinks, deeper and less amenable to organizational
control, which makes it more difficult for leaders to restrain their
followers. The stakes in ethnic conflicts are less negotiable, evidenced
in outbidding by hardline elites and by massacres. Ethnic divisions raise
the question of whether a state should be a state, as opposed to how
it should be run. Barry's argument makes sense in two respects. Inter-
ethnic divisions that have become inter-national divisions are less amenable to consociational engineering, or to consociational engineering
alone. And pure class conflict is rarely as intense or as violent as pure
ethnic conflict.

The rest of Barry's implicit political sociology of cleavages is less
obvious than he thinks. Not all ethnic divisions generate rival nationalities, though they are more likely to do so than other divisions. If
ethnic communities agree on the territorial integrity of a state or region,
then creating and managing consociation need not be insuperably
difficult, as it is not, for example, in Belgium and Switzerland. Prose-
lytizing religious communities may be more mutually existentially
threatening to collective and individual identity than endogamous

ethnic communities. Institutional compromises over the management of linguistic policies may be easier to obtain than over religious matters.[61] After all, linguistic groups need not listen to or read others' religious proclamations. And agreeing on programs of government may be easier between representative ethnic parties, or within a descriptively consociational catch-all party, than between parties divided by ideology or class.

In fact, it is rare for any complex state or region not to have multiple cross-cutting cleavages. Standard pluralist theory has it that cross-cutting cleavages dampen down the intensity of each cleavage – for example, ethnic divisions will dilute class divisions and vice versa – and multiply the bases on which people can be mobilized for coalitions. It suggests that, in this political environment of multiple and less-aligned group members, there will be less need for consociational politics. That is true when it is true, and it is also possible that a sustained period of consociational institutions may generate such a configuration. But its empirical likelihood appears to depend on the supposition that all cleavages are equally salient for significant numbers of cross-cut individuals.

There appear to be many cases, however, where cross-cutting cleavages do not reduce the intensity of a dominant antagonistic cleavage. Class divisions may lead to party differentiation within national, ethnic, or religious communities without reducing the intensity of the conflict between them. Indeed, where communities have been mobilized behind rival nationalisms or rival sectarianisms, this is almost true by definition. In these circumstances, standard pluralist or integrationist recipes are unlikely to work, and consociational prescriptions may be appropriate, even if they may not be easy to achieve.

However, consociationalists can accept pluralist reasoning up to a point. In the absence of a control system and where there are two national, ethnic, or religious communities, and where one is disproportionately concentrated in the dominant economic and subordinated economic strata respectively, we can legitimately expect conflict to be more likely, and more violent. This is why Lijphart has argued that approximate socio-economic equality between segments is a significant conducive factor in making and sustaining a consociational settlement – presumably because the political system will not be loaded with major redistributive conflicts between communities.

This does not mean that the futility thesis is correct, that consociationalism only works in societies that are mildly divided. That moderate

conflict makes consociation easier can hardly be denied. That it is the
product of resolved struggles is scarcely a criticism: it is, or can be, a
part of a resolution. Does the formation or existence of consociation
prove that the cleavages in question were moderate in nature? Northern
Ireland, Lebanon, and South Africa might suggest otherwise. Perhaps
the cleavages were moderating, as a result of mutual recognition of a
stalemate, but that is another matter. Consociation, it bears emphasis,
is not peddled as a panacea – at least not by its careful exponents. And
the suggested inapplicability or "inaptness" of consociational arrangements where deeply redistributive as well as profoundly symbolic and
existential identity questions are at stake is just not proven – consider
Lebanon, Bosnia-Herzegovina, and Northern Ireland. And even if it
were proven, consociationalists would at least be able to advocate
appropriate constitutional and political designs for moderate conflicts.

### (b) The Domestic Political Regime: Political Culture and Institutions

Publics that are disposed towards accommodation and power sharing
will reward political leaders and parties that promote these objectives.
But this point simply echoes Daalder's argument about the importance
of prior traditions of accommodation. What about the more problematic cases of ethnic communities that are not disposed by history or
culture – or the present facts of their relations – to be well disposed
towards consociational settlements and their maintenance? Here, the
contribution of Eric Nordlinger remains helpful, though it needs
restatement. According to Nordlinger, "the presence of conflict-regulating motives, in combination with conciliatory attitudes and the top
leaders' political security, constitutes a sufficient explanation for elite
conflict-regulating behaviour [and] the structured predominance of
elites vis à vis non-elites within their own conflict groups is a necessary
condition for conflict-regulating outcomes."[62] In Nordlinger's view, one
or more of four conflict-regulating motives is necessary: the desire to
ward off external states (on which see below); the desire to acquire or
obtain governmental offices and power;[63] the desire to avoid bloodshed
(Lijphart's self-denying prophecy); and the desire to obtain or increase
prosperity (which is most likely when each community has an extensive
commercial class). The first, third, and fourth of these are instrumental
and statesmanlike considerations that would generate and maintain a
consociation. Nordlinger's second point, however, is more controversial,

for it implies the necessity of secure and autonomous elite predominance over a politically deferential or organizationally encapsulated
following.[64] Plainly, where publics are neither deferential nor encapsulated, sufficient numbers may nevertheless support a consociational
regime – though, of course, the regime will be more vulnerable to the
withdrawal of their electoral support and to the mobilizing appeals of
undeferential and extremist ethnic or communal "outflankers."

It therefore seems better to argue that structured elite predominance
facilitates the making of a settlement, rather than being a necessary
condition. Nordlinger identifies four conditions that generate such
predominance: (1) general apolitical quiescence; (2) politically acquies-
cent followers; (3) patron-client relations; and (4) mass parties with
extensive organizational capabilities. The first three of these seem less
and less likely to be available because of worldwide modernization
processes – even if they are differential in their impact, and even if
patron-client politics will persist in the developing world in the future.
It is, therefore, organized mass parties with confident and secure leaders
that are typically the politically critical variable.

This reasoning in turn generates a key institutional-design question.
What systems of electoral and party law create the right environment
for such parties to be able to generate consociations? Where consociational parties – i.e., single parties that are consociational in their
internal make-up and policy positions – already exist, it is best to leave
the electoral and party laws alone even if they are not based on pure
PR. Lijphart, however, has been a consistent advocate of party-list PR
to facilitate appropriately consociationally disposed parties and leader-
ships – suggesting that such systems give leaders control over their
parties' candidates (and therefore over their internal party rivals), as
well as obtaining transparent proportionality. But such systems, unless
accompanied by high thresholds, also create incentives for dissidents
to create their own parties and thereby encourage outflanking and
possible system breakdown. Intra-ethnic competition may be as dangerous to a consociation as inter-ethnic competition if hardline extremists become ascendant within one or more communities. Preferential
PR systems, such as the single transferable vote, however, may well
assist moderate parties (as opposed to hardline parties) within ethnic
communities. That is because moderate parties and their candidates are
more likely to obtain lower-order voting preferences (transfers) from
the voters of their ethnic rivals.[65]

Complete (as opposed to weak) consociations seem much less likely under party-list PR systems. Moreover, party-list PR alone cannot guarantee a power-sharing executive: for that to happen there have to be either norms or rules attached to executive formation. Other formulas may be more likely to discourage the creation of significant anti-system, ethnically exclusive, parties without breaking democratic or consociational norms. If the *de facto* and *de jure* thresholds in the electoral system and in access to the executive both require parties to be of a generally large size and willing to abide by the rules of the game, then the incentives for party fragmentation may be reduced. It may be possible to have laws on party registration and formation that temporarily protect existing parties – for example, laws that prevent parties from forming within parliament or prevent legislators from changing their party allegiances without resigning their offices – without institutionalizing a cartel. Systems in which voters directly choose the executive through preferential PR systems, and in which the legislature's rules require a well-formed executive to enjoy at least weak consociational support, may be worth considering. Then voters would in effect be faced with a choice: vote for a representative executive that will work or vote for executive chaos.[66]

### (c) The External and International Environment

Three factors have been identified in the literature on the relations between a political system's external relations and its likelihood of adopting and maintaining consociational practices: size, shared threats, and foreign policy loads. I will add a fourth that has not previously been addressed: international norms.

Small demographic size is regularly invoked as a variable facilitating consociation.[67] This idea is inductively generated through observing the small populations of Lebanon, Austria, the Netherlands, Belgium, Switzerland, Suriname, and the Netherlands Antilles (and some would now add Luxembourg, Liechtenstein, South Tyrol – and, perhaps in the future, Northern Ireland, Bosnia-Herzegovina, and Macedonia). Lijphart distinguishes four possible effects of small size. The direct internal effect is that political elites all know one another, interact regularly, and thereby negotiate more easily without too much constituency pressure. The direct external effect is that small states are likely to feel externally threatened and be more induced towards internal accommodation. The indirect internal effect is that smaller states are easier to govern. The indirect external effect is that the country's low international salience creates a lighter foreign policy load.[68]

The hypothesized internal effects are less warranted than they appear. What matters, presumably, for successful elite interaction is psychological and political closeness rather than geographical distance. "Great hatreds, little room" was Yeats's memorable line about intra-Irish ethno-religious relations. Lijphart himself, drawing on Cyprus,[69] speculates that there may be directly negative effects from too small a population, as it makes a dearth of political talent more likely. But this, too, seems unwarranted; political talent has existed in abundance in Cyprus and Northern Ireland: it has just not been deployed until recently in a sustained politics of accommodation. The hypothesis of the greater governability of the small is surely not obvious: governing Lebanon is surely more daunting than governing France.

The external effects seem better warranted, but even here there are plausible counter-hypotheses. The direct external effect surely operates independently of size. That is because shared external threats give domestic elites significant incentives to accommodate one another's communities whatever the state's population happens to be (if size matters here it is because the smaller unit is geopolitically weaker). The direct effect, as Lijphart recognizes, surely also requires the threats to be shared – since only in that way can the belief that "my internal rival is my external enemy's enemy" generate the appropriate dispositions for coalition. The formation of the Lebanese *pacte nationale* in 1943 is a case in point. It was formed largely by Maronite and Sunni elites in opposition to the (Free) French mandatory authorities' coercive attempt to avoid decolonization. Analogous effects operated in 1958 when a political crisis re-equilibrated the Lebanese consociation as key elites sought to avoid external penetration of their state. The disappearance of sufficient shared threats, and the partisan alignment of local communities with external powers such as Israel, Syria, and Iran, was both cause and consequence of the breakdown of the Lebanese settlement in 1975. Agreement to weaken both Israeli and Syrian influence in the country arguably lay behind the making of the Ta'if Accord. As for the indirect external effect, it might be suggested that small states may well experience foreign policy overload, and, conversely, that a light foreign policy load might make the domestic indulgence of political antagonism easier. Within regional units of government, as opposed to sovereign states, local elites have blocked power-sharing deals even though they have no serious international responsibilities – for example, the Ulster Unionists in Northern Ireland between 1974 and 1998.

No consociational theorist maintains that a small population size is a necessary condition of consociational success. Consociational transitional arrangements worked in South Africa between 1993 and 1996, despite a population of nearly 40 million. India, which is now probably the state with the world's largest population, and Canada, which has a population of over 30 million, have both been seen as having had at least semi-consociational pasts and possible futures. The EU, which encompasses over 450 million people, has consociational and confederal practices, especially in foreign and security policy.

Perhaps, therefore, there are better ways to express the intuition behind the apparent correlation between consociation and small-sized polities. One is that the elites of great powers, as opposed to small powers, are more likely to be reluctant to embrace consociational decision making because of security imperatives that arguably call for less consensual decision making and more energetic discretionary executive power. This reasoning lies behind the arguments of those who want to create a vigorous and energetic apparatus for the foreign and security policy making of the EU. The second is that great and regional powers may be more willing to impose domestic arrangements on small powers that they would not dream of imposing on themselves. The United States and European powers used vigorous coercion and inducements to promote consociational settlements in Bosnia-Herzegovina and Macedonia. In the last century, the European powers intervened to create autonomy and rights packages for Christian minorities within many of the former provinces of the Ottoman Empire – packages that they did not always or even generally apply to their own religious minorities. Similarly, the centres of sovereign unitary states may be willing to induce local elites to agree to consociational autonomy or federal settlements in small, localized regions without re-engineering their core states, for example, Great Britain and Northern Ireland, and Italy and South Tyrol.

There is a last way in which external relations may matter in the genesis of consociations, and that is through the direct and indirect effects of international norms. There are, of course, diverse readings of the history of international norms and actions. The received understanding of the Westphalian system[70] was that sovereign states were to leave one another alone in their domestic cultural zones. In other words, their sovereignty gave them the right coercively to assimilate or integrate minorities within their borders. On some interpretations, sovereignty even included the right to commit genocide. This reading of the Westphalian system and its practices, however, has never been entirely without challengers. The Treaty of Westphalia protected some religious power sharing. Moreover, in the 1920s, after the collapse of the Habsburg, Ottoman, and Czarist empires, some new European states that had been recognized at Versailles signed minority-rights treaties that in principle could have been regulated by the League of Nations. These treaties bound them not to abuse their minorities and in some cases required them to maintain or develop semi-consociational practices (notably in religious, educational, and linguistic matters). The result, of course, was hardly a success story – and indeed the United Nations was partly constructed in a deliberate rejection of these experiments. But the post-decolonization international law of self-determination, and the politics of recognition that arose in post-communist successor states, have prompted a revival of efforts to lock new states into systems of minority protection – and in turn this has provided some external shield for minorities that advance consociational demands.

Other indirect effects of international norms and interventions are apparent. There are international proscriptions against genocide and expulsion. There are norms of some significance that reward states that are democratic and that make non-democratic regimes potential pariahs. There are additional proscriptions against coercive assimilation. There remain strong biases in the state system against secession and partition. The conjunction of these norms leaves international organizations and great powers – when they intervene in national, ethnic, and communal conflicts – usually confined to promoting one of three repertoires of conflict regulation: (1) territorial autonomy and/or federation; (2) integration; or (3) consociation. In some scenarios, to prescribe integration – for example, in Bosnia-Herzegovina, Macedonia, Northern Ireland, or Cyprus – is to prescribe the partisan victory of one community over another. The upshot is that the normative prohibition, if not factual exclusion, of certain options that were once standard may create leverage in favour of consociational arrangements in small political systems.

There are at least three current experiments in what are termed "complex consociations" – Northern Ireland, Bosnia-Herzegovina, and

Macedonia – that illustrate the above tentative suggestions. All involve the four consociational institutions of executive power sharing, proportionality, autonomy, and veto rights; but they also involve international efforts to resolve national self-determination disputes; international involvement in the mediation, negotiation, arbitration, and implementation of peace settlements; and cross-border or confederal relationships (and sometimes institutions) for national minorities with their kin in other states. They are somewhat less frequent than the international promotion of autonomy settlements, but their presence in our times is suggestive.

Four elements make these emergent cases "complex." First, they are political settlements that specifically attempt to address national self-determination disputes between communities – i.e., where there is an opposition between at least some secessionists and some unionists or federalists – by institutionally recognizing more than one people, nation, or society and providing constitutional architecture within which more than one people can co-exist, durably if not necessarily permanently. The settlements may involve defining the state as multinational, recognizing national minorities as well as majorities, organizing referendums to ratify such settlements in more than one jurisdiction, or providing mechanisms to trigger referendums. Second, they are political settlements that simultaneously involve peace processes – mechanisms, confidence-building measures, and institutional and policy transformations that are intended to halt conflict and to terminate future violent recurrences.[71] They therefore involve the restructuring of security systems and the adoption of measures intended to end secessionist (and anti-secessionist) paramilitarism, as well as new human-rights protection mechanisms. Third, these settlements involve at least one other conflict-regulating strategy or principle in their design. This is most obvious in cases that combine consociation and territorial autonomy, as is illustrated by the attempted settlements in Northern Ireland and Bosnia-Herzegovina. But this point requires further elaboration.

"Complex" consociations involve at least one additional strategy *other than consociation*. Excluding those strategies to which no minority community's leaders would freely give their assent – namely, genocide, expulsion, assimilation, and hegemonic control – in practice means that "complex" consociations involve the combination of consociational strategies with one or more other strategies such as territorial autonomy, arbitration, integration, and possibly "downsizing."

Consociations, for example, may be combined with territorial autonomy. Northern Ireland has territorial autonomy from Westminster. The federation of Bosnia-Herzegovina has territorial autonomy for Serbs, Bosniacs, and Croats. Macedonia will have territorial autonomy for Macedonian Albanians. Consociations may have arbitration mechanisms for resolving disputes between the partners, such as impartial courts, commissions, international judges, or international commissions. Consociations may have elements of integration, such as common citizenship equality laws and constitutional and institutional designs that permit the voluntary integration of communities. And, not least, they may have mechanisms that enable the secession of the relevant unit of consociational governance, or, alternatively, a procedure for enabling the central state to "downsize." Northern Ireland illustrates this point, but, by contrast, there is no such provision in the cases of Bosnia-Herzegovina or Macedonia.

A fourth and last element of complexity is international involvement in the making, ratification, and maintenance of the relevant consociational or autonomy settlements. This may involve neighbouring states, regional powers, great powers, the UN, or regional organizations such as the Organization for Security and Cooperation in Europe (OSCE) or the EU. International involvement may be critical in organizing and monitoring ceasefires, in providing good offices for the making of settlements, in designing implementation arrangements, and in providing default mechanisms to arbitrate disputes. The levels of institutionalization may vary. Domestic incorporation of international human and minority rights standards does not necessarily challenge the sovereignty of the state. Institutionalized cross-border cooperation and the formation of bodies with executive powers in more than one formally sovereign jurisdiction, by contrast, do entail at least a pooling – if not necessarily a diminution – of sovereignty. High commissioners appointed by great powers are indistinguishable from the prefects of protectorates. In summary, "complex consociation" is distinguished by the existence of policies, institutions, and constitutional arrangements that address an antagonistic self-determination dispute, incorporate peace processes, involve elements of at least one other major domestic conflict-regulating strategy, and, lastly, enlist external or international powers in the making, implementation, and maintenance of the settlement.

The claim here is that these relatively novel emergent configurations are likely to proliferate in future crisis zones. That is not to suggest that they lack precedents; for example, the Cypriot constitution of 1960 had many of the elements of a complex consociation. It is to suggest that there are reasons why these hybrids are emerging simultaneously and in a more widespread manner. The small-polity effect and changes in the norms of the international order may be the keys to such formations.

## CONCLUSION

The rival moral and political evaluations of consociation are unlikely to be resolved and are probably not amenable to decisive confirmation or falsification by evidence. Anti-consociationalists fear that consociation will bring back racism, fundamentalism, and patriarchy, whereas consociationalists fear that integrationists will provoke avoidable wars and are biased in favour of dominant communities.[72] The intensity with which this debate has raged attests to the influence of consociational thought. It certainly belies the claim that consociationalism is irrelevant.

The test of concepts, taxonomies, and theories in the social and legal sciences is twofold, i.e., whether they serve worthwhile explanatory or normative purposes. The claim of this study is that the exponents of consociation, when their case is put carefully, can successfully rebut the wilder charges made against their moral and political positions. Consociations, simple or complex, are certainly difficult to love and celebrate – even if their makers often fully merit intellectual, moral, and political admiration. They are, after all, usually cold bargains, even if they may be tempered by political imagination. Ardent secessionists and uncompromising unionists might profitably be counselled that their efforts may land them with these systems if they fail to win on the battlefield.

As for the explanation of consociations, it is fair to say that, while significant preliminary work has been done, a comprehensive comparative historical analysis of consociational settlements and their outcomes remains to be completed. It will be no bad thing if further consociational research and practice reduces, by no matter what small amount, the tides of national, ethnic, religious, and communal blood that regrettably seem certain to flow in our times.

## NOTES

1 The United States Institute of Peace provided support to the author for the research behind this manuscript, and the Rockefeller Foundation provided him with a residential fellowship at Bellagio, Italy, in the winter of 2002. A longer version of this chapter was presented at the University of Western

Ontario, London, Ontario, in November 2002, and in a revised form at the Cultural Diversity in a Globalizing World conference in Hawaii in February 2003. The chapter consists of segments of a work in progress. Appreciation is owed to John McGarry, Arend Lijphart, Katharine Adeney, John H. Aldrich, Tozun Bahcheli, Florian Bieber, Matthijs Bogaards, Shelley Deane, Kristin Henrard, John A. Hall, Jim Hughes, Margaret Moore, Jack H. Nagel, Sid Noel, Jurg Steiner, Gwen Sasse, Steve Wilkinson, and Stefan Wolff, and all my colleagues at the Asch Center at the University of Pennsylvania. These arguments were compelled into existence by the conviction that it is important to rebut now conventional criticisms of consociational theory and practice, for which some of my own friends and teachers are responsible, e.g., Brian Barry, Ian S. Lustick, Donald L. Horowitz, and Rupert Taylor. Changing their minds is part of the chapter's agenda.

2 Arend Lijphart, *The Politics of Accommodation* (Berkeley: University of California Press 1968); Arend Lijphart, "Consociational Democracy," *World Politics* 21, no.2 (1969): 207–25; Arend Lijphart, *Democracy in Plural Societies: A Comparative Exploration* (New Haven, Conn.: Yale University Press 1977); Arend Lijphart, *Power-Sharing in South Africa* (Berkeley: University of California Press 1985).

3 "Power sharing" is not a synonym for consociation because there are other than consociational ways to share power: e.g., through federation, intermittent and temporary coalitions, alternating governments, the separation of powers, and generally "collegial" institutions. See Randall Collins, *Democratization from the Outside in: A Geopolitical Theory of Collegial Power* (Stanford, Calif.: Stanford University Press 1999). Each of the types of power sharing listed above can be deployed in consociational formats. What makes consociational power sharing distinctive is that it mandates power sharing across communities through formulae of proportionality and autonomy.

4 For further discussion, see John McGarry and Brendan O'Leary, *The Northern Ireland Conflict: Consociational Engagements* (Oxford, U.K.: Oxford University Press 2004).

5 Donald Horowitz, *Ethnic Groups in Conflict* (Berkeley: University of California Press 1985), 256.

6 Rupert Taylor, "The New South Africa: Consociational or Consensual Power-Sharing," *ASEN Bulletin* 8 (2004): 14–18; Rupert Taylor, "Consociation or Social Transformation?" in John McGarry, ed., *Northern Ireland and the Divided World: Post-agreement Northern Ireland in Comparative Perspective* (Oxford, U.K.: Oxford University Press 2001), 36–52; Joseph Ruane and Jennifer Todd, *The Dynamics of Conflict in Northern Ireland:*

*Power, Conflict and Emancipation* (Cambridge, U.K.: Cambridge University Press 1996).

7 Paul R. Brass, *Ethnic Conflict in Multiethnic Societies: The Consociational Solution and Its Critics* (New Delhi: Sage 1991), 338.

8 Taylor, "Consociation or Social Transformation?," 40.

9 Brass, *Ethnic Conflict in Multiethnic Societies,* 346n.11.

10 For a typical libertarian-conservative statement of the jeopardy thesis, see Thomas Sowell, *Preferential Policies: An International Perspective* (New York: Quill 1990).

11 Brass, *Ethnic Conflict in Multiethnic Societies,* 334 (my emphasis).

12 Ibid., 334, 339.

13 Courtney Jung and Ian Shapiro, "South Africa's Negotiated Transition: Democracy, Opposition, and the New Constitutional Order," *Politics & Society* 23, no.3 (1995): 273–4, 293; Samuel P. Huntington, *The Third Wave: Democratization in the Late Twentieth Century* (Norman: University of Oklahoma Press 1991).

14 Brian Barry, "The Consociational Model and Its Dangers," *European Journal of Political Research* 3 (1975): 393–413; Brian Barry, "Review Article: Political Accommodation and Consociational Democracy," *British Journal of Political Science* 5 (1975): 477–505.

15 M.P.C.M. Van Schendelen, "The Views of Arend Lijphart and Collected Criticism," *Acta Politica* 1 (1984): 19–55.

16 Brass, *Ethnic Conflict in Multiethnic Societies,* 340. Since Brass uses Great Britain for his argument rather than the United Kingdom, one must assume that his exclusion of Northern Ireland from his endorsement of its adversarial politics is deliberate (or else, like some Americans, he fallaciously equates Great Britain with the United Kingdom). If Northern Ireland is considered part of the United Kingdom political system, which it has been, the merits of adversarial politics are much less obvious. See Brendan O'Leary and John McGarry, *The Politics of Antagonism: Understanding Northern Ireland,* 2nd ed. (London: Athlone Press 1996). As for the United States, the claims for the integrative effects of adversarial politics with respect to native Americans and the descendants of slaves have been unconvincing to successive cohorts of foreign observers of the country from Tocqueville to Myrdal. Their stories are an integral part of the critical histories of American political development. See Rogers M. Smith, *Conflicting Visions of Citizenship in U.S. History* (New Haven, Conn.: Yale University Press 1997).

17 Brass, *Ethnic Conflict in Multiethnic Societies,* 341.

18 Sue Halpern, "The Disorderly Universe of Consociational Democracy," *West European Politics* 9, no.2 (1986): 181–97.

19 Ronald Kieve, "Pillars of Sand: A Marxist Critique of Consociational Democracy in the Netherlands," *Comparative Politics* 13, no.3 (1981): 313–37.

20 Ian S. Lustick, "Lijphart, Lakatos and Consociationalism," *World Politics* 50, no.3 (1997): 88–117.

21 Cambridge, Mass.: Harvard University Press 1991.

22 Arend Lijphart, "The Politics of Accommodation: Reflections – Fifteen Years Later," *Acta Politica* 19, no.1 (1984): 9–18; Lijphart, *Power-sharing in South Africa*, 83–117.

23 Anthony D. Smith, *The Nation in History: Historiographical Debates about Ethnicity and Nationalism* (Oxford, U.K.: Polity Press 2000), 51–78.

24 John Stuart Mill, "Considerations on Representative Government," in H.B. Acton, ed., *Utilitarianism, On Liberty, and Considerations on Representative Government* (London: J.M. Dent 1988). John Stuart Mill, *On Liberty and Other Writings* (Cambridge, U.K.: Cambridge University Press 1989). In *On Liberty* and *Considerations on Representative Government*, Mill, like Tocqueville, was much more concerned about the tyranny of the ignorant and of conformist puritanical, ignorant, and unlettered masses. In *Considerations*, however, he famously decreed the unlikelihood of multi-national or bi-national states (391–8).

25 Otto Bauer, *The Question of Nationalities and Social Democracy*, ed. Ephraim Nimni, trans. Joseph O'Donnell (Minneapolis: University of Minnesota Press 2000).

26 Arend Lijphart, "The Evolution of Consociational Theory and Constitutional Practices, 1965–2000," *Acta Politica* 37 (2002): 11–22.

27 W. Arthur Lewis, *Politics in West Africa*, the Whidden Lectures, (Toronto and New York: Oxford University Press 1965).

28 For examples of this reasoning, see S.J.R. Noel, "Canadian Responses to Ethnic Conflict: Consociationalism, Federalism and Control," in John McGarry and Brendan O'Leary, ed., *The Politics of Ethnic Conflict-Regulation: Case Studies of Protracted Ethnic Conflicts* (London: Routledge 1993), 41–61; Milton Esman, "Power Sharing and the Constructionist Fallacy," in Markus Crepaz, Thomas A. Kolbe, and David Wilsford, ed., *Democracy and Institutions: The Life Work of Arend Lijphart* (Ann Arbor: University of Michigan Press 2000), 91–113.

29 Michael Walzer, *On Toleration* (New Haven, Conn.: Yale University Press 1997), 22.

30 Halpern, "Disorderly Universe," 190.

31 These distinctions may be clarified by placing them on the Nagel spectrum. See Jack H. Nagel, "Expanding the Spectrum of Democracies: Reflections on Proportional Representation in New Zealand," in Crepaz et al., *Democracy and Institutions*, 113–27.

32 Lijphart recognizes this, describing "joint decision making" as the key characteristic of power sharing. See Arend Lijphart, "Multiethnic Democracy," in Seymour Martin Lipset, ed., *The Encyclopedia of Democracy* (London: Routledge 1995) 853–65. My analysis suggests that some objections to Lijphart's classifications may be dismissed: for example, Horowitz's objection that none of the four developing countries identified by Lijphart as having followed consociational practices – namely, Lebanon, Malaysia, Surinam, and the Netherlands Antilles – had grand coalitions because each group was represented by more than one set of leaders. Donald L. Horowitz, *Ethnic Groups in Conflict*, 575.

33 Donald L. Horowitz, "Constitutional Design: An Oxymoron?" in Ian Shapiro and Stephen Macedo , ed., *Designing Democratic Institutions* (New York: New York University Press 2000), 253–84; Jung and Shapiro, *South Africa's Negotiated Transition*, 269–308.

34 Lijphart, *Democracy in Plural Societies*, 130–4.

35 The offer of such institutions, it is important to add, came intermittently from the u.k. government; but even if nationalists had not had a wider agenda, not even a plurality of Ulster Unionists was then prepared to share executive power with them.

36 Rein Taagepera and Matthew Soberg, *Seats and Votes: The Effects and Determinants of Electoral Systems* (New Haven, Conn., and London: Yale University Press 1989), 273–5; Arend Lijphart, *Electoral Systems and Party Systems: A Study of Twenty-seven Democracies* (Oxford, u.k.: Oxford University Press 1994), 25–30.

37 Brendan O'Leary, "The Nature of the British-Irish Agreement," *New Left Review* 233 (1999): 66–96.

38 My thanks to Matthijs Bogaards for obliging me to address this matter (personal communication).

39 Where one segment stays constantly in the executive and alternates its partners from other segments, it may seem plausible to label such a phenomenon a "diachronic grand coalition," but this, I submit, looks too much like conceptual stretching.

40 Donald V. Smiley, "French-English Relations in Canada and Consociational Democracy," in Milton Esman, ed., *Ethnic Conflict in the Western World*

(Ithaca, N.Y.: Cornell University Press 1977). S.J.R. Noel cites historian Frank Underhill as saying that the great Canadian invention of the nineteenth century was the "composite bi-racial, bi-cultural party, uniting both French and English voters" (Noel, "Canadian Responses to Ethnic Conflict," 49).

41 I have benefited from discussions with Matthijs Bogaards. Our positions are not, in my view, very different.

42 The second and third criteria are Bogaards's; the first and last are mine.

43 O'Leary, *Consociation*.

44 Arend Lijphart, "Foreword: One Basic Problem, Many Theoretical Options – And a Practical Solution?" in John McGarry and Brendan O'Leary, ed., *The Future of Northern Ireland* (Oxford, U.K.: Clarendon Press 1990), vi–viii.

45 See, e.g., Will Kymlicka, *Multicultural Citizenship: A Liberal Theory of Minority Rights* (Oxford, U.K.: Oxford University Press 1995); Will Kymlicka, *Finding Our Way: Rethinking Ethnocultural Relations in Canada* (Don Mills, Ont.: Oxford University Press Canada 1998); Will Kymlicka and Wayne Norman, ed., *Citizenship in Diverse Societies* (Oxford: Oxford University Press 2000).

46 Adriano Pappalardo, "The Conditions for Consociational Democracy: A Logical and Empirical Critique," *European Journal of Political Research* 9 (1981): 365–90; Eric Nordlinger, *Conflict Regulation in Divided Societies* (Cambridge, Mass.: Centre for International Affairs, Harvard University 1972).

47 Two of Lijphart's critics, Lustick and Bogaards, observe the changes in the numbers of conducive conditions he identifies over successive publications. Lustick makes fun of the changes, but, rather than seeing them as indicative of inconsistency on Lijphart's part, they should be viewed as an appropriately flexible and explicit effort to refine theory through accepting logical and empirical criticism.

48 Arend Lijphart, "The Power-sharing Approach," in Joseph P. Montville, ed., *Conflict and Peacemaking in Multiethnic Societies* (Lexington, Mass.: Lexington Books 1989), 497–8.

49 Lijphart, *Democracy in Plural Societies*, 55.

50 Lijphart, *Democracy in Plural Societies*, 55.

51 For a lucid exposition of the Nash equilibrium, see Ken G. Binmore, *Fun and Games: A Text on Game Theory* (Lexington, Mass.: D.C. Heath 1992), xxix, 602.

52 Pappalardo, "Conditions," 369.

53 In Bosnia-Herzegovina, before the war that accompanied its independence, the demographic composition of the population (in 1981) was 40 per cent Bosniac (of Muslim origin), 32 per cent Serb, and 18 per cent Croat (with the remaining 10 per cent identified as "Yugoslavs" or as members of other ethnic groups or of mixed origins) – S.P. Ramet, *Nationalism and Federalism in Yugoslavia, 1962–91*, 2nd ed. (Bloomington: Indiana University Press 1992), 181 (calculated from Table 22). A combination of Bosniacs and Serbs or Bosniacs and Croats would thus constitute a clear majority, while a Croat-Serb coalition was within credible reach of a majority. This tripolar situation, in which no one segment had a demographic or electoral majority, but in which any combination of two could credibly hope to have one, became explosive. For accounts of the civil and international war that followed and its aftermath, see Richard Holbrooke, *To End a War* (New York: Random House 1998); and Sumantra Bose, *Bosnia after Dayton: Nationalist Partition and International Intervention* (New York: Oxford University Press 2002).

54 Hans Daalder, "On Building Consociational Nations: The Cases of Netherlands and Switzerland," *Legislative Studies Quarterly* 3, no.2 (1971): 11–25. Sceptics suggest that this idea may simply displace the key question: the continuation of elite accommodation in open democratic conditions may deserve explanation as much as its origins. See Rudy Andeweg, "Consociational Democracy," *Annual Review of Political Science* 3, no.1 (2000): 509–36.

55 Gerhard Lehmbruch, "Consociational Democracy in the International System," *European Journal of Political Research* 3 (1975): 377–91.

56 Nordlinger, *Conflict Regulation*, 42–53.

57 McGarry and O'Leary, *Understanding Northern Ireland*.

58 Lijphart, "Evolution of Consociational Theory," 20n3.

59 See McGarry and O'Leary, *Understanding Northern Ireland*; McGarry and O'Leary, *The Northern Ireland Conflict*. That is one of our arguments concerning Northern Ireland.

60 Barry, "Review Article: Political Accommodation," 502–3. Horowitz makes a similar claim: "European [as opposed to Asian or African] conflicts are less ascriptive in character, less severe in intensity, less exclusive in their command of the loyalty of participants, and less pre-emptive of other forms of conflict" (*Ethnic Groups in Conflict*, 571–2).

61 David Laitin, *Language Repertoires and State Construction in Africa* (Cambridge, U.K.: Cambridge University Press 1992).

62 Nordlinger, *Conflict Regulation*, 119.

63 Horowitz's claim that "no mechanism can be adduced for the adoption or retention of consociational institutions, particularly no reason grounded in electoral politics" ("Constitutional Design," 258) is unwarranted. Politicians may have both instrumental incentives and other reasons to make and maintain consociational institutions. Horowitz's claim startlingly contradicts the claim of other consociational critics (and that he has also made) that the making and preservation of consociations provides incentives for politicians to maintain and reinforce group differences and bestow patronage based on quotas.

64 Nordlinger, *Conflict Regulation*, 78–87; see also Pappalardo, "Conditions," 380–2.

65 Paul Mitchell, Brendan O'Leary, and Geoffrey Evans, "The 2001 Elections in Northern Ireland: Moderating 'Extremists' and the Squeezing of the Moderates," *Representation* 39, no.1 (2002): 23–36; Paul Mitchell, "Transcending an Ethnic Party System? The Impact of Consociational Governance on Electoral Dynamics and the Party System," in Rick Wilford, ed., *Aspects of the Belfast Agreement* (Oxford, U.K.: Oxford University Press (2001), 28–48.

66 Within regional consociations or protectorates, the relevant publics may enjoy the luxury of irresponsibility: they may be able to vote for chaos knowing that direct rule from the centre or international rulers will likely take over from the local executives. Voters in independent and sovereign consociations have greater reasons to be circumspect.

67 Lijphart, *Plural Societies*, 65–70.

68 Lijphart, *Politics of Accommodation*, 59ff., 122ff.

69 Lijphart, *Plural Societies*, 139; Lijphart, *Power-sharing in South Africa*, 123.

70 The system of state sovereignty that developed in Europe after the Treaty of Westphalia (1648).

71 John Darby and Roger MacGinty, ed., *The Management of Peace Processes* (Basingstoke, U.K.: Palgrave 2000).

72 McGarry and O'Leary, *The Northern Ireland Conflict*, chapter 1.

# 2

# Between Stability and Collapse: Internal and External Dynamics of Post-agreement Institution Building in Northern Ireland

## STEFAN WOLFF

On 14 October 2002 the British government suspended devolved government in Northern Ireland for the third time. Unlike the previous two suspensions, on 11 August 2001 and 21 September 2001 – which were only "technical" twenty-four-hour suspensions to allow the political parties in Northern Ireland to resolve a deadlock over the decommissioning of weapons in possession of the Irish Republican Army (IRA) and Sinn Féin's membership in the executive – this suspension, similar to the very first one on 11 February 2000, had no time limit attached to it.

Despite assurances of continued commitment to the peace process as a whole from the British and Irish governments and from the political parties in Northern Ireland, the future of the Agreement[1] concluded on 10 April 1998 was once again put in serious doubt. The difficulties that have repeatedly arisen since 1998 – and, in a sense, ever since the idea of power sharing as a mechanism to resolve the conflict in Northern Ireland was first introduced in the early 1970s – suggest one of the following three explanations as the underlying causes for the failure of power sharing to deliver sustainable peace:

1 Power sharing, or at least the particular form it takes in the institutional structures established under the Agreement since 1998, is unsuited as a mechanism for conflict resolution in Northern Ireland.

2 At fault are not the institutional structures, on which wide agreement was reached among the conflict parties and which were endorsed in referenda in both Northern Ireland and the Republic of Ireland. Rather, it is the lack of leadership, vision, and skills, primarily among Northern Ireland's politicians but also, to a lesser degree, among the governments in London and Dublin, that have resulted in a lasting crisis.

3 Certain structural shortcomings of the institutions established under the Agreement have been exacerbated by this lack of leadership, vision, and skills and have, needlessly, led to these institutions' decreasing ability to function.

In my analysis of the situation in Northern Ireland, the third explanation is the most credible and comprehensive, as well as the one that can potentially point to a way out of the almost permanent crisis in which the Northern Irish peace process has found itself over the past several years. I argue that, while far from perfect, power sharing is the only viable approach to conflict resolution in Northern Ireland, and the Agreement reached in 1998 provides a reasonable framework for such an approach – but only if some of its structural shortcomings are addressed and only if political leaders rise to the challenges that the negotiation and implementation of such a revised agreement would bring with it, so that they begin to put the long-term interests of Northern Ireland before their own short-term constituency interests. This second requirement is a tall order, but its achievement can be significantly facilitated by appropriate revisions to the current Agreement, combined with the right combination of pressures and incentives from the governments in London and Dublin, and not least in Washington.

There are five parts to my examination of power sharing in Northern Ireland. I begin with a brief outline of the structure of the power-sharing institutions that were set up under the 1998 Agreement. This is followed by a discussion of the rationale behind opting for a power-sharing settlement and the wisdom of adopting the particular institutional design found in the Agreement. I then turn to the problems encountered in the implementation and operation process, and examine in particular their underlying causes. Following this, I raise some normative concerns about the institutional structure of devolved government in Northern Ireland from the perspective of whether it is sufficiently democratic. In conclusion, I assess the future of power sharing in Northern Ireland.[2]

## POWER-SHARING STRUCTURES
## PROVIDED BY THE AGREEMENT[3]

The Agreement deals with three main issues: (1) democratic institutions in Northern Ireland; (2) the North-South Ministerial Council; and (3) the British-Irish Council, the British-Irish Inter-Governmental Conference, and "Rights, Safeguards and Equality of Opportunity."

Concerning democratic institutions, the Agreement provides for the establishment of a 108-member Assembly, to be elected by the single transferable vote system (STV) from existing Westminster constituencies. The Assembly exercises full legislative and executive authority over the powers previously held by the six Northern Ireland government departments. Subject to later developments, the Assembly could take on responsibility for other matters in accordance with the Agreement. To ensure that all sections of the community can participate in the work of the Assembly, and to protect them in their rights and identities, the following safeguards were included: specific procedures for the allocation of committee chairs, ministers, and committee membership in proportion to party strength in the Assembly; the primacy of the European Convention on Human Rights (ECHR) and any future bill of rights for Northern Ireland over any legislation passed by the Assembly; arrangements to ensure that key decisions are taken on a cross-community basis (parallel consent and weighted-majority voting procedures); and the creation of an Equality Commission. Crucial for the operation of the Assembly is that its members register their identity as Nationalist, Unionist, or Other, in order to have a measurement of community support for any vote carried out under either the parallel consent or the weighted-majority procedures.

Under the Agreement, a committee for each of the main executive functions of the Northern Ireland administration was established. Chairs and deputy chairs of these committees are allocated proportionally according to the d'Hondt system,[4] while membership in the committees is in proportion to party strength in the Assembly. The responsibilities of the committees include administrative scrutiny, policy development, consultation, and initiating legislation with respect to the departments with which they are associated. Their powers include considering and advising on departmental budgets and initiating annual plans in the context of overall budget allocation; giving detailed consideration at the committee stage to relevant legislation; and initiating inquiries and making reports. In addition to these permanent committees, the Assembly has the right to appoint special committees as required.

Executive authority on behalf of the Assembly rests with the first minister and his or her deputy and up to ten ministers with departmental responsibilities. Following the election of the first minister and deputy first minister on a joint ticket, the posts of ministers are allocated to parties according to the d'Hondt system. An Executive Committee, comprising all ministers (including the first minister and deputy first minister), handles all issues that cut across the responsibilities of two or more ministers in order to formulate a consistent policy on the respective issue. Ministers have full executive authority in their departments within a policy framework agreed on by the Executive Committee and endorsed by the Assembly. Ten departments for the government of Northern Ireland were agreed among the pro-Agreement parties in December 1998: agriculture and rural development; enterprise, trade and investment (including tourism); health, social care, and public safety; finance and personnel; education; employment and learning; the environment; regional development; social development; and culture, arts, and leisure.

Legislation can be initiated by an individual member of the Assembly, a committee, or a minister. The Assembly can pass primary legislation for Northern Ireland in all areas where it has devolved powers. The passing of legislation is subject to decision by a simple majority of members voting (except for decisions that require cross-community support), to detailed scrutiny and approval in the relevant departmental committee, and to coordination with Westminster legislation. Any disputes over legislative competence are to be decided by the courts. In its relations with other institutions, the Assembly has to ensure cross-community participation.

A North-South Ministerial Council was agreed upon in order to institutionalize formal relationships between the executive organs of Northern Ireland and the Republic of Ireland. Its responsibilities include consultation, cooperation, and the implementation of decisions on issues of mutual concern. All decisions of the council have to be by agreement between the two sides, and their implementation is subject to approval by both parliaments. Six so-called implementation bodies for the North-South Ministerial Council were agreed on in December 1998: Waterways Ireland; the Food Safety Promotion Board; the Trade and Business Development Board; the Special European Union

Programmes Body; the North/South Language Body; and the Foyle, Carlingford, and Irish Lights Commission. Selected aspects of transport, agriculture, education, health, environment, and tourism were additionally agreed on as areas of functional cooperation.

Provisions in the third part of the Agreement are of only peripheral consequence for the structure of the power-sharing institutions, although arrangements with regard to rights, safeguards, and equality of opportunity have an impact on their operation.

## WHY POWER-SHARING AND WHY THIS PARTICULAR INSTITUTIONAL DESIGN?

These two questions are best answered through an examination of the nature of the Northern Ireland conflict and of previous attempts to resolve it.

The conflict is caused by incompatible conceptions of national belonging and the means to realize them. These two different conceptions are, on the one hand, the idea of a united Ireland pursued by Nationalists and Republicans, and, on the other hand, the Unionists' and Loyalists' desire for continued strong constitutional links between the province and Great Britain, within the United Kingdom. Historically, these two conceptions have been associated with two different religions – Catholicism and Protestantism. Religious labels have consequently played a significant role in the conflict, for they have made possible the systematic pursuit of discrimination and segregation. Yet this has not made the conflict into an ethno-religious one; nor have distinct linguistic identities (Gaelic and Ulster Scots) or differences regarding class, culture, and ideology overshadowed the fundamental divide between the two communities over the issue of national belonging. However, what turns these differences into additional dimensions of the principal divide over national belonging is that for decades they have exacerbated polarization between the two communities in Northern Irish society, leaving little or no room for cross-cutting cleavages and almost completely eradicating cross-communal political space.

Defining the Northern Ireland conflict thus as an ethno-national one has important implications for its analysis and for the critical examination of any attempt to settle it. First of all, different conflict parties and their relationships with one another need to be defined. Within Northern Ireland, conflict parties act within three political spaces, which are defined in communal or cross-communal terms.[5] The situation there must not be seen in isolation from the United Kingdom and the Republic of Ireland, which are both parties to the conflict as well as its principal mediators, and, as far as the United Kingdom is concerned, its principal arbitrator. Increasingly over the past two decades, factors in the international context have become more and more important as well – international connections of paramilitary groups, the influence of diasporas, and the consequences of European integration. In the current peace process, it has especially been the influence of the Irish diaspora in the United States and that of successive American administrations which has had a significant impact on developments in Northern Ireland.

The dynamics existing among and between these different internal and external actors can explain why a power-sharing dimension is crucial for any settlement to succeed. More generally, the need for power sharing can be derived from demographic and political power balances in Northern Ireland. Without a formal commitment to power sharing, the Nationalist/Republican community would, in all likelihood, have remained permanently excluded from the executive process in Northern Ireland for the foreseeable future, as was the case when a traditional majoritarian system of government was operated in the province between 1921 and 1972. Not to include any provision for power sharing in a peace agreement would thus make it unlikely, if not impossible, that Nationalist or Republican representatives would sign up to any deal. At the same time, the setting up of a collective executive branch of government as part of the power-sharing institutions (as opposed to, say, a committee-only system to run Northern Ireland) was of highly symbolic value for Nationalists and Republicans, provided that it ensured their mandatory inclusion in it.

This *conditio sine qua non* imposed on the peace process from one community is reflected in similar conditions put up by the other. In exchange for agreeing to the institutionalization of power sharing, Loyalists and Unionists demanded security guarantees – in other words, a proven (and, via the Mitchell Principles of Non-violence,[6] enforceable) commitment by Sinn Féin and the IRA to follow exclusively democratic means in the pursuit of their political strategies. This has become manifest, in particular, in the Unionist emphasis on decommissioning as a precondition for the workability of the institutions in their current form.

The specifics of the agreement concluded in 1998, which go far
beyond many power-sharing arrangements operating elsewhere, can be
explained by looking at both the previously failed, or partially successful, attempts to settle and/or manage the conflict, and by taking into
account the different pragmatic and symbolic needs of the individual
communities and the political parties within them.

To begin with the former, after the violent unrest in the late 1960s
and early 1970s and the subsequent imposition of direct rule on
Northern Ireland, a first attempt was made at establishing a power-
sharing government. This happened after a consultation process in
1973 and was followed by elections in Northern Ireland, which
returned a two-thirds' majority for a subsequently formed coalition of
the Unionist Party, the Social Democratic and Labour Party (SDLP),
and the Alliance Party. These three parties and representatives of the
British and Irish governments then met in December 1973 at
Sunningdale to hammer out the details of formalized cross-border
cooperation at the executive and legislative levels between the Republic
of Ireland and Northern Ireland. The resulting Sunningdale Agreement
became a major bone of contention both inside and outside the Northern Ireland Assembly. When a general strike against the new institutions
in the spring of 1974 brought the province to an almost complete
standstill, the executive resigned amidst increasing sectarian violence,
at which stage the British government reintroduced direct rule.

The major lesson learned from this early failure of power sharing
was that there could be either power sharing in Northern Ireland or
cooperation with the Republic, but not both. While subsequent power-
sharing/devolution schemes did not amount to much, an Anglo-Irish
Agreement was concluded in 1985. It excluded political parties in
Northern Ireland from the ensuing process of cooperation between the
two governments. While this newly found level of trust and collabora-
tion marked a significant step forward in British-Irish relations, it did
little to resolve the conflict in Northern Ireland. Nevertheless, it established a reasonably efficient framework of conflict management and
thus contributed to paving the way towards the 1998 Agreement. The
experiences accumulated over more than two decades of attempts at
conflict management thus form one part of the background against
which the Agreement concluded in 1998 must be seen.

In addition, the different pragmatic and symbolic needs of individual
communities and the political parties representing them at the negotiation

table also considerably shaped the specific form that the Agreement finally took. Many of the safeguards that are built into the Agreement, including the specific voting procedures in the Assembly and the need for the Assembly to approve any decision taken by the North-South Ministerial Council, were designed to satisfy both communities' need to be able to exercise a veto over issues that they consider of particular importance for their own communal interests. The choice of the d'Hondt principle for the appointment of individual ministers to the executive was required to ensure cross-communal representation without excluding any of the major parties in each communal party bloc. However, this was also necessary from a more pragmatic standpoint, namely, to avoid protracted bargaining over executive appointments. Having STV as the electoral system was meant to satisfy the demand for relative proportionality in the composition of the Assembly while at the same time strengthening the moderate centre by allowing the indication of preferences on the ballot paper and thus, it was hoped, encouraging cross-communal vote transfers between supporters of moderate parties.

The establishment of both the North-South Ministerial Council and the Council of the Isles sought to address specific "external" dynamics. North-South cooperation was one of the key demands of the Nationalist and Republican community, while the Council of the Isles is a mechanism that, from a Unionist and Loyalist perspective, facilitates the anchoring of this specific Irish dimension in the broader context of the British Isles. It thus carries a distinct notion of strengthening the links between Northern Ireland and other parts of the United Kingdom (even if the council also includes the Republic of Ireland).

Clearly, this is not a comprehensive list of all the specifics of the institutional design provided in the Agreement. However, it lists the most significant and, to some extent, the unusual elements. What is important to note is that this design was not arbitrary or accidental. It was arrived at after tough and drawn-out negotiations, even though successive drafts of the Agreement were almost exclusively produced by civil servants in the Northern Ireland Office[7] in cooperation with their counterparts in the Irish Foreign Ministry and negotiated between them and the major players: the Ulster Unionist Party (UUP) the SDLP, and Sinn Féin. This is not to say that it was the only possible outcome, but rather that all the parties that eventually signed up to it, regardless of the actual amount of their involvement in the negotiations leading up to it, invested considerable time and effort to arrive at this particular result.

The referendum held in Northern Ireland on the Agreement on 21 May 1998 saw a 71 per cent "Yes" vote, with an overwhelming majority of Nationalists and Republicans and a much smaller majority of Unionists and Loyalists endorsing the compromise reached. Subsequent elections confirmed this difference between the communities. The Nationalist SDLP and the major Republican party, Sinn Féin, both represented the undisputable pro-Agreement attitudes of one community (even though their rationales for doing so differed, with the SDLP seeing the Agreement as a long-term if not permanent settlement and Sinn Féin regarding it as merely a stepping stone towards Irish reunification). For their part, the generally pro-Agreement UUP and Progressive Unionist Party (PUP) faced stiff opposition from an almost equal number of Assembly members representing the Democratic Unionist Party (DUP) and a small number of other anti-Agreement Unionists. Both cross-communal parties, the Alliance Party and the Women's Coalition, represented decidedly pro-Agreement attitudes.

### Inter-community and Intra-community Dynamics

With the return of power sharing to Northern Ireland, intra-community dynamics acquired a whole new dimension. Electoral support became more important, and more profitable, for a larger number of people. As one of my interview subjects (an Assembly member) put it, "a relatively high and regular salary, an office at Stormont, staff who work for you and the status you acquire as an Assembly member do not necessarily corrupt you, but they make you want to keep all these things and you are suddenly prepared to walk the extra mile to retain the support of your electorate." However, what he also admitted was that the willingness to put in this extra effort did not necessarily extend to all Assembly members and "did not mean that there was automatically a greater preparedness to compromise and make concessions to ensure the survival of the very institutions that deliver all these perks."

This, however, is not necessarily a contradiction. The situation in Northern Ireland is such that all political parties compete for a strictly limited pool of votes within their own political space. There is a relatively clearly defined number of Unionists and Loyalists and the same is true of Nationalists and Republicans. Crossover voters between the two are extremely rare, even though the electoral system in Northern Ireland would easily allow, and was adopted to facilitate, vote transfers between supporters of moderate parties across communal boundaries. However, to the disappointment of the moderate centre, "vote transfers between UUP and SDLP were only around 10 per cent either way – this is not enough for us to promote compromise and emphasize that we have more in common with 'them' than with other parties in our own community, even though this might well be the case." Quite apart from the fact that one reason for this low number of transfer votes may be the lack of a targeted campaign to encourage transfer votes, it also shows that the emphasis of electoral politics has decidedly shifted from inter-community to intra-community competition. With the dominant view being that there are too few chances to attract voters from the other side, election campaigns become intra-community events and lead to increasing polarization and radicalization, essentially strengthening hardliners at the expense of moderates in each community. The lack of transfer votes thus becomes a self-fulfilling prophecy.

Another likely consequence of this is that the political space in which cross-community parties can operate and gain votes becomes ever smaller, and there is a real risk that both the Alliance Party and the Women's Coalition will be squeezed out of or substantially reduced in their presence in the Assembly if there is no significant change in the political climate.

While these overall dynamics of polarization hold true for both communities, their underlying reasons are somewhat different. In the Nationalist and Republican community, the problem is not the split between pro- and anti-Agreement factions, since both Sinn Féin and the SDLP are supportive of it. However, Sinn Féin has overtaken the SDLP in the number of seats won in the general elections for Westminster and in the 2003 Assembly elections, confirming fears among Unionists that Sinn Féin would become the strongest "Catholic" party in the Northern Ireland Assembly and so make it virtually impossible to form an executive. The reasons for the growing support for Sinn Féin are various. According to most of the people I interviewed, it is perceived (and in fact is) the younger and more dynamic party; it has more charismatic leaders, who command respect and loyalty in their community; and (during periods between suspensions) it has managed to turn two difficult ministries – health and education (which together account for about 60 per cent of the total budget of Northern Ireland) – into a true public relations asset, so that, much more than the SDLP, they are seen as delivering government. Sinn Féin also benefits from its public commitment to the Agreement and the peace process, especially among members of the younger generation, who have no personal experience or recollection of some of the worst IRA violence. At the same time, the electoral and political pressure under which the SDLP found itself within its own community was aggravated by a crucial lack of cooperation from the UUP. More engagement between them, and more joint political initiatives coming from the first minister and deputy first minister, would not only have helped increase governmental efficiency but also improved the perception and public visibility of the SDLP. The increasingly hawkish stance taken by David Trimble as UUP leader – and thus implicitly as first minister – contributed to the erosion of support for the SDLP and bolstered support for Sinn Féin.

Within Unionism, the major problem is that there is deep scepticism about whether all the concessions that the Unionists (in their view) have made in the Agreement have paid off in terms of an end to IRA violence and a genuine commitment by Sinn Féin to the peace process and to democratic politics. Although the IRA (and, for that matter, the Ulster Volunteer Force (UVF) as well) have maintained their ceasefires, with the result that the number of deaths from sectarian violence has decreased since 1998, violence remains a feature of Northern Ireland society. The violence, as many Unionists and Loyalists told me, is believed by many in their community to be orchestrated by paramilitaries on both sides, including the IRA. However, orchestrated violence in the form of rioting and clashes between hostile mobs is not its only manifestation. The number of non-fatal shootings and assaults has dramatically increased since 1998 (from 216 in 1998 to 330 in 2001), and around 60 per cent are committed by Loyalist paramilitaries. It also needs to be noted that the majority of these acts are directed at members of the paramilitaries' own community or at rival paramilitary groups within it, such as the feud between the UVF and its main rival, the Ulster Defence Association (UDA).

Against this background of continued violence, four events have been particularly damaging: the uncovering of an alleged IRA gun-smuggling operation in Florida; the arrest of three suspected IRA members in Colombia (subsequently charged with training Marxist guerrillas); the break-in at the Special Branch offices at Castlereagh Police Station in Belfast, during which sensitive documents were stolen, an act attributed to the IRA; and the uncovering of an alleged spy ring operated by Sinn Féin and the IRA at the Northern Ireland Office. Regardless of the substance of any of these incidents, they have confirmed the fears of a majority of Unionists and Loyalists, who had already been wary of the commitment of Republicans to peaceful democratic politics, and they have triggered the latest crisis and the suspension of the devolved institutions in Northern Ireland.

The decreasing trust that Unionists have in the institutions to which the UUP signed up in 1998 has undermined the electoral support which the party used to command and has made the position of its leader extremely difficult, for he is fighting a two-front battle in his community: against challenges to his authority within his own party, and against increased electoral support for the DUP. However, part of the problem – in fact, the main reason, according to many of the people I interviewed – is that David Trimble and the UUP have failed to demonstrate a clear commitment to the institutions established under the Agreement, and they have not sold the advantages of the Agreement to their own community. One Unionist interviewee noted that it is difficult and potentially counterproductive to "emphasize over and over again that the Union has been secured and that there is an IRA ceasefire" when the price for this has been to sit in government with Sinn Féin. But it is equally true, as another Unionist put it, that "the advantages of devolved government for Unionists go beyond securing ties with Britain and having achieved an IRA ceasefire and subsequently the beginning of decommissioning."

Making local decisions locally may sound banal, but better representation of farmers and fishermen, and of tourism and other sectors of industry, have brought direct benefits to the people of Northern Ireland, as have the ability to establish direct contacts with Washington and Brussels and open offices there, and the ability to coordinate directly with Dublin the harmonization of cross-border policies. To some extent, the problem for many Unionists is to accept that these are things won in exchange for power sharing, even though they benefit Nationalists and Republicans too. Thus, many Unionists and Loyalists perceive the situation as one in which they have given more and received

less than the Nationalists and Republicans have. It is obviously unhelp-
ful in such a situation when one party, the DUP, because of its lack of
commitment to the power-sharing institutions established in 1998, puts
most of its efforts into discrediting its partners in government and
attempts to prove that the institutions, at least in their current form,
are inoperable and disadvantageous for Unionists and Loyalists. Even
though the DUP has more recently softened its goal from destroying
the institutions to reforming them, it has electorally benefited the most
from Unionist and Loyalist fears about power sharing and consequently
it has done nothing to alleviate these fears.

Thus, the persistence of inter-community differences has exacerbated
intra-community party competition, which since 1998 has hardened
opposition among Unionists and Loyalists to the institutions created
under the Agreement. The lack of Unionist and Loyalist support for
the Agreement remains the gravest threat to its future. This, however,
is not to put all blame on the political elites of the Unionist/Loyalist
community, for Republicans have contributed a great deal to this
community's fears. While there may have been "lack of appreciation
of how significant a step it was for the IRA to actually begin decommissioning," as one Unionist admitted, recent events have made it at
best difficult for Unionists and Loyalists to believe that Republicans
are genuinely committed to peace.

### The Ambiguous Role of the Institutions: Delivering Devolved Government versus Delivering Peace (and Decommissioning)

In contrast to devolution in other parts of the United Kingdom, notably
Scotland and Wales, devolution in Northern Ireland was more a by-
product of conflict resolution than part of a comprehensive devolution
strategy. The fundamental goal of implementing a specific and different
form of devolved government in Northern Ireland was to provide the
framework for a political process in which a conflict about different
conceptions of national belonging could be de-escalated below the
threshold of violence and, in the long term, be fundamentally transformed. This explains the complexity of the institutions in Northern
Ireland and the multitude of safeguards built into their operation.

However, different priorities among the parties committed to the
Agreement, and even more so among all the conflict parties, meant that
early on in the implementation process of the Agreement – and in fact

even before the institutions were properly set up – they had become hostages of a political process in which division and distrust, rather than shared vision and joint commitment, dominated political strategy and tactics. For most Republicans and many Nationalists, the symbolism of the institutions, especially the executive and the North-South Ministerial Council, made them an easy object for political bargaining (or, more cynically speaking, blackmail) in the hands of Unionists. Undoubtedly, this strategy worked to some extent. Each major crisis and each suspension of the institutions resulted in progress on the decommissioning front. However, what has not been seen, or has not been seen clearly enough, is that there was a price to be paid in terms of an increasing disillusionment among Republicans and Nationalists, leading many of them to wonder "whether Unionists will ever share power fairly and accept sitting in government with Nationalists and Republicans," as one Nationalist phrased the widely shared frustration over "Unionist obstructionism."[8]

On the one hand, it is only right and proper that Unionists insist that all parties in government abide by the Mitchell Principles of Non-violence and that "it is unacceptable that one party in government has a private army at its disposal that it can use in the political bargaining process." Yet, regardless of whether and which formal or informal links exist between Sinn Féin and the IRA, the linking of decommissioning to the functioning and survival of the executive, the Assembly, and the North-South Ministerial Council was, in the words of one Loyalist, "a disastrous mistake on the part of Unionism, as it enabled Republicans to determine the pace of progress and blame any lack thereof on Unionists."

From this perspective, the power-sharing institutions in Northern Ireland created under the Agreement have become a "political football used by various parties for anything but the delivery of good governance." The inability to separate the two purposes of devolution – achieving sustainable peace and delivering good governance – sufficiently from one another is particularly felt among parties in the cross-communal space. It has also led to a situation in which both the public perception of the institutions and the views that many senior politicians on both sides of the communal divide have towards them are essentially negative. Ironically, this is so "because the institutions did not achieve what they were not created for."

Trying to turn the institutions into an instrument to achieve decommissioning before delivering governance has dealt several serious blows to the implementation process. It raised hopes among Unionists and Loyalists that were unlikely to be fulfilled in the short term and thus exacerbated their underlying fears of having been sold out to Sinn Féin and the IRA. At the same time, Republican opposition to accepting early on that decommissioning was part of the spirit, if not the letter, of the Agreement has played into the hands of Unionist hardliners.

### The Role of the Governments: Addressing Issues versus Accommodating Parties

It would be unfair, however, to blame only the political parties in Northern Ireland for the successive crises that the Agreement and thus the entire peace process has faced. At the very least, the British government, in its handling of the difficulties of the peace process, has facilitated patterns of political behaviour among the parties in Northern Ireland that were far from conducive to constructive crisis management.

The major criticism that must be levelled at the British government and its partners in Dublin and Washington is that they have absolved the parties in Northern Ireland from taking responsibility for their actions, either individually or collectively. By threatening and executing suspension on four occasions and postponing or cancelling elections to the Northern Ireland Assembly, the government in London took responsibility for the failures of individual parties and politicians, as well as for the institutional shortcomings exacerbated thereby, rather than forcing them to address these in a constructive manner. For example, rather than dealing with the fact that the voting system in the Assembly could all too easily be used to create a deadlock, the Alliance Party was pressured to redesignate three of its members as Unionist to create a large enough "Unionist" majority to elect David Trimble and Mark Durkan as first minister and deputy first minister in November 2001.

The other problematic aspect of British government policy in this context is that the government too often tried to salvage the peace process by making concessions to individual parties. This tactic worked quite well at first, but it also reinforced the behaviour pattern of seeking individual reward for specific parties rather than for collective bodies, such as the executive. By engaging individually with the political parties, the British government undermined any sense of collective responsibility among those sitting together in the executive. While it would obviously be wrong to blame the British government directly for all the problems in the peace process, it is not unrealistic to assume that some of the underlying structural and personal shortcomings could at least have been minimized in their impact by the adoption of different policies. In the end, this might not have prevented the need for a review of the institutions created under the Agreement, but it could have provided for an environment more conducive to such a review's successful conclusion and implementation.

### NORMATIVE CONCERNS AND THEIR PRAGMATIC IMPLICATIONS

The structure of the power-sharing institutions in Northern Ireland raises five principal normative concerns from the point of view of how democratic this system of government actually is. On top of these normative concerns, the lack of some basic democratic mechanisms also has some acute pragmatic implications that cast serious doubt on the long-term sustainability of this system of government.

The first concern relates to the very mechanism of suspension. This is problematic from two angles. First, it was not part of the original Agreement concluded in 1998 but was subsequently rushed through the British Parliament in February 2000 to enable the then secretary of state for Northern Ireland, Peter Mandelson, to suspend the institutions, pre-empting the resignation of David Trimble after just three months in office. Second, it makes a mockery of a political process that supposedly brings government closer to the people of Northern Ireland but in fact depends on the consent of the British government, which at any time can revoke the powers it transferred to the democratically elected politicians in Northern Ireland in institutions that have been approved in a referendum by more than 70 per cent of the people there.

Obviously, on the one hand, the pragmatic rationale behind introducing suspension was to give the British government a means to step in and prevent the serious damage to the peace process that would result from the collapse of the institutions. On the other hand, the existence of this fail-safe device has perhaps not focused the minds of politicians in Northern Ireland hard enough on making the institutions work within the existing framework, and has "allowed the creation of crises in which one could prove that one remained a true believer in the cause, Republican or Unionist."

The second and third normative concerns are closely linked and relate to the peculiar way in which the executive is appointed. While it is normal for power-sharing systems to prescribe cross-communal partic- ipation at least in the executive branch of government, it is less common to find the d'Hondt rule operating in these circumstances. In Northern Ireland, its application means two things: that there is virtually no opposition, certainly no effective opposition, and that it is close to impossible for the electorate to vote the parties that are in government out of it. Earlier, I explained the pragmatic rationale behind this procedural choice, but this does not mean that one should ignore its implications. At the very least, the current arrangement means that there is little real need for a joint program of government and subsequent collective commitment to its implementation.

This and two further normative concerns, namely, a real possibility for the creation of party fiefdoms in individual departments[9] and the *division* rather than the *sharing* of power in the executive, also suggest that there is only limited collective or individual accountability in the executive and that the political process in the institutions is dominated by the executive. While executive domination is generally a feature that is favoured, if not required, by proponents of consociational power sharing, because it allows political elites to make necessary compro- mises without immediately exposing themselves to wider accountability, in the context of Northern Ireland it has had the opposite effect – of making political elites less prepared to compromise. In fact, by effec- tively guaranteeing the same four parties a place in government for the foreseeable future, sectarian divisions in the institutions, and by exten- sion in society, have been entrenched rather than broken down, making compromise across the communal divide not only less necessary and desirable but in fact potentially dangerous in terms of compromising a party's electoral support.

It is the very idea of consociational power sharing to put limits on majoritarian democracy by implementing institutional designs that guarantee minority representation and include safeguards protecting minorities against abuse by majorities. The particular design of insti- tutions in Northern Ireland was an attempt to address the concerns of both communities there. From that perspective, it was a necessary condition for the peace process to move forward. Subsequently, this same design has proved difficult to implement and operate, throwing the future of the entire peace process in doubt.

## THE FUTURE OF POWER-SHARING
## IN NORTHERN IRELAND

*Resolving Existing Problems within the Current Institutional*
*Framework or Renegotiating the Current Framework*
*to Resolve Existing Problems?*

This question was crucially linked to the timing and outcome of the elections in Northern Ireland in November 2003. If the impasse that occurred in 2002 could have been overcome before the elections, it would have allowed the institutions of devolved government to be restored and pro-Agreement parties to be strengthened. However, this did not happen. Instead, a carefully choreographed sequence of events that was supposed to lead to the restoration of devolved government collapsed when the Ulster Unionist Party was not satisfied with the degree of transparency of a crucial round of IRA decommissioning and refused to rejoin the Northern Ireland executive. When the British government went ahead and called the elections anyway, the result was a sea change in the composition of the Northern Ireland Assembly, with the DUP and Sinn Féin emerging as the strongest parties.

Over the following nine months, it proved impossible to put the institutions in Northern Ireland back on track. Intensive negotiations over the summer of 2004 involving the DUP and Sinn Féin (mediated by the British and Irish governments, since the DUP continued to refuse to engage in direct talks with Sinn Féin) led to top-level negotiations at Leeds Castle, Kent, in September. The key problems facing the negotiators were to achieve a complete decommissioning of paramilitary weapons and an end to all paramilitary activity, on the one side, and reforms of the institutions established under the Agreement that would protect the basic bargain achieved in 1998 and at the same time enable the DUP to sit in government with Sinn Féin, on the other. When it emerged that the IRA was prepared to accept decommissioning and an end to its activities, the focus of the negotiations shifted to the DUP's preparedness to play an active and constructive role in the devolved government.

Though no agreement was reached at Leeds Castle, it appears that significant progress was made and that a formula is within reach which might allow the parties to overcome the hurdles still existing before a restoration of the power-sharing institutions in Northern Ireland is possible. In order to do so with better prospects of success than in

previous attempts, however, they will have to address the structural
flaws of the Agreement, with the aim of achieving an inclusive and
representative political process – one that is not devoid of safeguards
and also one in which safeguards cannot be used to destroy the process.

## New Structures for Internal and External Power Sharing?

On the basis of the foregoing analysis, it is possible to point to some
key revisions that are, in my opinion, necessary to ensure greater
stability in any reformed power-sharing institutions in Northern Ireland.
The following remarks are based on the assumption that a restoration
of power-sharing institutions, regardless of their specific design, will be
aimed at resolving the underlying conflict of national belonging
between two communities with diametrically opposed visions in this
respect. This also means that the conflict must be truly settled, in the
sense of giving people a sense of permanence and predictability of their
political future, rather than placing them in a situation in which the
possibility of fundamental change on the basis of a decision taken by
a 50 per cent + 1 "majority" hangs over them like a sword of Damocles.
Achieving that goal will make it necessary to rethink power-sharing
designs both on an internal and on an external level.

On the internal level, two key changes appear to be necessary: in
relation to the d'Hondt rule and to the parliamentary voting system.
For the d'Hondt rule, there are two options: either to scrap it completely or to extend it to the appointment of the first minister and
deputy first minister. Scrapping it would mean that, instead of mandatory representation in the executive of all those parties with a sufficiently high number of votes, a voluntary coalition would be able to
run Northern Ireland with only one condition imposed on it, namely,
that it be a cross-community body (i.e., include at least one party from
each of the two communities). This would greatly enhance the accountability of ministers to the Assembly and also to the electorate, and it
would mean that a sense of collective responsibility within the executive
would be strengthened. It would also increase opportunities for the
smaller cross-community parties and at the same time create an effective opposition in the Assembly. Such a redesign would have to be
complemented by provisions for a constructive vote-of-no-confidence.
Yet, despite some of its apparent advantages, significant parts of the
current political elite in Northern Ireland would find it difficult to go
down this path.

The alternative to scrapping the d'Hondt procedure is to extend it to the appointment of first minister and deputy first minister. Again, this would have to be complemented by the qualification that the strongest party overall nominates its candidate for the position of first minister, while the strongest party in the other community nominates its candidate for deputy first minister. This way, representation in the two posts remains cross-communal (i.e., even if the two strongest parties overall are from within the same community, each community will obtain only one of the two top posts). This might be more appealing to Sinn Féin and the DUP, in that it would not require them to vote for each other's candidate, as is the case under present arrangements. The UUP, too, might find this aspect attractive, especially if the party believes that it stands a good chance of recovering its former position by outperforming the DUP at the next elections. For the SDLP, this scenario is clearly the least promising in terms of its future participation in government, if, as is generally predicted, Sinn Féin maintains its lead in the next Assembly elections. However, the problem with this change lies elsewhere, namely, that the parties would have to agree to it and agree to deliver their constituencies with them. With the clear implication that this might give Sinn Féin not only renewed representation in the executive but also one of the two top posts within it, any Unionist leader would be hard pressed to sign and sell such a deal. Nevertheless, in combination with some of the other reforms suggested below, this could be a possible way forward, since it would reflect an increasing desire for stronger separation among significant parts of Northern Ireland's population and their political representatives.

In terms of changing parliamentary voting procedures, it would be a constructive step forward if the parallel consent mechanism for key decisions was removed and replaced by qualified majority voting, with a sufficiently high threshold (e.g., three-fifths or two-thirds of Assembly members present and voting). This would still ensure that no decision could be taken against significant opposition in one of the two communities. It would also mean that the principle of designation could be removed – a small but significant symbolic step towards breaking down sectarian divisions in the Assembly.

In order to increase their acceptability and long-term contribution towards lasting peace in Northern Ireland, these reforms of power sharing at the internal level would have to be combined with revisions of the current arrangements at the external level. Though potentially an explosive issue in the short run, if the United Kingdom and the

Republic of Ireland formally moved to some form of joint authority over Northern Ireland,[10] in the long run an additional level of safeguards would be established for both communities, something that they are unlikely to achieve under the current institutional design. While that design includes a mechanism for potentially changing the constitutional status of Northern Ireland from membership in the United Kingdom to unification with the Republic of Ireland, Nationalists and Republicans can never be sure that they will muster the necessary majority to achieve this, nor can Unionists and Loyalists be sure that they will always have enough support to prevent it from happening. Thus, formal external power sharing, if added to a revised internal formula, would accomplish two things: it would make internal revisions less painful by adding another layer of governance addressing community-specific concerns, and it would establish a sense of (satisfactory) permanence, predictability, and security for both communities, regardless of any actual or impending changes in the demographic balance between them. Combined with the proposed revisions at the internal level, this would also facilitate further separation of the two communities and simultaneously aid their closer individual integration into the nation-states of their choice (i.e., the United Kingdom and the Republic of Ireland). Such a revised combination of internal and external power sharing would therefore actually address the underlying conflict of national belonging in a much more effective way than either form of power sharing can on its own. Both forms may individually be able to contain the conflict in a relatively effectively way over some period of time, but the history of conflict resolution in Northern Ireland, from Sunningdale to the Anglo-Irish Agreement and to the Agreement of 1998, shows that there are limits in their ability to make a significant contribution to its long-term resolution. This is perhaps the most important lesson to draw from the current crisis and the previous failures, and its implications should be seriously considered if power sharing is indeed to have a future in Northern Ireland.


NOTES

1 Rather than engaging in a debate over whether it should be called the "Good Friday Agreement" or the "Belfast Agreement," I will simply use "Agreement" whenever making reference to this document.

2 This analysis draws largely on research conducted in Northern Ireland during the summer and autumn of 2002, and in some sections on previously published work. I am grateful to many people in Northern Ireland, London, Dublin, and Washington for allowing me to interview them, notably, John Alderdice, Quentin Davies, David Ervine, Stephen Farry, David Ford, Eilis Haughey, Colin Irwin, Steven King, Allan Leonard, Patricia Lewesley, Chris McCartney, David McClarty, Ned Nolan, and Peter Weir. Six individuals in different locations wished to remain anonymous.

3 For studies of the background to and details of the Agreement, see John McGarry and Brendan O'Leary, *The Northern Ireland Conflict: Consociational Engagements* (Oxford, U.K.: Oxford University Press 2004), chapter 9; Jörg Neuheiser and Stefan Wolff, ed., *Peace at Last? The Impact of the Good Friday Agreement on Northern Ireland* (New York and Oxford, U.K.: Berghahn 2003); Rick Wilford, ed., *Aspects of the Belfast Agreement* (Oxford, U.K.: Oxford University Press 2001); and Stefan Wolff, *Disputed Territories: The Transnational Dynamics of Ethnic Conflict Settlements* (New York and Oxford, U.K.: Berghahn 2003), chapter 7.

4 The d'Hondt system, named after its nineteenth-century Belgian inventor, Victor d'Hondt, is a proportional method of allocating seats or offices to parties by means of sequential choices. For a discussion of this method and its application in Northern Ireland, see Brendan O'Leary, Bernard Grofman, and Jorgen Elkit, "Divisor Methods for Sequential Portfolio Allocation in Multi-party Executive Bodies," *American Journal of Political Science*, 49:1 (2005): 198–211.

5 The cross-communal space is ambivalent. Even though the two main parties in it, the Alliance Party and the Women's Coalition, do not define themselves exclusively but rather aspire to bridge the communal divide, their political outlook mostly favours the retention of the existing constitutional links with Great Britain.

6 A set of six principles set forth in the 1996 Report of the Committee on Decommissioning chaired by U.S. Senator George Mitchell. Acceptance of these principles committed the negotiating parties to peaceful and democratic means of resolving political issues and the total, independently verifiable disarmament of all paramilitary organizations.

7 The department of the British government responsible for Northern Ireland affairs, with offices in London and Belfast. It is headed by the secretary of state for Northern Ireland, a British cabinet minister.

8 The illegal banning of Sinn Féin ministers from attending meetings of the North-South Ministerial Council imposed by First Minister David Trimble is perhaps the most obvious example in support of this view.

9 The problem of party fiefdoms could be relatively easily resolved if the Assembly committees assigned to each of the executive departments took a more active role in monitoring ministerial performance.

10 On this widely under-researched mechanism of conflict resolution, see Stefan Wolff, *Disputed Territories*. On its application to Northern Ireland, see Brendan O'Leary et al., *Northern Ireland: Sharing Authority* (London: Institute for Public Policy Research 1993).

# 3

# Significant Events in the Northern Ireland Peace Process: Impact and Implementation[1]

## LANDON E. HANCOCK

Despite continuing political difficulties over the implementation of the Belfast Agreement of 1998, the peace process that led to the Agreement remains very much alive. It is particularly notable that not even the British government's suspension of the Northern Ireland Assembly in October 2002 and the postponement of new elections led to an abrogation of the ceasefire and the resumption of hostilities. This suggests that the peace process in Northern Ireland has acquired a degree of resilience that is conspicuously lacking in other peace processes where post-agreement difficulties have led to the resumption of violence – as in the aftermath of the failed Oslo Accord. If research can identify which events in the peace process have helped to bring about this resilience, and why, it might be possible to apply the findings to other peace processes and power-sharing agreements, current and future.

The purpose of this chapter is to examine the various events associated with the peace process in Northern Ireland[2] to determine which had the most impact on the day-to-day lives of the general population. The nature and quality of these "significant" events will then be examined in the light of their impact on the social atmosphere and social structure, especially with respect to post-conflict peace building and implementation. The general argument is that, for an event to have a significant impact, it must affect the population both at the moment of its announcement and over time through some form of implementation.

## A NOTE ON METHODS AND TERMINOLOGY

The data for this analysis are derived from three sources: a small series of in-depth, open-ended interviews with local community representatives from both sides of the conflict; a collection of editorials and some opinion pieces from Northern Ireland's two morning dailies, the Belfast *News Letter* and the *Irish News*, spanning the course of the peace process from August 1994 to October 2001; and the results from the community relations sections of attitudes surveys conducted by the Social and Community Planning Research (SCPR) group and the Northern Ireland Life and Times (NILT) from 1989 to 2000.

The reasoning behind the use of three different sets of data is to allow the strengths of each set to help compensate for the weaknesses of the other two. The interviews were designed to collect a great deal of rich data about the impact of significant events in terms of how much the community was affected and what types of impact were more prevalent. The editorial data were designed to determine the impact of certain events in terms of communal response, given the notion that certain newspapers both reflect the values of their readership community and attempt to direct those values on occasion.[3] The survey data were designed to measure the impact of events on the general populace, in effect testing whether the events uncovered by the interview and editorial analyses could be generalized to the entire population. Overall, the survey collection consists of nine separate surveys conducted by two groups. The first subset is the Northern Ireland Social Attitudes (NISA) survey, which was run as a subset of the British Social Attitudes (BSA) survey. The second subset, the Northern Ireland Life and Times survey, was created as a joint project between Queen's University Belfast and the University of Ulster.

## INTERVIEW RESULTS

The interviews concentrated on respondents' perception of which events were most important to the political, social, and personal aspects of the peace process. The three types of event are defined as event, policy, and agreement. The purpose of these distinctions is to differentiate between single things that happened, a plan of action implemented by a party, and an agreement between two or more parties. The level of impact reflects whether a particular event had a political impact on the process, a social impact on the everyday lives of the general population, or a personal impact on the respondent or someone close to the respondent.

A rough content analysis of the interview responses reveals that the most significant event was the 1994 paramilitary ceasefires. The most significant policy appears to have been the decision to release the paramilitary prisoners. However, this response may have been skewed because of the close affiliation of several interview subjects with the ex-prisoner movement, possibly leaving the Patten Report on policing as the most significant policy. The most significant agreement by far was the Belfast Agreement,[4] with the Anglo-Irish Accord of 1985 a distant second.

In terms of impact, the Belfast Agreement, ceasefires, and the Patten Report tie for first. However, several interview responses indicated that, while the ceasefires may have had a large initial impact, their impact faded over time as normalization took place. For instance, one respondent stated that she[5] had forgotten about the impact of the ceasefires, while another lamented that people forgot about how far they had come because of the time involved and the slow pace of change. Additionally, two interview subjects, when commenting on the significance of the ceasefires, indicated that the withdrawal of British forces from the streets of Belfast, and to a lesser extent across the province, provided a powerful follow-up impact to the ceasefires. Therefore, it seems reasonable to include the demilitarization and normalization results in the ceasefire results (as the former were directly precipitated by the latter), which makes the ceasefires the number-one event. Also, the withdrawal of British forces and the removal of checkpoints were responses to the success of the ceasefires in dampening violence. This link between the two is alluded to by Roger MacGinty and John Darby, who note that "the ending of mainstream paramilitary violence led to the relaxation of some security measures and improvements in the quality of life, particularly in those areas hardest hit by the violence."[6] Therefore, it is reasonable to assume that the demilitarization would not have taken place without the ceasefires, and thus these effects can be lumped together to some extent in our analysis.

Although the evidence suggests that the ceasefires were the most significant event in terms of affecting daily lives, the overwhelming preponderance of responses identifying the Belfast Agreement in the personal and political areas suggests that the Agreement may be either

more significant or equally significant, with some difference in the type
of impact. It therefore seems prudent, when moving to some of the
descriptive responses, to examine respondents' reasons for choosing the
Agreement alongside the reasons given for choosing the ceasefires.

For the ceasefires, there were a number of interesting comments
regarding their perceived political, social, and personal impact. One
respondent stated:

Personally, I give thanks for the ceasefires, because while we have a somewhat
imperfect peace if you like this past seven or eight years, I would prefer to
look at it more positively ... there's a lot of people alive today who would
probably otherwise be dead, had the ceasefires not been in place. And I get
frustrated sometimes at politicians continually sniping at the imperfect nature
of the ceasefires, if you like. But surely you have to take consolation in the
fact that, imperfect though they may be, they're better than what went before.

Another respondent indicated that the ceasefires were "the point that
turned things from an extremely negative situation to a very positive
one," politically, socially, and personally. Going on to describe the
social impact, she said:

Within three or four days there was a great sense of relief and I think that
went right through all communities in Northern Ireland. And so the impact of
it in society's terms was one of a sigh of relief ... The second impact was to
engender, for the first time in a long time, hope. And the third effect was to
start to create expectation of a different life. So the hope and expectation were
for people at a personal level, a family level, and at a community and society
level, of hope that this would be it, if I remember rightly the feeling at the
time. That this would stick, that this would be the end of fear and violence.
And on the other side it was hope of a better quality of life. And probably
expressed in many ways through peoples' hope for their children. That there
would be a new future there, of freedom from fear, freedom from violence and
expectation of a better future.

A third respondent concurred, adding that "it was the first time in my
life that I was ever going to be able to live without fear of getting
bombed or shot."

The main recurring theme here is the great sense of relief, and the
lifting of a sense of fear, that everyone felt. Although the ceasefires did

not end all of the violence, and although "punishment" attacks continued, the feeling that one would be randomly targeted for no more
reason than one's communal affiliation did end, bringing with it this
sense of relief and some optimism for the future.

The sentiments expressed about the impact of the Agreement were
similar regarding optimism for the future, but without the overall lessening of fear or sense of relief that were imparted by the ceasefires. One
respondent noted: "The Good Friday Agreement has had the biggest
impact, certainly in my lifetime, on people in Northern Ireland. There
are those of us who are very much in favour of the Agreement [who]
were given a great sense of euphoria that this was the beginning of the
end. People would have mechanisms by which we could resolve our differences." Some respondents pointed to the importance of the referendum
on the Agreement. Since it was held about a month after the signing, on
22 May, it gave the population a sense of ownership that had been lacking in previous agreements. As one respondent noted, the Agreement was
important "because it was done by the people. What I mean by that is
that is it was voted on by the people. It was our first, I mean. Up until
then the Anglo-Irish Agreement was imposed, by both governments ...
so it was a softening up to see how people would react to it."

Another respondent put it best when she described the most significant
events as "the double thing of the ceasefires and the Good Friday Agreement." When asked to explain why, she replied: "The ceasefires were
significant in that they broke with the past of violence, not necessarily
for good. But they were a major threshold. Therefore, if you interpret
peace as being the absence of violence, which it's not, they had incred-
ible significance. And they opened the door on the possibility of a way
forward. The Good Friday Agreement structured, described, put into a
political context and political possibility that way forward. So it was
like, if you want, the ceasefires were the beginning of the end and the
Good Friday Agreement was the end of the beginning."

## EDITORIAL RESULTS

In order to verify the results from the interview pool, this section
provides a content analysis of the editorial data using the series of
events, policies, and agreements uncovered by the interviews. For each
editorial, only the first time the sought-out phrase appeared in the text
was counted. In addition, for events with more than one name, a second

Table 1
Comparison of interview and editorial counts

| Event/Item | Interviews | Editorials | Event/Item |
|---|---|---|---|
| Good Friday Agreement | 22 | 318 | Ceasefires |
| Ceasefires | 8 | 280 | Good Friday Agreement |
| Patten & Policing | 5 | 61 | Patten & Policing |
| Prisoner Releases | 5 | 24 | Omagh Bombing |
| Anglo-Irish Accord | 3 | 23 | Anglo-Irish Accord |
| Omagh Bombing | 1 | 10 | Prisoner Releases |
| Quinn Brothers Murder | 1 | 3 | Quinn Brothers Murder |

Table 2
Pearson correlation of interview and editorial-event counts

| | | Interview Count | Editorial Count |
|---|---|---|---|
| Interview Count | Pearson Correlation | 1 | .773* |
| | Sig. (2-tailed) | | .041 |
| | N | 7 | 7 |
| Editorial Count | Pearson Correlation | .773* | 1 |
| | Sig. (2-tailed) | .041 | |
| | N | 7 | 7 |

* Correlation is significant at the 0.05 level (2-tailed).

name was added to the search (for instance, "the Good Friday Agreement" and "the Belfast Agreement"). The term "policing" was included as an alternative in the search on the Patten Report to make sure that all instances dealing with the issue of police reform were found. The overall results of this content analysis are shown in Table 1, which shows the number of editorials that mention each event at least once from August 1994 to October 2001, alongside the results gained from the interviews. The differences in Table 1 show that the ceasefires are transposed with the Agreement as the number-one and number-two events, while the prisoner releases and the Omagh bombing are transposed as the number-four and number-six events. A possible reason behind the transposition of the prisoner releases and the Omagh bombing was alluded to above, namely, that the interview pool may have been prejudiced towards seeing the prisoner release issue as more prominent. The transposition of the ceasefires and the Agreement does little to negate the findings of Table 2, which shows a significant correlation of .773 (p < .05, n = 7) between the interview and editorial counts of the events.

It can therefore be said with some degree of confidence that the first two events listed in both the interview and the editorial counts – the paramilitary ceasefires and the Agreement – were likely to be the two most significant events of the peace process. In order to determine this further, the next section will turn to the analysis of large-scale attitude surveys to see if the interview and editorial patterns are reflected in the wider society. Before we do so, however, it is interesting to note some of the references the editorials made regarding the top two events and how these references echo some of the interview statements.

For the ceasefires, there are two editorials that are interesting. This is because they are both from the predominantly Protestant newspaper, the Belfast *News Letter*, both describe an aspect of the daily impact of the ceasefires, and both were written some four and six months after the implementation of the ceasefires. The first appeared on 13 January 1995 and was entitled "Another Sign of Normality." It stated:

The announcement by the Chief Constable Sir Hugh Annesley that army patrols will be removed from the streets of Belfast during daylight is official confirmation of what has become, by a gradual process, normal practice since the ceasefire announcements ...

The withdrawal of troops to barracks is a sensible decision, so long as the security forces remain willing and able to counter any renewed threat of terrorism or to react speedily to events which endanger the security of the country or put individuals at risk.

This editorial shows support for the demilitarization effort that followed the ceasefires, but that support was tempered by the caution that the security forces remain able to return to the streets if necessary. This caution was also evident in the next major editorial on the same subject, which appeared on 25 March. It begins with the following announcement: "For the first time in 25 years, troops will be off the streets of Belfast from today onwards. Only time will tell whether the decision by security chiefs is a wise one, but there can be little doubt that it is yet another sign of rapidly changing times in the city."

The editorial cautions that the move may be a "sop" to Sinn Féin but adds, as before, that the army should be available if needed. The one very interesting point for my analysis is in the final paragraph, which states: "In the meantime, most people will agree that the ceasefires have created a new environment for everyone in Northern Ireland.

People who have longed for peace for 25 years are optimistic that the peace will hold. The freedom from violence and the absence of troops on the streets are fully compatible with that new optimism." Clearly, more than just a few interview participants felt that the cease-fires had a positive impact on their lives and on Northern Irish society as a whole.

In terms of the Agreement, there was a similar outpouring of enthusiasm for its possibilities, tempered with distrust of the opposing side and sometimes of politicians in general. For the Protestant side, the *News Letter* concentrated on the democratic aspect of the Agreement, promoting it as the only workable solution, despite difficulties in its implementation. For example, the following editorial from 23 February 2000 addresses both issues:

Every Ulster Prod who voted Yes to the Good Friday Agreement was accepting the primacy of the democratic process, and endorsing the view that if a majority at any stage wish it to be so, then and only then will Ireland be united, regardless of their personal preference.

The Good Friday Agreement, which does much to encourage a sense of allegiance among northern Catholics while institutionalising closer co-operation and understanding between the two entities, remains the best formula yet devised for ending centuries of debilitating antagonism between two significant cultures sharing one small island.

The mainly Catholic newspaper, the *Irish News,* was consistently more upbeat in its coverage of the Agreement, calling for a strong "yes" vote in the referendum. In an editorial that appeared on 21 May (the day before the referendum), the *Irish News* promoted the Agreement as the path to peace and reconciliation, benefiting both communities: "For arguably the first time in the history of the state, there is a realistic possibility of those of all religions and none uniting behind a common aim. The cause is that of peace and reconciliation, and there are overwhelming grounds for believing that it can be achieved through the vehicle of the Good Friday agreement." After discrediting attacks on the Agreement and its supporters by anti-Agreement forces, most notably the Reverend Ian Paisley, the editorial concluded:

In any event, it is much more appropriate to concentrate on the positive benefits which the entire community will receive from the ratification of the Good Friday agreement.

The referendum amounts to a choice between retreating into the shadows of bitterness and marching confidently into a fresh era in which new relationships can be constructed.

Reaching an accommodation between different traditions can never be an easy process, but an equitable solution is within our grasp. A strong yes vote tomorrow is the key.

It is clear that both newspapers see the Agreement as a watershed event, one that has the potential to transform Northern Irish society and to set the stage for the long-term peace which had, until that point, eluded both peacemakers and ordinary citizens.

## SURVEY RESULTS

The interview and editorial results suggest that the ceasefires and the Agreement were the most significant events of the peace process. However, to explore this argument further, we will examine the survey data using longitudinal analysis to determine whether some years showed more significant changes in attitudes than others.

When we look back at the results from the interviews and editorials, some clues regarding which questions might be more useful to examine come to light. In both the interview and editorial data, the ceasefires are described as reducing or removing a climate of fear and having an impact on the social atmosphere. The descriptions were sharp and focused when describing the lessening of the sense of fear, but they were more diffuse when describing the creation of a sense of hope. This may be because a ceasefire is an absence of violence, not a positive plan for resolving conflict or rebuilding society. The type of change that could affect the sense of hope more significantly is one that provides structures for governance and for future relations between the two communities.

In order to explore this idea more fully, it was necessary to choose questions from the surveys that express perceptions of both a change in atmosphere and changes in political structures. To test whether the significance of the paramilitary ceasefires uncovered by the interview and editorial data can be generalized to the wider population, this section will first examine three questions drawn from the community relations portion of the attitudes surveys:

1  whether the respondent believes that current relations between Protestants and Catholics are better, worse, or the same as five years in the past;

Table 3
Analysis of variance across 1994 ceasefires

|                                              | N | F      | Significance |
|----------------------------------------------|---|--------|--------------|
| Relations are better than 5 years ago        | 9 | 60.532 | <.001        |
| Relations will be better 5 years from now    | 9 | 17.018 | 0.004        |
| Religion will always make a difference       | 9 | 4.855  | 0.063        |

2 whether the respondent believes that relations between Protestants and Catholics five years into the future will be better, worse, or the same as current relations; and

3 whether the respondent believes that religion will always make a difference in the way people feel about each other.

Of these three questions, the first two examine the nature of the current social atmosphere, and the third speaks more to the social structural elements because of the way that religious identity has been embedded in aspects of Northern Irish society and in the conflict. In other words, for religion to become less important, certain imbalances in the educational systems and access to jobs would have to change, not just atmospheric changes leading to less fear on the streets. Therefore, it seems likely that, if the ceasefires prove significant, this would be reflected more in the questions addressing atmospheric changes than in those addressing structural changes.

It is clear from the responses in Table 3 that 1994 constituted a watershed year for changes in perceptions regarding inter-communal relations. Table 3 shows the results of an analysis of variance (ANOVA) for answers to these three questions across the break-point of the 1994 ceasefires. In this ANOVA, as with all of the others used in this chapter, the variance in responses within the two sets of answers, before and after the break-point, is compared to the variance in answers across the break-point. A statistically significant finding indicates a long-term change in responses across, or after, any selected break-point. The ANOVA for the response to question 3 – that yes, religion would always make a difference – shows a significance of .063 (n = 9), indicating no significant change. However, the ANOVAs for the other two measurements are a significant .004 (n = 9), indicating a sharp upward shift in the percentage of people who subsequently believed that relations would improve, and a highly significant <.001 (n = 9), indicating a strong upward shift in the percentage of people who subsequently believed that relations had improved. In sum, the paramilitary ceasefires proved to be a significant break-point in attitudes regarding relations between Catholics and Protestants, with both questions 1 and 2 reflecting a perceived improvement and the expectation of a continued improvement in inter-communal relations. The lack of a significant change in the responses to question 3 indicates that this perception of improvement had more strength in the area of an improvement in the social atmosphere than in the area of an improvement in social structures relating to inter-communal relations.

An investigation of the Agreement's significance to the general populace calls for a different type of question than those used to investigate the significance of the paramilitary ceasefires. Given that the Agreement codifies political relations between the two communities and affects both the structure of Northern Irish society and the rules by which the province may change its constitutional status, it seemed appropriate to focus on questions surrounding Northern Ireland's status within the United Kingdom and the possibility of its reunification with the Republic of Ireland.

The questions chosen for this analysis were:

4 What is your preferred long-term policy for the future of Northern Ireland?
5 How likely do you think a united Ireland will be in the next 20 years? ·

For question 4, the choices were to remain in the United Kingdom, to reunify with Ireland, or to create an independent state. For question 5, the choices ranged from very likely, quite likely, even chance, quite unlikely, and very unlikely. As with the choices available in all of the survey questions, the ranges represented in these questions indicate that, to some extent, an increase in one answer will result in a decrease in others. Therefore, this analysis will concentrate only on those changes that are most pertinent, reflecting a shift in attitudes at odds with existing communal expectations.

Regarding question 4, on Northern Ireland's long-term preferred policy, there are two interesting findings. Table 4 shows a significant drop in those preferring to remain in the United Kingdom and a significant rise in those preferring to create an independent state, indicating a possible willingness among some Protestants to reunify eventually with the Republic of Ireland.

Table 4
Analysis of variance across 1998 agreement

|  | F | Significance |
|---|---|---|
| Prefer a long-term policy of remaining in UK | 12.937 | 0.009 |
| Prefer a long-term policy of independent state | 69.897 | <.001 |
| Believe a United Ireland quite unlikely in 20 yrs | 28.969 | 0.001 |
| Believe an even chance of a United Ireland in 20 yrs | 19.945 | 0.003 |

Table 4 shows a clear change in belief and in preference regarding the structural future of Northern Ireland, based on the results of an analysis of variance test on four variables using the 1998 Agreement as the break-point. The significant shifts upward in the independent-state preference and downward in the United Kingdom preference (<.001 and .009 respectively, n = 9) indicate a direct change in preference from one to the other, as noted by the insignificant finding of .081 (n = 9) in the remaining choice of reunification with Ireland. If we look at the results from question 5, the belief that such reunification would take place took a dramatic shift upward, as evidenced by the significant (.001, n = 9) decrease in the belief that a united Ireland was quite unlikely and the (.003, n = 9) increase in the belief that there was an even chance of the creation of a united Ireland in the next twenty years.

The analyses of variance tests show that there were two significant changes that correspond both in time and in type with the most significant events as outlined by the interview and editorial results. These findings support the earlier findings that the ceasefires and the Agreement were the most significant events in the peace process in terms of their impact on the general population. The meaning of their impact will be covered in the next section.

## ANALYSIS

It seems clear that each of the events studied has had a significant impact on the perceptions and attitudes of Northern Ireland's populace. However, it does appear that the focus of the effect was different for each event. For the paramilitary ceasefires, the most significant impact was on the perceptions of improved relations between Catholics and Protestants, followed by a lesser impact on the perception of the course of Northern Ireland's future. In definitional terms, the impact of the ceasefires could be said to be more atmospheric (affecting the social atmosphere) than structural (affecting the social and political structure).

For the Agreement, the strength of significant measurements is reversed. In definitional terms, therefore, the impact of the Agreement could be said to be the opposite of that of the ceasefires, namely, that the Agreement had more impact on the social and political structure and less on the social atmosphere. So what we can see here is that the ceasefires had a stronger social impact on everyday life while the Agreement has had a stronger impact on the perception of a viable future. In some sense, this difference in emphasis of impact reflects the earlier quote from one of the interviews that the ceasefires were the "beginning of the end" and the Agreement was the "end of the beginning."

The ceasefires produced an environment wherein peace could be pursued by creating a sense of hope and a return to a kind of normality in everyday life that had not existed for twenty-five years. According to several of the interview subjects, the ceasefires engendered an immediate sense of hope and relief. Their longer-term impact was in engendering a sense of normality that was reinforced by the British government's response of pulling the army off of the streets and lifting some of the more onerous and visible security responses. Examples of this include the reduction of security checkpoints and random searches in city centres and the removal of barriers from in front of some police and army stations.

It is possible to see why the impact of the ceasefires was felt more in the realm of improved inter-communal relations than in perceptions of Northern Ireland's future. As the "beginning of the end," the ceasefires had much more of an impact on everyday life and interaction, while doing little to address the structural issues of how Northern Ireland was to be governed and how people would participate in that governance to make their lives better in the future. The hope that they would be able to do so was certainly created, but there was still uncertainty about how that hope would be realized.

By contrast, the signing of the Agreement spoke directly to the structural issues of how Northern Ireland would be governed and how Protestants and Catholics would resolve inter-communal differences in the future. Therefore, it is understandable that the most significant changes are visible in responses to questions regarding the future of Northern Ireland and its long-term preferred policy.

Conversely, the impact of the Agreement on daily life was much less than that of the ceasefires. Eventually, the implementation of the Agreement, including the convening of the Northern Ireland Assembly and Executive, would – if successful – allow for a long-unheard local voice in government affairs. But, at the time of the signing of the Agreement and the subsequent referendum, these were only promises for the future.

## IMPACT AND IMPLEMENTATION

According to the results of our analysis, the primary impact of the ceasefires was on the social atmosphere while the primary impact of the Agreement was on the social and political structure. What this means is that, although the atmospheric impact of the ceasefires was positive in terms of a reduction of general fear and relief, translating into some perception of improved future relations between the two communities, this atmospheric impact was not enough to "build forward upon." Essentially, the space generated by the ceasefires was necessary for the transformation of Northern Ireland's environment to one that would make the Agreement possible; but, without the Agreement, the ceasefires themselves could not sustain the peace or create a new society. The ceasefires, as one interview respondent put it, brought a sense of relief and a sense of hope – hope that at long last there could be peace in Northern Ireland.

By contrast, the importance of the Agreement was to create a framework that people could use to translate their sense of hope into an action plan for the future. As one interview respondent put it: "You know you can't reconcile an Irish republic to Britain, but I feel the Good Friday Agreement, complex though it is, it does offer the best way of peaceful coexistence ... People would have mechanisms by which we could resolve our differences." The Agreement was consistently described as something that was "imperfect" – not an end in itself but a vehicle that could help the two parties resolve their continuing differences in a peaceful manner. The Agreement was described as creating a new structure, a new set of politics, and as "our Magna Carta" – all references to a break with past structures and the creation of new structures by which the two communities could govern themselves and interact peacefully. Along with these sentiments, several respondents and editorials referred to the Agreement as a "chance for peace," suggesting that it was seen as part of a continuing process –

and that once it had been signed and approved, people would still have to expend effort to "make it work."

Essentially, the lessons of this inquiry are that a successful peace process seems to require events with certain qualities. Events should have both atmospheric and structural qualities to change both the social atmosphere and the social and political structure. Atmospheric events help to create the space for the impact of structural events. And both types of events seem to require not just a significant impact on a large segment of the population at the time when they occur but also an extended period of implementation to allow the first blush of that impact to sink in and have a long-term effect.

In terms of measurement, we can see that the significant results of the associated analyses of variance represent not only an immediate impact but also the longer-term impact of the successful implementation of an event, like the Belfast Agreement, or the long-term impact of normalization that resulted from the paramilitary ceasefires. We can thus conjecture that, of necessity, to be successful, an event or policy must not only have an immediate impact but also produce a sustained effort to maintain that impact and, one hopes, to translate it into popular support for the peace process.

## NORMALIZATION AND IDENTITY SALIENCE

The normalization that resulted from the ceasefires was one of the key factors leading to a changed environment. Within this changed environment there was a reduction in the threat perceived physically by individuals and existentially to the diametrically opposed communal identities held by most of the population. With the reduction in threat, individuals indicated that they no longer felt the need to defend these identities and were thus free to engage in other activities and allow other roles or identities to assume more importance in their daily lives. This process is described by Sheldon Stryker and Robert T. Serpe as identity-widening.[7] That is, it allows for a shift in identity-salience hierarchies, with a reduction in conflict-oriented communal identities vis-à-vis their more neutral subnational counterparts.

The reduction in personal threat engendered by the ceasefires was strengthened and codified by the structure of the Agreement, which provided a legal framework that was designed to protect both communal identities and allow for differences to be resolved in an atmosphere of safety and security for both communities. This codification of identity-protection in the Agreement helps to secure the reordering of identity-salience hierarchies, protecting the gains made by the ceasefires and contributing to a social sense of de-escalation – even if that sense is not reflected by the political parties.

## CAUTIONS AND RECOMMENDATIONS

It appears that the peace process in Northern Ireland has been generally successful in generating a sense of support through the enacting of specific measures that affect the everyday lives of the general population and through long-term implementation efforts. Although the events described here do not represent the transformation of the conflict, or the transformation of relationships between the two communities, they could represent the beginning of such a transformation.

In order to maintain support for the peace process and to provide the space for further shifts in identity salience – and, ideally, conflict trans-formation – the government of Northern Ireland should focus on two specific policy aims. The first should be to reduce the focus on highly contentious concerns, such as decommissioning and police reform, and to increase the focus on the bread-and-butter issues of education, jobs, and health care. The highly contentious issues are not going to disappear, nor are they going to become easier to solve. However, the more the politicians from leading parties continue to predicate their partici-pation in government on these issues, to the detriment of bread-and-butter ones, the more they will tend to contribute to a sense that the peace process is stalling instead of moving forward.[8]

A second major policy area that should be tackled by political actors at all levels is the increasing perception on the part of the Loyalist community that it is not benefiting equally from the peace process. In line with the findings, one can argue that some of the economic benefits following normalization and deriving from the peace process are a form of implementation. Therefore, the growing perception by Protestants that they are not benefiting enough economically from the peace pro-cess may be a part of the reason why the Loyalist enclaves in North and East Belfast continue to be flashpoints of violence. It is not so much the reality of monetary or economic benefits that are of issue in this case; it is the perception by these communities that they are being left out or exploited for political or economic gain, often by middle-class

Unionist politicians. The overwhelming sentiment in these communities is that they were on the front lines of the fight during the Troubles but, after doing the "dirty work," they have been tossed aside.[9] A concentrated effort to assist these communities, especially from a participatory and information-eliciting standpoint, could go a long way towards ameliorating feelings of alienation and persuading Loyalists that they have a future in a new Northern Ireland.

### LESSONS FOR OTHER PEACE PROCESSES

While circumstances in other conflicts and other peace processes are too varied to make specific recommendations, a few general lessons may be drawn. First and foremost, it should be recognized that, in order to secure the support of the population for any peace process, the public needs to feel the positive effects of that process on a daily basis. This usually means a return to – or the creation of – a sense of normal life, with a reduced level of threat to the communal identities of all sides. Differing circumstances in different conflicts will determine the type of impact sought or available, but some generalizations can be made. The first is that, for any ceasefire to have a long-term impact, it should be followed as rapidly as possible by some form of normalization. This would probably entail the removal of some security forces from the streets and the dismantling or scaling back of checkpoints and security sweeps. While it could be argued that security "demobilization" only plays into the hands of spoiler groups, it could also be argued that continuing high levels of security would probably do little to deter spoilers and would fail to convince the subordinate community that positive changes are permanent.

A second generalization has to do with the types of agreements made and their relation to the communal identities of the parties to the conflict. One of the key effects of the Belfast Agreement was to lessen the threat felt to communal identities by most of the Catholic/Nationalist/ Republican community and much of the Protestant/Unionist/Loyalist community. The idea that both these communal identities were given explicit legitimacy within the framework of the Agreement allowed these identities to be reduced in salience vis-à-vis other less polarized identities. While terms of normalization may differ greatly depending on circumstance, policy makers should pay attention to the identity needs of communities in conflict and attempt to address these needs in a manner that reduces the perceived threat to the identities of these communities. Finally, policy makers should try to take into account the needs of the communities at large, and not just the political activists who support the parties at the table, because the support of a majority of all of the people is needed in order to sustain any peace process over the long haul.

## NOTES

1 The research for this chapter was supported by a Peace Scholar award from the United States Institute of Peace. The views expressed are those of the author and do not necessarily reflect the views of the Institute of Peace.

2 For further studies of the Northern Ireland peace process, see John Darby and Roger MacGinty, "Northern Ireland: Long Cold Peace," in John Darby and Roger MacGinty, ed., *The Management of Peace Processes* (London and New York: Oxford University Press 2000); Sean Farren and Robert F. Mulvihill, *Paths to a Settlement in Northern Ireland* (Gerrards Cross, U.K.: Colin Smythe 2000); and Eamonn Maillie and David McKittrick, *Endgame in Ireland* (London: Coronet Books 2002).

3 Adriana Bolívar, "The structure of Newspaper Editorials," in M. Coulthard, ed., *Advances in Written Text Analysis* (London: Routledge 1994).

4 The Belfast Agreement is also commonly called the Good Friday Agreement. The former is used here, except in direct quotes from interview responses or other sources.

5 In order to protect the identity of respondents, the female personal pronoun is used in all cases.

6 Roger MacGinty and John Darby, *Guns and Government: The Management of the Northern Ireland Peace Process* (New York: Palgrave 2002).

7 Sheldon Stryker and Robert T. Serpe, "Commitment, Identity Salience and Role Behavior," in W. Ickes and E.S. Knowles, ed., *Personality, Roles and Social Behavior* (New York: Springer-Verlag 1982); Sheldon Stryker, "Identity Theory: Developments and Extensions," in K. Yardley and T. Honess, ed., *Self and Identity: Psychosocial Perspectives* (New York: Wiley 1987).

8 This sentiment, first expressed in early September 2002, has become more important with the October 2002 suspension of the Assembly by the British government – the fifth such suspension in the four years since the Agreement was signed.

9 Michael Hall, *Reinforcing Powerlessness: The Hidden Dimension of the Irish Troubles* (Newtonabbey, County Antrim: Island Publications 1996).

# 4

# Power Sharing after Yugoslavia: Functionality and Dysfunctionality of Power-sharing Institutions in Post-war Bosnia, Macedonia, and Kosovo[1]

## FLORIAN BIEBER

Three of the conflicts following the disintegration of Yugoslavia brought about internationally mediated institutional (re-)arrangements in Kosovo, Bosnia, and Macedonia that include elements of power sharing. International actors have thus promoted power sharing as a key structuring principle for post-conflict institution building in diverse societies. The institutional frameworks emerging from the different peace settlements have been varying in their effectiveness both in governing the respective countries and territories and in promoting accommodation between the different national groups.

This chapter will examine different institutional systems based on power-sharing arrangements in the five cases: Bosnia, its two entities (the Bosniac-Croat Federation and Republika Srpska, the Serb Republic), Macedonia, and Kosovo. The main focus will be on arrangements pertaining to the various parliaments and governments, special mediating procedures, and minority vetoes. All except one of the current institutional arrangements of power sharing were made recently. In May 2001 Hans Haekkerup, the special representative of the secretary general (SRSG) of the United Nations (UN), who is the civilian administrator of Kosovo, imposed the Constitutional Framework for Kosovo. In August 2001 the parliamentary parties of Macedonia – following intense international mediation – signed the Ohrid Framework Agreement, which led to constitutional changes at the end of 2001 that transformed some crucial aspects of power sharing. The constitutions of the two Bosnian entities underwent major revisions in April 2002, after a constitutional court decision declared parts of the previous constitutions unconstitutional under the state constitution. The high representative (HR), Wolfgang Petritsch, the international overseer over the civilian aspects of the peace process, eventually imposed these revisions although the parties themselves had largely agreed to them. The Bosnian state institutions are older, having been established at the peace negotiations in Dayton, Ohio, in the winter of 1995.

## POWER SHARING "PLUS" AND POWER SHARING "MINUS"

Power sharing in deeply divided societies can encompass a range of different measures to accommodate ethnic (or other) diversity. It would be flawed to conceptualize power sharing as a rigid catalogue of institutions and legal protections that have to be accommodated in order to qualify as power sharing. Already the variety of tools put forth by scholars of power sharing point to the absence of an agreed set of instruments.[2] Moreover, in divided societies around the world, there is a wide variety of institutions. Thus, in order to avoid making the term power sharing meaningless, it is important to limit its meaning rather than attempt to encompass all types of regimes for the protection of particular groups in a given state.

The concept of power sharing contains two specific components: "power" and "sharing." Any system that seeks to share resources between different groups in a society will have power at its core. Power sharing requires that the authority of the state be administered jointly, and not by only one narrow constituency. When either devising a power-sharing system or examining an existing case, it is important to make sure that the institution (usually, we are talking about specific institutions which are the expression of power sharing) actually has power. Without power, there can be no power sharing. The second component implies that this power is shared. It is not divided, which would mean that different groups divide tasks and do not consult and cooperate when making decisions. It also does not mean that one group holds power and asks others for advice but can disregard the advice if it wishes. Sharing requires the consent of a broad representation of groups in a given system.

When determining a narrow definition of power sharing, we can draw on Arend Lijphart's definition of a consociational arrangement, which is more limited than power sharing in general.[3] Lijphart identifies the following five main criteria of a consociational arrangement: (1) grand coalition, i.e., the inclusion of all major groups in government; (2) proportional representation of all relevant groups in parliament and public administration; (3) inclusion in government of the major groups; (4) veto rights; and (5) a high degree of autonomy.[4] In order to distinguish between consociation (power sharing plus) and power sharing minus, these points have to be interpreted more broadly than in the original definitions offered by Lijphart. Autonomy, for example, can be understood more broadly as decentralization – a tool of power sharing – without implying that this decentralization necessarily would have to be "ethnic" decentralization alone. Similarly, grand coalitions have to be broad and inclusive but not necessarily built on the basis of ethnic parties. Additionally, non-dominant groups do not necessarily need to have an absolute veto right to fulfil the criteria of a power-sharing arrangement. In fact, as I will argue later, an unconditional veto right may be an obstacle to effective power sharing. Furthermore, proportional representation in parliament and public administration should be distinguished, since they require different tools and have different functions in a society. Proportional representation in parliament – not always necessary if strong veto rights are given to the groups – ensures representation and participation in decision making. Representation in the administration has strong implications for the sense of "ownership" that previously underrepresented groups might have in the state.

The above criteria could be categorized by two aspects. First, they define the features of the layers of governance in a given political system. Second, they are defined by elements of inclusion and cooperation. In some elements of an institutional arrangement, inclusion and representation are more important, while cooperation carries more weight elsewhere. Arguably, both need to be present at all levels. However, as Table 1 shows, they can be given different weight in the institutional system.

Because of limitations of space, this chapter will focus only on the first three elements: parliamentary representation, broad government, and veto or co-decision power. The power-sharing systems under consideration vary greatly in the different institutional mechanisms employed to "manage diversity," reflecting different processes of their

Table 1
Power sharing between inclusion and cooperation

|                                                           | Inclusion | Cooperation |
|-----------------------------------------------------------|-----------|-------------|
| Parliamentary Representation                              | ✓         |             |
| Broad Government                                          |           | ✓           |
| Veto or Co-Decision Power                                 |           | ✓           |
| Proportional Representation in Public Administration      | ✓         |             |
| Decentralization/Autonomy                                 | ✓         |             |

establishment as well as divergent interethnic dynamics. Nevertheless, a comparison between the three cases is not only appropriate but useful in understanding post-conflict institutional design and in assessing the effectiveness of power-sharing arrangements.

In addition to structural similarities, such as size and geographic location, the three cases share other attributes. Bosnia, Kosovo, and Macedonia all belonged to Yugoslavia. The Yugoslav legacy has left an imprint on the management of inter-ethnic relations, in view of the elaborate system of non-democratic power sharing and minority rights which the country had instituted and which was supported at the international level).[5] Additionally, all three have seen major institutional reforms as part of the process of ending violent conflict. The current arrangement has been largely authored and/or mediated by international actors: the United States (for Bosnia), the UN (for Kosovo), and the European Union (EU) (for Macedonia). In all three cases, although less so in Macedonia, international actors have also been part of the implementation of the arrangements, adding a further level of complexity to the systems in place.

The power-sharing arrangements in Kosovo, Bosnia, and Macedonia belong to the types of system that were deliberately designed. They did not evolve over time on the basis of older institutional traditions, nor did they come into being "coincidentally"; rather, they were conceived to manage ethnic relations. This puts them in the same category as the plans for Cyprus and the arrangements in Belgium and Lebanon.

The deliberate effort behind the arrangements does not imply that they are necessarily based on a comparative study of institutional arrangement in post-conflict societies or that they are informed by scholarship – although this has been the case for some of the mechanisms in place. Neither does it imply that the legacy of earlier institutions did not "slip" into the post-conflict institutions. This applies equally to the pre-war institutions in all three cases, as well as to the personal institutional experience of the outside designers of the arrangements.[6]

## WHO IS REPRESENTED IN PARLIAMENT?

Parliaments in divided societies play a dual role. First, they are the institutions where laws are passed. Second, they are the principal body of representation for communities. Parliament allows groups and individuals to formulate concerns, shape the political agenda, and supervise the work of the executive. In order to ascertain the role of parliament in power-sharing arrangements, one needs to take into consideration the way in which the diversity in the given society is represented, how much power the parliament has as a whole, and how much power the different communities hold within it. The first aspect describes the element of representation, while the latter shapes the participation of communities. The latter is usually defined in negative terms – that is, in terms of preventing exclusion through mutual vetoes – as will be discussed later. Turning to the mechanisms of representation, one can identify four commonly used instruments: (1) electoral systems; (2) electoral districts; (3) thresholds; and (4) reserved seats.[7]

In an examination of election processes, the two crucial considerations are (a) who should be represented and (b) what should be represented. The choice of election procedures can have a profound impact on who will be represented in parliament, and with what strength. A general assumption of power-sharing systems is that parliaments should strive to be generally representative of all groups, that they should not exclude some communities or grossly over-represent others – though, in the case of small minorities, a degree of over-representation or positive discrimination may sometimes be desirable. The question of what should be represented is considerably more difficult to manage, and the subtle influence of electoral systems is often hard to assess. Here one has to consider whether the goal of the electoral process is to represent adequately the groups as groups or whether the electoral process should be conducive to cooperation, the aim being the electoral success of either moderate candidates and parties (those not primarily campaigning on the basis of ethnic identity) or cross-communal forces.[8]

Electoral systems offer a wide variety of tools for determining who will be elected, though the different systems will not be examined in detail here. It is sufficient to note that the conventional dichotomy of

majoritarian and proportional electoral systems does not indicate the
variety of subsystems available. Generally, a form of proportional representation has the advantage that most major groups can be expected
to be represented in the parliament, while majoritarian systems tend to
favour the strongest party, candidate, or (by extension in deeply divided
societies) ethnic groups, in the respective electoral district.[9]

Closely tied to the electoral system are the size and demography of
electoral districts. While the size is often determined by the electoral
system chosen, the location in relation to the population distribution
is not. On the one hand, in cases of gerrymandering, majority parties
can design electoral districts to ensure that minorities are consistently
excluded. On the other hand, the shape of electoral districts can be
designed to create coherent minority or group-based districts.

The threshold is another important tool for engineering the electoral
process. Most Western democracies have electoral thresholds to prevent
a fragmentation of parliamentary representation into many small parties. The height of the threshold varies from less than 1 per cent
(Netherlands) to 10 per cent (Turkey). While thresholds may be desirable for the functionality of parliaments, they possess the inherent
danger of excluding minorities. This occurs almost automatically where
the minority's share of the population falls below the threshold,[10] but
it can also occur where the minority's party spectrum is fragmented –
that is, where several parties compete for minority votes and each gains
less than the threshold. To counter this particular obstacle to the
representation of minorities, either the threshold can be lowered for all
parties participating in elections or minority parties can be exempt from
the threshold or face a lowered one.

Finally, reserved seats in parliament are the electoral tool providing
the most certain guarantee for community representation. The seats set
aside can be filled (a) by minority representatives, chosen by minority
organizations; (b) by holding separate elections for minorities for those
seats; or (c) by assigning the reserved seats to the minority parties with
the highest votes. In a number of cases the minorities can also participate and compete in the elections for the remainder of the seats, thus
gaining additional representation. Generally, this tool is in use for
smaller minorities when other mechanisms are less likely to ensure
adequate representation.[11]

All the cases under study here have adopted a variation of proportional representation for the election of their parliaments.[12] Presidential

elections are held in a first-past-the-post system in Bosnia and the Serb Republic, and in a two-round run-off in Macedonia. In Kosovo and the Bosniac-Croat Federation, the president is elected by parliament. Thresholds in all five cases are low, allowing for a high number of parties to enter parliament. In Bosnia and Macedonia the threshold is 3 per cent, whereas in Kosovo there is no threshold.

In addition to low thresholds, all but one – Macedonia – have special mechanisms to ensure adequate representation of communities through reserved seats. In Kosovo, ten seats are reserved for Serbs and an additional ten are reserved for other minorities (four Roma, three Bosniacs, two Turks, and one Gorani). Seats are allocated to the parties of the respective communities according to their share in the elections. Since these seats do not affect seats gained as part of the overall system of proportional representation, the Serb community was able to gain twelve additional seats in the 2001 election, as did three other minority parties. In Bosnia the reserved seats do not primarily apply to the smaller communities but do apply to all three recognized "constituent" peoples (Bosniaks, Serbs, and Croats), with additional seats set aside at some levels for "others" (including smaller minorities, such as Roma, and citizens not running as members of the three dominant nations). In the bicameral Bosnian state and Federation parliaments, there is one chamber, called the "House of Peoples," for representation of the communities. Bosniaks, Croats, and Serbs are equally represented in both "Houses of Peoples," with additional representation for "others" in the Federation house. In Republika Srpska, the Council of Peoples – elected by parliament – fulfils a similar function but has fewer powers.[13] Additionally, the lower chambers of both institutions have mechanisms to guarantee group inclusion: both are required to have at least four members from each of the three communities, whereas the state parliament must have two-thirds of its representation from the Federation and one-third from Republika Srpska, which – owing to the geographically concentration of communities – translates into some degree of ensured inclusion of all three groups.

In none of the five cases is representation of the groups ensured through separate electoral lists, nor do the minorities have separate elections for the reserved seats. Instead, seats are assigned to the strongest parties or candidates of the respective community, according to proportional representation. If there were separate electoral lists, the electors would be forced to identify themselves openly with one particular community, and both international and domestic actors have generally considered this undesirable. In Kosovo, for example, the OSCE rejected ethnic lists, even though such lists were part of the Rambouillet plan: "... Security and ethical consideration prevented us from conducting such an ethnic registration."[14] In Kosovo, and in Bosnia for the election of the House of Representatives of the Federation of Bosnia and Herzegovina, for the presidency and vice-presidency of Republika Srpska, and for the National Assembly of Republika Srpska, the parties or candidates have to declare their ethnicity to benefit from the reserved seats. The ballot papers in Bosnia, however, do not indicate the ethnicity of the candidate.[15]

Reserved seats – the tool used for group inclusion in parliaments in four of the five cases – are also employed in neighboring Montenegro (for Albanians) and Croatia (for Italians, Hungarians, and Serbs), albeit with some variation of the mechanisms. While leaving less room for manipulation than other tools and offering predictable results, the reservation of seats is also a blunt tool with considerable disadvantages. First, it frequently contains an element of positive discrimination (as in Kosovo), which easily attracts the resentment of the majority. Thus, although it may increase representation, it does not necessarily promote participation or cooperation. Second, it may complicate the electoral process when there are other factors to be considered, such as the geographic distribution of mandates. For example, in the Bosnian Federation House of Peoples, the deputies have to represent equally the whole entity and the cantons in which they are elected. The ensuing complexity can reduce voter confidence in the electoral process. Third, the system encourages voters to vote for candidates of their own ethnicity rather than for members of other groups.

One alternative to reserved seats would be to look at the voters rather than those elected. Thus, instead of prescribing that a specified number of seats in parliament have to be filled by one ethnic group (which always raises the problem of the number of votes not corresponding to those eventually elected), voters could choose between multiple lists for the respective communities.

Additionally, the electoral system itself offers a range of other ways to influence representation, which have been largely underutilized in the cases under consideration here. Only Bosnia, in 2000, experimented with electoral engineering. While some aspects (open lists, multi-member constituencies) have been kept, others have been abandoned (preferential voting).[16]

## ARE THERE GRAND COALITIONS?

Since governments are the primary institutions of executive power, no power-sharing arrangement would be complete without broad group representation at the governmental level.[17] Governments require cooperation, being usually formed among like-minded parties on a joint (pre- or post-electoral) platform. While representation can be legislated, as has been demonstrated above in the discussion of parliamentary representation, legislating cooperation can be considerably more challenging.

A legal framework can achieve representation of all major groups in government by means of three tools, or options. The first option assigns a numerical or proportional key, according to which the different groups have to be included in government. The second option requires that there be deputy ministers of different group membership in every ministry in order to ensure that each ministry is run – or at least contains some degree of oversight – by all groups. Finally, a range of procedural rules can avoid the concentration of power within one community. Such mechanisms include rotating the prime ministership or presidency (as in Switzerland).

The willingness to form a coalition for joint decision making and inclusion, however, requires that the major parties participating in the government's formation consent to include the "other." Otherwise, legislated representation runs the risk of being just that – representation – causing the government to resemble a small-size replica of parliament. Grand coalitions are particularly difficult to form when only one dominant party represents each group, since this limits the range of possible variations. Furthermore, in post-conflict societies – such as four of the five[18] considered here – the parties that will be participating in one government have frequently been at war with each other during the conflict, making cooperation particularly difficult. In effect, the emphasis on elite cooperation in theories of consociationalism is put to the test in the executives of the post-conflict states of former Yugoslavia.[19]

The Bosnian entities and state institutions, as well as Kosovo, have legal requirements for representation of different communities. Whereas this has been an aspect of Bosnian state-level governance since its inception, the entities were only recently required to include non-dominant communities in their governments. In the Federation, Serb participation has been minimal and in the Serb Republic the first Bosniac minister joined the government only in 2001.

In the two Bosnian entities and in Kosovo, a set number of ministries have to be run by members of the non-dominant groups. Additionally, at the state level in Bosnia and in the Federation, two deputy ministers of the other groups are assigned to every minister. A similar mechanism is employed for the presidency: at the state level, a three-member presidency rotates in regular intervals, whereas, in the two entities, the two vice-presidents have to be from a different group than the president. Macedonia has no formal requirements for a grand coalition. Nevertheless, since its first freely elected government was formed following the 1990 elections, parties representing the Albanian community have been included in government. Here, as in Bosnia, it has been general practice to include a deputy minister from a different group than the minister.

In addition to the aforementioned danger of government emulating the dynamics within a parliament, difficulties can arise from the above arrangements. The mechanism of appointing deputy ministers has in practice frequently led to the creation of powerless positions, without influence over the workings of the respective ministries. In the absence of a defined division of tasks, the deputies run the risk of being mere window-dressing. Intra-governmental dynamics can also lead to an "ethnification" of ministries. Here, ministries cater to the needs and demands of the community of the minister and compete with other ministries.[20] In other cases, such as in Montenegro and Yugoslavia, minority ministers are appointed to ministries for minorities – positions that are primarily of symbolic importance rather than reflecting participation in decision making.[21]

A key difference between Macedonia on the one hand and Kosovo and Bosnia on the other is the nature of governmental coalition building, which can partly be related to the difference between the informal tradition versus the formal requirement of grand coalitions. In Macedonia there have been pre-election coalitions, or at least partnerships, between Macedonian and Albanian parties; thus, a change of the governing majority party has also brought to power a new minority party. This has meant that, in addition to an ample degree of inter-ethnic electoral campaigning and competition, there has been campaigning between the parties of each community. In Kosovo, despite the short history of only one election, the record of non-cooperation between Serb minority and Albanian majority parties suggests that, in the medium term also, both pre- and post-election coalitions are unlikely. The participation of minorities is thus the fulfillment of a legal requirement rather than part of the political process of coalition building.

Bosnia has had only one experience with a broad cross-party coalition, the Alliance for Change. However, this did not come about until the 2000 elections were concluded, and it involved the heavy-handed intervention of international actors (Office of the High Representative [OHR], OSCE, U.S. embassy).[22] The ten-member coalition disintegrated in less than two years, and its member parties subsequently lost the October 2002 elections. In the case of Bosnia, the key challenge has been that each community (with the partial exception of Bosniacs) has given overwhelming support to just one national party. Thus, coalition building has been hampered by a lack of choice: cross-cutting, issue-oriented coalition building is not possible and intra-group competition is considerably less than in Macedonia.

The nature of a grand coalition poses a particular challenge that can be met only with difficulty by institutional engineers, because it requires political actors who are willing to cooperate. In addition to reserving governmental positions directly, as in Bosnia and Kosovo, change is most likely to come from change in the party system (which in turn can be partially influenced by the electoral rules).

## WHAT KIND OF VETO?

Veto rights constitute an important aspect of power-sharing arrangements, but at the same time they can have the most serious negative repercussions on the functioning of any institutional arrangement. The aim of veto rights is to prevent the non-dominant groups from being out-voted in the parliament or in the executive. This chapter will focus only on veto rights within parliament, since they are generally more comprehensive and crucial in regard to legislation. While broad representation both in parliament and in government ensures participation and co-decision making, it does not prevent out-voting. Thus, veto rights can ensure that groups in a power-sharing system are indeed participating in the existing arrangement.

Veto rights in the cases in question can be found at the levels of the parliament, the government, and even the presidency. These group rights are rarely absolute – that is, it is not possible for one member of the respective group, or often even a simple majority, to block all decisions. In most cases, veto rights have considerable limitations or qualifications in order to limit the danger of immobilizing the decision-making process. One can observe two commonly used limitations. First, the threshold: there must be a stipulated minimum number of deputies or government members of a group opposing a given decision in order to block it. Second, a number of different instruments exist to limit the areas in which a veto can be used. In addition to these two limitations, most veto arrangements have mechanisms for overcoming a deadlock in the decision-making process caused by the veto. This mediation process can remove the decision from the respective institution (e.g., parliament) and transfer it to another (e.g., constitutional court) or it can propose a compromise measure for consideration by the institution in which the veto was first raised.

Turning first to the degree of support required to block decisions in Bosnia, Kosovo, and Macedonia, we have to distinguish between a joint veto of all minorities and the option of one community to veto decisions. In Macedonia, the veto right is not given to any one community in particular; instead, it is given to "the majority of votes from the present representatives who belong to communities which are not a majority in Republic of Macedonia."[23] Kosovo, *de facto*, gives only Serbs, and not the other smaller communities, the possibility of delaying legislation. It stipulates that one deputy, with the support of five others, can object to a parliamentary decision, triggering a mediation process.[24] But, since only Serbs have ten guaranteed seats in parliament, the five-member support clause in fact means that a majority of Serbs would have to object to the law. The relative flexibility of the framework, however, allows for support by deputies who do not belong to the same community as the deputy submitting the objection. Theoretically (though not realistically, at present), Albanian members of parliament could support the objection of a Serb or other minority MP. In reality, the current regulation means that only the Serb minority has the possibility of delaying legislation, while other smaller minorities would need support from other minorities (or the majority) to secure such a procedure.[25]

In Bosnia and its entities, each community by itself has the right of veto. In both entities a two-thirds majority of the respective community's deputies is required in the House of Peoples (Federation) and Council of Peoples (Republika Srpska) to block legislation. At the state level, only one-third from each entity can block a law in either of the two chambers of parliament. Additionally, a majority of one of the three peoples can also veto legislation.

A greater challenge to veto rights than the numerical threshold is the definition of the field of legislation or decision making where such a veto right is applicable. The most generous interpretation of the veto right would allow community representatives to block any decision. Since such an interpretation would allow for the veto of decisions that could in no way negatively affect the respective community, it opens the door to misuse. There is a general need to balance the protection of the community with preventing misuse for a political agenda unrelated to community concerns. However, whereas such a balance can easily be conceptualized in theory, the reality highlights the near impossibility of achieving a middle ground. Of the five cases under discussion here, Macedonia has the most restrictive approach to veto rights. The constitutional amendments of November 2001 stipulate that the consent of a majority of the deputies representing non-dominant groups is required only in the following areas of decision making: culture; use of languages; education; personal identification; use of symbols;[26] and local self-government.[27] In all other areas of legislation, minority support is not required in order to pass laws.[28] The advantage of such a relatively restrictive regulation is that it can help prevent blockage of the entire decision-making process. Furthermore, it limits the areas in which ethnicity is formally part of parliamentary procedure. Nevertheless, this limitation contains the inherent danger that other decisions that might have a profound impact on minorities, such as economic policy or infrastructural development, are excluded and thus are beyond the reach of the minorities' veto.

The constitutions of Kosovo and the two Bosnian entities have taken a middle ground between leaving room for flexible interpretations of the veto powers and suggesting a limitation. All three constitutions, as well as the Bosnian state constitutions, allow for the use of vetoes in cases where the "vital interest"[29] of the respective group is affected. The stipulation of a vital interest, if not further qualified, suggests that the veto right is limited to decisions of major importance and that not every decision, even one that adversely affects one group, is subject to minority veto rights. Such an interpretation, however, can be nothing more than a recommendation, since vital interests can be interpreted broadly, leaving room for the vetoing of virtually any decision. This has been a considerable problem at the state level in Bosnia, and so the constitutional amendments imposed on the two entities in 2002 have sought to address the matter. The definition of vital national interests used in both the Federation and Republika Srpska is as follows: exercise of the rights of constituent peoples to be adequately represented in legislative, executive, and judicial authorities; identity of one constituent people; constitutional amendments; organization of public authorities; equal rights of constituent peoples in the process of decision making; education, religion, language, and promotion of culture, tradition, and cultural heritage; territorial organization; and public information systems.[30]

This list clearly limits the realm of the veto rights, as in the Macedonian case (although with a broader range of fields). However, a concluding point undermines the limitations imposed above: "Other issues [can be] treated as of vital national interest if so claimed by 2/3rd of one of the caucuses of the constituent peoples in the House of Peoples."[31] Thus, the same majority required to veto a decision is also able to declare that the respective issue falls within the competence of such a veto right. Consequently, the list of areas in the above definition of vital interest can still be seen merely as a recommendation, rather than as a limitation on the veto right. Hence, theoretically, a major departure from the above definition in invoking the veto right would not be counter to the legal definition but could later be used by the media or other parties to criticize the respective group for interpreting the veto too broadly. Considering the current state of inter-ethnic relations in the two Bosnian entities, where the media and interest groups are also ethnically divided, the self-limiting aspect of the vital interest definition is unlikely to be effective.

The constitutional framework in Kosovo contains a similar delimitation: "A motion may be made on the grounds that the law or provisions discriminate against a Community, adversely affect the rights of the Community or its members under Chapters 3 [Human Rights] or 4 [Minority Rights], or otherwise seriously interfere with the ability of the Community to preserve, protect or express its ethnic, cultural, religious or linguistic identity."[32] This definition differs significantly from that of the Bosnian entities, since it does not state who has the competence to interpret when a decision seriously interferes with the community rights. Considering the primacy of the SRSG as the civilian administrator, it is plausible to assume that his office, rather than a Kosovo institution, would have the final word in determining the appropriateness of such an objection. While this does not affect the ability to put forth an objection to a law or decision, it might affect the outcome of the mediation procedure.

All the cases mentioned here have attempted to limit veto rights by proposing issue areas where such rights can be invoked. Nevertheless, the fluid nature of group interests has made it difficult to impose such limitations. In fact, Kosovo and Macedonia, the two systems that have generally weaker power-sharing institutions than the Bosnian state and the Federation, have also greater limitations on the breadth of the veto rights. The nature of the limitations on these two systems points to the fact that the institutional mechanisms in Kosovo and Macedonia are primarily conceived as elements of minority rights' protection rather than as a power-sharing arrangement per se.

The third and final dimension to veto rights is how to attempt to overcome the conflict between communities once a veto is invoked. A mediation process is part of the arrangement in all five cases. This is motivated by the obvious concern that a veto without mediation puts an end to the respective decision or law and thus can lead to a blockage of the decision-making process; also, if there are no instruments to bridge policy gaps, the use of the veto can exacerbate inter-ethnic relations. The mediation procedure usually involves a small body (less than ten members) with representation of all communities in question that are seeking to negotiate a compromise. In the case of Kosovo, first the parliamentary presidency seeks to develop a compromise. If that fails, a panel consisting of one member from each community in question (for instance, the Albanian and a minority community) and one member appointed by the SRSG will propose a solution (by majority vote) to the assembly.[33] Similarly, in the Bosnian parliament, a three-member panel (one Bosniac, one Serb, and one Croat) is charged to mediate. Since the panel is required to arrive at a consensus to propose a solution to the dispute, the case can be referred to the constitutional court if there is disagreement.[34] The same procedure is foreseen for the House of Peoples in the Federation and the Council of Peoples in Republika Srpska.[35] In Macedonia, the Committee for Relations between Communities is intended to serve as a permanent forum for mediating conflicts arising in parliament. The committee will have the task of resolving controversies arising from decisions that require majority consent from the minority deputies but fail to get it.[36] The committee itself can decide with a simple majority – which requires

cross-community coalition building because the Macedonians and
Albanians each hold only seven of the nineteen seats, while all other
minorities have one seat.[37]

In the cases under examination here, the attempts to limit or qualify
the veto right point to the difficulty, which Arend Lijphart describes,
that the decision-making process may be paralysed as a result of these
rights. Lijphart dismisses this danger all too lightly, arguing that – based
of the rationality of the political parties and their interest in promoting
the decision-making process – the parties will refrain from using the
veto rights.[38] However, in post-conflict societies, and with a political
system that is contentious in itself, as in the cases here, such an
assumption is not valid. Although the effectiveness of limitations to the
veto rights will have to be examined empirically elsewhere, the above
analysis of the legal framework suggests that these limitations do not
accomplish much.

## LOOKING BEYOND POWER SHARING

The above overview of the different mechanisms and approaches to
power sharing in parliament and government in Bosnia and its entities,
in Kosovo, and in Macedonia highlights both the variety of tools
available and the challenges in creating a working power-sharing system
that includes the different communities and renders the political system
workable.

Other aspects, not discussed in detail here – such as the symbols of
power sharing (for instance, whether the state is conceived as multinational, civic, or a nation-state), autonomy, and participation in the
administration (especially in the police) – are equally crucial in render-
ing power sharing workable.

With the exception of Macedonia, all the systems have a high degree
of formal "design" in their power-sharing systems but little actual practice of power sharing. As highlighted in the different sections of this
chapter, the key difficulty arises from the fact that representation is
considerably easier to achieve through constitutional design than cooperation. While representation is a prerequisite for participation, it does
not necessarily lead to cooperation between representatives of the different communities. It is here that a tool to change both the political elites
and the political choices of the population is necessary in order to alter

the patterns of cooperation and conflict in these societies. Instruments for changes in this area have to be sought beyond the theories of power sharing. Proponents of "imposed" power sharing will not only have to look more closely at the best practices in power-sharing systems around the world, but also will have to work in close conjunction with the "bottom-up" approach of proponents of social transformation in order to achieve democratic and cohesive plural societies.

### NOTES

1 I would like to thank Matthijs Bogaards for his helpful comments on the first draft of this chapter.

2 See Timothy D. Sisk, *Power Sharing and International Mediation in Ethnic Conflicts* (Washington: USIP 1996), 34–45.

3 On the relationship between power sharing and consociationalism, see Matthijs Bogaards, "The Uneasy Relationship between Empirical and Normative Types of Consociational Theory," *Journal of Theoretical Politics* 12, no.4 (2000), 395–423.

4 Arend Lijphart, *Democracy in Plural Societies: A Comparative Exploration* (New Haven, Conn., and London: Yale University Press 1977), 25.

5 See Vanessa Pupavac, "Socialist Federal Republic of Yugoslavia's Multi-ethnic Rights Approach and the Politicisation of Ethnicity," *Human Rights Law Review* 5, no.2 (2000), 3–8.

6 On this issue, see Florian Bieber, "Institutionalizing Ethnicity in former Yugoslavia: Domestic vs. Internationally Driven Processes of Institutional (Re-) Design," *Global Review of Ethnopolitics* 2, no.2 (2003): 2–16. More generally, see John M. Owen IV, "The Foreign Imposition of Domestic Institutions," *International Organization* 56, no.2 (2002), 375–410.

7 Adopted from Kristian Myntti, *A Commentary to the Lund Recommendations on the Effective Participation of National Minorities in Public Life* (Åbo, Finland: Institute for Human Rights, Åbo Akademi University 2001), 15–27.

8 This choice describes the primary differences in the divergent approaches of Arend Ljiphart and Donald Horowitz to power-sharing systems.

9 Ben Reilly and Andrew Reynolds, *Electoral Systems and Conflict in Divided Societies*, Papers on International Conflict Resolution, no.1 (Washington, D.C.: National Academy Press 1999).

10 Only coalitions of several minorities could overcome the threshold.

11 On these issues, see also European Commission for Democracy through Law (Venice Commission), "Electoral Law and National Minorities" (Strasbourg, 12 January 1999. CDL-MIN [99] 1 rev. 2).

12 Until 2002, Macedonia used a mixed PR and Single Member District (SMD) system.

13 As the Council of Peoples is elected by parliament, the system in Republika Srpska cannot be considered bicameral.

14 Peter Erben and Jarrett Blanc, *Electoral Processes and Stability in Post-Conflict Societies: The Ongoing Experience of Kosovo/Federal Republic of Yugoslavia* (Organization for Security and Cooperation in Europe, Mission in Kosovo, Department of Election Operations 2002).

15 Both in Kosovo and in Bosnia, however, the ethnicity of most candidates can be identified by the names. In Bosnia, Serb parties generally use Cyrillic script on the ballot papers, while Bosnia and Croat parties use the Latin script.

16 On this, see Florian Bieber, "Regulating Elections in Post-War Bosnia: Success and Failure of Electoral Engineering in Divided Societies" (paper presented at the workshop on Electoral Laws in Post-War Societies, in Beirut, Lebanon, 27–28 September 2002).

17 Lijphart considers it to be the most important element of consociationalism. See Lijphart, *Democracy in Plural Societies*, 25–31.

18 Since Macedonia did not experience a full-fledged war, the term "post-conflict societies" is only partly applicable.

19 See Lijphart, *Democracy in Plural Societies*, 99–103; and Matthijs Bogaards, "The Favourable Factors for Consocational Democracy: A Review," *European Journal of Political Research* 33 (1998): 480.

20 This has been the case, for example, in the election campaign in Macedonia between the Ministry of Justice and the Ministry of Interior (RFE/RL *Newsline*, 20 August 2002).

21 There is the additional danger that these ministers cater primarily to their minority rather than to all communities.

22 Željko Cvijanović, "The Last Year of the Dayton Accords" (AIM, 6 June 2001).

23 Amendment X (16 November 2001), Article 69, Constitution of Macedonia. This new veto mechanism is not yet fully operational.

24 9.1.39, Constitutional Framework for Provisional Self-Government, May 2001.

25 Since minorities can gain additional seats through the PR system, the number of six votes required could be reached by one single minority other

than Serbs, but, considering the 2001 election results and current demographics, this is unlikely. For Serbs, the 2001 results (22 Serb MPs) mean that less than a third of Serb deputies would suffice to trigger a mediation process.

26 Amendment X (16 November 2001), Article 69, Constitution of Macedonia.

27 The law regulating local self-government requires both a two-thirds majority and majority consent of the minorities. Amendment XVI (16 November 2001), Article 114, Constitution of Macedonia.

28 The two-thirds requirement for a number of laws and decisions taken by parliament does, however, require some minority participation in other fields as well.

29 Article 9.1.39, Constitutional Framework for Provisional Self-Government, May 2001; Article IV, 3, e, Constitution of Bosnia-Herzegovina (21 November 1995).

30 Amendment XXXVII, Definition of Vital Interests, Decision on Constitutional Amendments in the Federation of Bosnia and Herzegovina, OHR, 19 April 2002; available at: www.ohr.int.

31 Amendment XXXVII, Definition of Vital Interests, Decision on Constitutional Amendments in the Federation of Bosnia and Herzegovina, OHR, 19 April 2002; available at: www.ohr.int.

32 9.1.39, Constitutional Framework for Provisional Self-Government, May 2001.

33 9.1.40, 9.1.41, Constitutional Framework for Provisional Self-Government, May 2001.

34 IV, 3, f, Constitution of Bosnia-Herzegovina, 21 November 1995.

35 Article 18, Constitution of the Federation of Bosnia-Herzegovina, June 1994.

36 This committee has not yet been established. It is therefore not clear how effectively it will operate once formed.

37 Amendment XII.1, Article 78, Constitution of Macedonia, 16 November 2001.

38 He argues that there are three reasons why the minority veto is unlikely to be invoked: (1) since all communities have the veto right, the fear of having their own initiatives blocked limits its use; (2) the availability of the veto itself provides a sufficient guarantee, making the actual use superfluous; and (3) the recognition of possible deadlock in institutions. Lijphart, *Democracy in Plural Societies*, 37.

# 5

# Post-conflict Reconstruction: Constitutional and Transitional Power-sharing Arrangements in Bosnia and Kosovo

PATRICK J. O'HALLORAN

This chapter examines the constitutional and transitional power-sharing arrangements in Bosnia-Herzegovina (hereafter Bosnia) and Kosovo. It is a comparative analysis of post-conflict governance and issues of implementation of the 1995 Dayton Accord in Bosnia and of United Nations (UN) Security Council Resolution (1999) in Kosovo.

## POST-CONFLICT RECONSTRUCTION AND THE POLITICAL PILLAR

Post-conflict reconstruction comprises all activities associated with the social and political re-engineering of a state, including, but not limited to, the following: developing political institutions, civil society, and responsible and accountable leadership; the disarmament, demobilization, and reintegration of soldiers; security sector reform; demining; the professionalization of military and police forces; the reconstruction of social infrastructure, such as schools and roads; economic development; and the improvement of public policy and administration.

Implicitly or explicitly, post-conflict reconstruction in Bosnia and Kosovo has tended to involve the imposition of a generalized version of the Western state and economic model – liberal democracy and a market economy – onto a post-conflict (and formerly communist) state. Post-conflict reconstruction, thus understood, is seen as comprising a number of "pillars." The joint project of the Center for Strategic and International Studies and the Association of the United States Army (CSIS/AUSA), for instance, identifies four pillars: security; justice and reconciliation; social and economic well-being; and governance and participation.[1] The subject of this chapter is the governance and participation or "political" pillar. It should be remembered, however, that studying one pillar in isolation from the others is only conceptually possible; in reality, they are interdependent and meld into one another. For example, security sector reform is generally regarded as the most essential element of immediate post-conflict reconstruction since, without a secure and stable social environment, economic and political reconstruction is problematic if not altogether impossible.

The political pillar includes tasks that are intended to further the development of liberal-democratic governance and establish the three components of democratic government (executive, legislature, and the judiciary). Other governance tasks are to define national identity, citizenship status, state languages, religions and symbols; establish transitional governments (international, national, and permanent); and (where federalism is mandated) establish both federal and provincial government executives, civil services, legislatures, and independent judiciaries. Participation tasks are those related to the planning, monitoring, and execution of elections, the formation of political parties, the development of independent media, and the building of civil society.

The political pillar also includes designing power-sharing relationships, both constitutional (between ethnic groups and between the state and local governments) and transitional (between international actors and the state). If political power is defined as the ability to make autonomous decisions and the capacity to protect vital interests, political power sharing can be understood as the distribution of these two elements among the various actors.[2] The section that follows examines the political pillar of post-conflict reconstruction in Bosnia and Kosovo. Specifically, it examines the constitutional plan for power sharing and power-sharing arrangements during the transition phase from international to local governance.

## CONSTITUTIONAL ARRANGEMENTS: BOSNIA

The General Framework Agreement for Peace in Bosnia and Herzegovina, known as the Dayton Peace Agreement or Dayton Accord (hereafter the Accord), was initialled in Dayton, Ohio, on 21 November 1995 by the presidents of Croatia, Bosnia-Herzegovina, and the Federal Republic of Yugoslavia and formally ratified in Paris on 14 December 1995.[3]

Annex 4 of the Accord contains the constitution, in which Bosnia is established as a federal state with two constituent entities, the Bosniac-Croat Federation (composed of Bosnian Muslims and Croats) and Republika Srpska, composed of Serbs, comprising 51 per cent and 49 per cent of the territory respectively. The constitution assigns equal legal status to both written forms of the Serbo-Croat language (Cyrillic and Latin) and to the three main religions: Islam, Orthodox Christianity, and Roman Catholicism. It sets forth the fundamental democratic founding principles of the state and the rights of citizens, the structure of government institutions, the composition of electorates, the distribution of power and responsibilities between the Bosnian state and its constituent entities (federalism), and the constitutional-amending procedure. Specifically, for example, it defines the six "common institutions" of the Bosnian state: the presidency, the parliamentary assembly, the Council of Ministers, the central bank, the Constitutional Court, and the standing committee on military matters.

The constitutional adhesive that is supposed to cement the multiethnic Bosnian state together is power sharing, through the mechanisms delineated in the constitution. Bosnia, in effect, was designed to be a weak federation in which mechanisms based on ethnic criteria would operate throughout all levels of government. Federal power, for example, was devolved in a way that was intended "to provide security to all three minorities and therefore provide a crucial mechanism for institutionalizing support for a multi-ethnic society."[4]

In addition to the federal distribution of land and power, the constitution mandates five mechanisms of power sharing: (1) an ethnically based distribution of seats in parliament; (2) a rotating presidency; (3) legislative conditions that require support for bills across ethnic lines; (4) an ethnically based legislative veto over matters of vital interest; and (5) an electoral process based on proportional representation and party lists.[5]

The parliamentary assembly of Bosnia consists of two chambers, the House of Peoples (upper chamber) with fifteen delegates, and the House of Representatives (lower chamber) with forty-two members. The respective upper chambers of the entities nominate the delegates to the Bosnian upper chamber, while the members of the lower chamber are elected in their respective entities. The interests of the three identity groups are protected by a number of mechanisms, all premised on a one-third rule of ethnic representation. Both chambers, their chairs, and the presidency are organized so that the Serbs, Croats, and Bosniacs share the available seats. In the House of Representatives, the member ratio is twenty-eight Federation members to fourteen Republika Srpska members. In the House of Peoples, the delegate ratio is ten Federation (five Croat and five Bosniac) delegates to five Republika Srpska delegates. All legislation requires the approval of both chambers and "all decisions in both chambers shall be by majority of those present and voting."[6] Paragraph 3(d), however, states that "the Delegates and Members shall make their best efforts to see that the majority includes at least one-third of the votes of Delegates or Members from the territory of each Entity." When a piece of legislation fails to secure this distribution of ethnic-group support, it is referred to a commission formed by the respective chambers' chairs, and, if this attempt also fails, the legislation will pass nevertheless as long as the "dissenting votes do not include two-thirds or more of the Delegates of Members elected from either Entity."

The Bosnian executive consists of a tripartite rotating presidency and a Council of Ministers. The three members of the presidency (one from each ethnic group) are elected by direct vote. Each holds the title of head of state for eight months. The Council of Ministers and its chair, the prime minister, are appointed according to ethnic and entity criteria. The prime minister is nominated by the presidency and must be approved by the House of Representatives. The prime minister nominates the other ministers, who must also be approved by the House of Representatives. Deputy ministers are nominated by the prime minister and "shall not be of the same constituent people as their Ministers."

Another mechanism to protect national interests is the concept of vital interests and the veto. Decisions proposed by the parliamentary assembly and the presidency may be declared to be "destructive of a vital interest of the Bosniac, Croat, or Serb people" by a majority of national delegates in the House of Peoples. If this invocation is opposed, the decision goes before a joint commission formed by the chair and three delegates (Bosniac, Croat, and Serb) and, failing this, before the Constitutional Court. Likewise, the presidency "shall endeavour to adopt all Presidency Decisions ... by consensus."[7] If a member of the presidency declares a decision to be "destructive to the vital interest of the Entity from the territory from which he was elected," the decision is then referred to the member's respective upper chamber, where a two-thirds vote against the decision can annul it.

The driving force behind political autonomy is the desire to protect national interests and cultural identity. The Bosnian constitution presents a framework for a multi-ethnic federal state that claims to guarantee constitutional protection of individual rights but, at the same time, establishes a government model that may be characterized as "cultural pluralist" – meaning that the political unit is not the individual but the ethnic group. Through the mechanisms noted above, the constitution develops a federal system of power sharing that fractions both the parliamentary assembly (House of Representatives and House of Peoples) and the presidency into ethnic blocs. These mechanisms of checks and balances – which were put in place as a means to guarantee ethnically neutral or equitable legislation – also tend to perpetuate identity-group politics. Consequently, the three groups lack an incentive to develop a multi-ethnic party system that promotes inter-ethnic voting. Moreover, the result of devolving power to the two entities has been to reify their territorial claims on the basis of the 1995 ceasefire line – but that line does not coincide with the identity groups' understanding of what was traditionally their national homeland. Hence, a loose federal structure has not dissipated their urge to reclaim lost territory; it merely discourages those who want to return to their pre-war homes.

Arguably, a unitary state based on shared homelands might have better resolved homeland issues within Bosnia by reducing the salience of ethnic-group territorial rights, thus eventually permitting people to return to their homes and, one hopes, recreating the country's pre-war multi-ethnic demographic tapestry. However, once a federation was established, these possibilities were effectively closed off. Bosnians and Croats are now unwilling to surrender their political autonomy, or the Serbs their *de facto* statehood. At the end of 1997, some two years into the state-building process, the Peace Implementation Council (PIC) chairman noted that Bosnia continued to suffer from a "lack of strong multi-ethnic political parties and a structured civil society."[8]

Cooperation on policy and structural issues within the federation, between the Bosniac-Croat Federation and Republicka Srpska, and between all three constituent peoples, has also been lacking. For example, there has been slow, if not entirely negligible, policy cooperation at the state level for the disbanding of unilateral ethnic-based institutions and the creation of joint ones such as a joint army and a joint police force, the adoption of a common legal system, and the sharing of fiscal and infrastructure responsibilities related to electricity, water, sewage, railway lines, roads, and telephones. The most persistent unilateral institution was the so-called Republic of Herzeg-Bosna (a Croat area within the Croat-Bosnian Federation).[9] On 19 December 1996 the Herzeg-Bosna Republic was supposedly dissolved, but vestiges of its institutions continue to exist.

The West would have preferred a unitary multi-ethnic liberal Bosnian state but was obliged for reasons of conflict resolution, given the military positions at the time of the ceasefire and the demands of the three groups, to present plans that carved up Bosnia into national territories, within a loose federal framework. The basic thrust of the constitution is thus cultural-pluralist, rather than multicultural, and it has not been able to operate successfully because of a lack of cooperation on the part of the three dominant ethnic groups. As a result, Bosnia has had less political autonomy than originally intended and there has been a continued usurpation of political power by the UN high representative (HR) and other representatives of the international community: "Although Bosnia remains formally a sovereign state, the extension of international mandates over the state has left little space for Bosnian state institutions to make or to implement policy."[10] In sum, the constitutional arrangements for power sharing in Bosnia have proven inadequate for resolving the conflict and promoting the development of a stable, independent, and democratic state.

## CONSTITUTIONAL ARRANGEMENTS: KOSOVO

The war in Kosovo ended on 9 June 1999 with the signing of the Kumanovo Agreement between the North Atlantic Treaty Organization (NATO) and the former Federal Republic of Yugoslavia. United Nations Security Council Resolution 1244 (1999),[11] adopted on 10 June, placed Kosovo under international administration, established the framework for post-conflict reconstruction, and created the United Nations Administrative Mission in Kosovo (UNMIK). Kosovo remained within Yugoslavia but was given back its former status as an "autonomous region" (which had been rescinded in September 1990).

The role of UNMIK was to provide "the whole spectrum [of] essential administrative functions and services covering such areas as health and education, banking and finance, post and telecommunications, and law and order."[12] UNMIK's principal areas of responsibility were: (1) institutions and democracy building, rule of law, and human rights, led by the Organization for Security and Cooperation in Europe (OSCE); (2) reconstruction, directed by the European Union (EU); and (3) civil administration, led by UNMIK's special representative to the secretary-general (SRSG) for Kosovo. Under UNMIK's auspices, joint administrative departments were formed in January 2000; the first step towards democratic representation was taken at the municipal level, where elections were held in October 2000; and a new Constitutional Framework for Provisional Self-government for Kosovo (hereafter the Constitutional Framework) was adopted on 15 May 2001.[13]

The Constitutional Framework defined the province as an undivided territory, declared liberal rights and freedoms, and established the provisional institutions of self-government, including the assembly, the presidency, the government, and the judicial system. It also defined (in Chapter 8) the "Powers and Responsibilities Reserved to the SRSG." These powers were broad and ensured that the SRSG maintained control and authority over all aspects of the post-conflict reconstruction project and the provisional government. General elections were held in November 2001, and in June 2002 the government of Kosovo met for the first time, after taking an oath of office in front of the SRSG. New municipal elections followed in October 2002.[14] The remaining stages of the UNMIK democratization project (as yet uncompleted) are to transfer authority to the provisional government and then to support the transfer to a permanent government.

Taken together, Resolution 1244 and the Constitutional Framework have seemingly created the conditions for the separation of Kosovo from Serbia and Montenegro (the successor state to the former Federal Republic of Yugoslavia). All of the necessary structures are in place: Kosovo has its own government, police, and judiciary; it issues its own postage stamps; and it uses the Euro as its currency instead of the dinar. The significance of these facts is not lost on the Kosovo Serbs. With only 10 of the 120 seats in the Kosovo assembly, where decisions are made by majority vote (with a quorum of forty), and only one of the seven seats on the presidency, the Serbs understandably feel powerless. Although the Constitutional Framework states that both of the communities in Kosovo shall have the right "to preserve, protect and express their ethnic, cultural, religious, and linguistic identities,"[15] the protection of "vital interests" is not included, as it is in the Bosnian constitution. Whereas the Bosnian model was based on one-third representation by each ethnic group within the government and presidency, the Kosovo model permits less representation. The result, in a democracy with an Albanian majority, is that Kosovo Serbs have to rely on their Albanian co-citizens and the Constitutional Court to ensure that their ethnic rights and interests are safeguarded.

## TRANSITIONAL ARRANGEMENTS: ACTORS, AUTHORITY, AND POWER SHARING

Constitutional mechanisms are only half of the power-sharing issue in post-conflict reconstruction. The other side of the same coin is the relationship and transition between the interim international administration and the provisional government. The CSIS/AUSA framework divides action on the political-pillar tasks into three phases: initial response, transformation, and fostering sustainability. The goal of the first phase is to determine the governance structure and establish the foundation for citizen participation. The second phase is designed to promote legitimate political institutions and participatory processes, and the third is to consolidate them (that is, to complete the transition to a system of stable, democratic government that is self-sustaining).

In the case of Bosnia, the first objective was achieved through the Dayton Accord, the second by way of the September 1996 elections, and the third objective has yet to be reached. In the case of Kosovo, developing provisional institutional structures was a mandate of the SRSG and was attained in May 2001, the second objective was achieved with the elections of November 2001, and, as in Bosnia, the third has yet to be reached.

The transition of authority should ideally be a fluid process whereby international administration diminishes over time while the authority of the provisional government (and sovereignty) increases. This is followed by a similar dynamic in the transition between provisional government and permanent government. Likewise, the ideal is for military activity to be intense at the beginning and then, over time, to diminish. In Bosnia, overall military activity has diminished, though there are still interventions (for example, to capture war criminals or to take action against biased media). Political interference and control, however, have grown over time, with the HR assuming more powers to pass legislation and to remove elected political figures whom he deems to be inhibiting progress. In Kosovo, military activity has also declined but the international political presence has remained as intense as ever.

Transitional arrangements in Bosnia, as outlined in Annex 2 of the constitution, included the appointment of a Joint Interim Commission (JIC) "with a mandate to discuss practical questions related to the implementation of the Constitution of Bosnia and Herzegovina ... and to make recommendations and proposals."[16] The JIC, however, "was little more than a high-level consultative body." The HR, as the authority responsible for overseeing the civilian implementation of the Dayton Accord, was, and remains, the principal actor in the political pillar of post-conflict reconstruction in Bosnia.[17] The HR is responsible for monitoring, facilitating, participating in, coordinating, and reporting on all civilian aspects of the Accord, including the "establishment of political and constitutional institutions in Bosnia-Herzegovina ... and the holding of free and fair elections."[18] He is nominated by the steering board of the PIC and is appointed by the UN Security Council. The HR is "the final authority in theatre regarding interpretation of [the Accord] on the civilian implementation of the peace settlement."[19] The HR initially had no legal powers to enforce compliance with the Accord. His role was "to facilitate the Parties' own efforts and to mobilize and, as appropriate, coordinate the activities of the organizations and agencies involved in the civilian aspects of the peace settlement."[20] The HR, in other words, was meant to respect the autonomy of the parties and to advise and guide them as to the impact of their decisions.

Over time, the powers of the HR, and those of other international actors, have been extended and augmented by decisions taken at the biyearly meetings of the PIC. The September 1996 elections were supposed to mark the full ownership of the democratic process by the Bosnians but, as the elections approached, they were recognized by the PIC as only a starting point for democratization, or a step in the right direction. At the PIC meeting in Paris in November 1996, the transition period was accordingly extended from one to three years by the addition of a two-year "consolidation period." The effect was to place Bosnia under international administration for another two years, thus reducing its capacity for autonomous decision making. "Rather than policy-making being the prerogative of the state and entity authorities, with the joint institutions there to ensure the international community's influence over areas of potential controversy, policy-making was to be retained by the international administration."[21]

At the December 1997 PIC meeting in Bonn, the HR's powers were again extended to allow him "to decide the time, location and chairmanship of meetings of the central institutions, to enact interim measures where the Bosnian representatives could not agree to Office of the High Representative policy, and to take action against non-compliant officials at both state and entity level."[22] Since December 1997 the HR has actively used his powers to enforce legislation and remove officials from office.[23] The transition to self-governance is slow and has generally been forced by the HR. Power sharing within the context of transitional (that is, not yet consolidated) government is structured so that Bosnia is nominally run by the Bosnian and entity governments but legally and actually by the HR and international committees.

Unlike Bosnia (or, more exactly, because of Bosnia), Kosovo was organized as an international protectorate from the beginning. Resolution 1244 provided the SRSG with all the necessary powers to control Kosovo's political, economic, and social structures.[24] The relationship between the international interim administration and the Kosovo government has remained essentially the same since 1999.

## TRANSFERRING AUTHORITY: DEMOCRACY THROUGH ELECTIONS

The goal of post-conflict reconstruction in south-east Europe is to establish an enduring democratic state. Democracy, however, comes in many forms and is generally applied in post-conflict situations by international bodies, such as the UN, which are comprised of states with varying interpretations of what democracy implies. Nevertheless, the model of Western liberal democracy tends to be the most influential. Yet Western liberal democracy assumes the existence of certain conditions that are not the norm in post-conflict states, such as, for example, that political majorities are temporary (hence today's minority can become tomorrow's majority), that voting will not follow ethnic lines, that group and individual rights will be balanced, that political opinions may be freely expressed, and that voters may vote as they please, without fear of retaliation. These may not be realistic expectations, however, in post-conflict ethnically divided states. If the creation of

Western-style democracy is nevertheless the goal, then the question becomes one of how to achieve that goal, which in turn raises questions about when and how to conduct elections, how to establish institutions of self-government, and when and through what process to transfer authority to local governments.

The transfer of authority from international administration to local governments in Bosnia and Kosovo was initially linked to the holding of democratic elections. The benchmark for both Bosnia and Kosovo was their demonstrated capacity to hold free and fair elections in a safe environment. This benchmark was later changed in Bosnia to the point in time at which the HR considered peace, liberal democracy, good governance, and a market economy to be self-sustaining. It would thus seem that the democratic prerequisites for a transfer to complete autonomy in Bosnia grew over time. Similarly, in Kosovo the SRSG does not yet consider the population ready to move from externally controlled, provisional self-government to self-rule.

In both Bosnia and Kosovo the holding of elections – almost regardless of the social conditions and expected ethnically biased outcomes – was considered an essential objective of the state-building project. In both cases it was assumed that the presence of democratic structures and the practice of democracy through voting would teach citizens and governments to be democratic. Elections were marked, however, by a lack of party pluralism and an abundance of voter intimidation. Following the November 2000 general elections in Bosnia, the SRSG reported that "the recent general elections ... demonstrated yet again how nationalist parties are willing to incite inter-ethnic fear and suspicion in order to preserve their power and privileges."[25]

Elections in post-conflict states, if held too early in the transition process, may entrench conflict and reify group/ethnic cleavages. In both Bosnia and Kosovo, it may be argued in retrospect, the timetable for democratic elections was unrealistic: in Bosnia, voting occurred nine months after the signing of the Dayton Accord, and in Kosovo the elections were held sixteen months after Resolution 1244. In both cases, international donor expectations increased the pressure for elections, before civic institutions were given a chance to replace ethno-nationalist ones.

The first opportunity for Kosovars to vote was on 28 October 2000. Organizing Kosovo for elections proved a difficult task, given both the social conditions and the bureaucratic system used by UNMIK to register voters. This raises the essential issue of what the basic conditions are for holding democratic elections and, thereafter, the granting of self-rule. In Kosovo, the decision was made by the SRSG to hold elections in spite of the continued violence and non-cooperation that characterized Kosovo's social conditions at that time. As Eric Chevallier writes, "la majorité des interlocuteurs de la MINUK [UNMIK] considéraient qu'il était déraisonnable d'organizer des élections dans le climat qui régnait au Kosovo, au motif que les conditions optimales propres à leur bon déroulement n'étaient pas réunies."[26] The result of the October 2000 elections[27] was to marginalize the Serbs who refused to participate. Ironically, the Serbs had refused to participate for fear of legitimizing a process that would marginalize them. Adding to the confusion, Belgrade at first supported Serb non-participation but, after the arrival of President Vojislav Kostunica, reversed its position and supported participation.

## CONCLUSION

In order for a people to embrace democracy, at some point they have to practise democracy and its rules of governance however imperfect they may be. Nevertheless, certain fundamental prerequisites regarding the salience of identity and ethno-nationalism must be fulfilled. If elections are held prematurely, under conditions of insecurity and when ethnic identity is the most salient political factor, the result will likely be the reification of ethno-nationalism with citizens voting in ethnic blocs.

Neither Bosnia nor Kosovo is politically autonomous or a stable democracy. In the October 2002 general elections in Bosnia, nationalist parties continued to reap the majority of votes of their respective ethnic groups, electoral participation was low (at 55 per cent of the 2.6 million eligible voters), and some 25,000 potential voters were turned away because they were not listed on official election registers.[28] In Kosovo the October 2002 elections were marred by violent incidents.[29] According to the SRSG, "Kosovo has not yet achieved the standards that either the international community or its own people demand."[30] Authority, consequently, has not yet been transferred to the provisional institutions.

From the examination in this chapter of the objectives and tasks of the political pillar of post-conflict reconstruction in Bosnia and Kosovo, and the outcomes to date, three general conclusions may be drawn. First, power sharing as a mechanism is likely to be ineffective unless the structural solution is accompanied by an ideational one. If the aim is to build a multinational civic state, for example, it is necessary to promote ideational change concerning citizenship, ethnic identity, and place (homeland). In Bosnia the Dayton Accord was weak with respect to explicitly addressing ideas, although the implementation process did make progress through initiatives designed to modify ideas by controlling the media, promoting civil society, developing state symbols, and supporting inter-group reconciliation. Addressing the rules, shared ideas, and practice of ethno-nationalist institutions fosters a transformation from ethno-nationalism to civic nationalism.

Second, constitutional power sharing is only one tool in the toolbox of post-conflict reconstruction mechanisms. To be effective, it must complement its political and social environment and be employed in unison with reconstruction mechanisms. The objective should be to provide some autonomy in decision making for minorities and guarantees for the protection of their cultural identity and interests, and to do so without obstructing the routine operations of government. Power-sharing institutions should also not obstruct the eventual development of a multicultural civic state.

Third, transitional arrangements should be designed to permit a state to become autonomous by meeting clearly defined milestones within a specified time-frame. Instead, in Bosnia the international administration has increased its authority over the government and expropriated the transition to democracy. In Kosovo the international administration continues to maintain tight control over the government.[31] The issues of when to transfer authority and how to identify and set benchmarks and milestones for self-rule are complex and case-dependent. What is clear, however, is that the international community should not wait for the processes of liberal democracy to reach Western standards before completing the transfer of authority. Furthermore, the transfer should be a fluid and gradual process, with local citizens gaining ownership of the process as the international presence diminishes.

NOTES

1 Association of the U.S. Army and Center for Strategic and International Studies, *Post-conflict Reconstruction: A Joint Project of the Center for Strategic and International Studies (CSIS) and the Association of the United States Army (AUSA)*, Task Framework (2001).

2 In his critique of power sharing as organized under the Dayton Accord, David Chandler cites these two elements – autonomy of decision making and security of vital interests – as the key to establishing a multi-ethnic Bosnia. David Chandler, *Bosnia: Faking Democracy after Dayton*, 2nd ed. (London: Pluto Press 1999), 66–89.

3 The Accord was the culmination of a number of preceding peace plans, agreements, and guiding principles. For the relevant documents, see Ministère des Affaires Étrangères, *Accords de Paix concernant l'Ex-Yougoslavie*, Documents d'actualité internationalie, February 1996 (Paris: La documentation Française 1996).

4 Chandler, *Bosnia*, 67.

5 The Accord also dealt with a number of other matters. It made Sarajevo a unified city; established a four-kilometre-wide corridor linking Sarajevo and Gorazde; and deferred, for international arbitration within a year, the issue of the town of Brcko and the Posavina corridor. It created a territory known as he "anvil" in northwest Bosnia (by transferring land from the Bosniac Federation to Republika Srpska) to ensure that the Serbs would have 49 per cent of the total territory; outlined the government structures and responsibilities of the respective entities; set a schedule for elections for the municipal, cantonal, entity, and federal levels; ordered the withdrawal and cantonment of military forces; and authorized the return of refugees and displaced persons.

6 The Constitution of Bosnia and Herzegovina, Articles IV(3)(c) and IV(3)(d) respectively.

7 Constitution, Article V(2)(c).

8 PIC chairman, "Summary of Conclusions," "Bosnia and Herzegovina 1998: Self-Sustaining Structures," Bonn Peace Implementation Conference 1997, Bonn, 10 December 1997 (OHR website).

9 The HDZ (Croat party) held majorities in cantons 2, 7, 8, and 10 and these cantons became the core of the so-called Herzeg-Bosna Republic. The existence of this republic was contrary to the Dayton Accord and was a barrier to the creation of the federation even after the September 1996 elections.

10 Chandler, *Bosnia*, 55.

11 United Nations S/RES/1244 (1999).

12 UNMIK homepage <www.unmikonline.org>, 2 August 2002.

13 Constitutional Framework for Self-Government UNMIK/REG/2001/9–15 May 2001.

14 Local elections were held on 26 October 2002. Democratic League of Kosovo (LDK) president Ibrahim Rugova won fourteen of thirty municipalities,

ethnic Serbs won in four. BBC, 27 October 2002 (www.balkantimes.com, 28 October 2002).

15 Constitutional Framework, preamble and 4(1).

16 Constitutional Framework, Annex 1(a) Transitional Arrangements, Annex 2 of Annex 4 (The Constitution).

17 The high representatives to date have been Carl Bildt, Carlos Westendorp, Wolfgang Petritsch, and Lord Paddy Ashdown.

18 Constitutional Framework, Annex 10, Article l(1).

19 Constitutional Framework, Annex 10, Article V.

20 Constitutional Framework, Annex 10, Article l(2).

21 Chandler, *Bosnia*, 53. The NATO and OSCE mandates were also extended in November.

22 Chandler, *Bosnia*, 54. (Based on PIC: Bonn Peace Implementation Council 1997, Bonn, 10 December, Office of the High Representative, XI, par. 2.)

23 For example, HR Carlos Westendorp removed Republika Srpska President Nikola Poplasen from office in March 1999 and in November 1999 HR Wolfgang Petritsch removed twenty-two elected Bosnian officials.

24 The SRSG's to date have been Bernard Kouchner, July 1999 to January 2001; Hans Hekkerup, February 2001 to December 2001; Michael Steiner, December 2001 to June 2004; Søren Jensen-Petersen, June 2004 to the present.

25 Report of the Secretary General on the United Nations mission in Bosnia-Herzegovina (UNMIBH), 30 November 2000. UNMIBH website, 31 January 2001.

26 Eric Chevallier, "L'ONU au Kosovo: leçons de la première MINUK," Occasional Papers, no.35 (Paris: European Union Institute for Security Studies, May 2002), 15.

27 Fifty-eight per cent for the moderate LDK and 35 per cent for ex-UCK (Kosovo Liberation Army; English: KLA) parties (27 per cent, Democratic Party of Kosovo [PDK]; and 8 per cent, Alliance for the Future of Kosovo [AAK]). Chevallier, "L'ONU au Kosovo."

28 Canada, Department of Foreign Affairs and International Trade/Department of National Defence, Weekly Briefing Note on Peacekeeping Ops (unclassified), 9–15 Oct 2002.

29 The mayor of Suva Reka of the Democratic League of Kosovo (LDK) was gunned down on Sunday 27 October 2002. Two weeks earlier, about "1000 Kosovo Albanians attacked (with stones and Molotov cocktails) a group of 50 Kosovo Serb returnees from Osojane Village." DFAIT/DND, Weekly Briefing Note, 9–15 October 2002.

30 UNMIK homepage <www.unmikonline.org>, 31 July 2002.

31 Three years after Resolution 1244, Kosovo Prime Minister Bajram Rexhepi stated that "Kosovo was now ready to take charge of its own affairs and should be allowed to join the international community of nations. Not so, according to the UNMIK officials. While considerable progress has been made in creating a democratic, multiethnic society, much work still remains to be done" (David Newman and Joel Peters, "Kosovo as the West Bank, Macedonia as Israel: If It Works in the Balkans, Could the 'State-in-Transition' Model Be Applied to the Israeli-Palestinian Conflict?" *Haaretz* (English edition), 30 October 2002).

# 6

# Power Sharing in a Police Car: The Intractable Difficulty of Police Reform in Kosovo and Macedonia

GORDON PEAKE

For a lasting peace to be achieved in a divided society, the existing police force must be radically reformed and its personnel retrained to orient them to a new style of policing. In peace processes throughout the globe, a core component has been the program to reconcile former foes by including their members in transformed police institutions in order to help head off the turbulent challenges that often accompany a peace process.[1] It is power sharing in microcosm. Participation is encouraged from members of historically under-represented ethnic groups so that the new police will better reflect the population as a whole. Irrespective of geographic location, the hope is the same – that, through a common uniform, a police force encompassing all members of historically distrustful ethnic groups can forge a new beginning in policing. Police reform is thus a key part of a wider raft of reforms to existing institutions during post-conflict reconstruction.

After discussing the need for reform, this chapter points out the great difficulties in translating rhetorical commitments into a workable reality. The difficulties are demonstrated by examining two examples from the southern Balkans: Kosovo (1999–present) and Macedonia (2001– present). Policing in these cases is shown to be a tough nut to crack. Both reform processes have received extensive support from donors, but major difficulties remain in translating the commitment to police reform into workaday practice. Although blending different ethnicities together in one uniform as police officers may be of high symbolic value, it requires much more than that to fundamentally alter a policing culture that has long been identified with one community rather than another. Similarly, it is not easy to increase confidence in policing in communities that have historically been excluded from the ranks of the police. In both Kosovo and Macedonia, new police forces thus face major obstacles in creating and cementing legitimacy for themselves in societies where many of the people have customarily regarded a uniformed officer as an emblem of fear rather than of succour or comfort. Legacies of distrust are hard to overcome, and it is difficult to create a lasting culture of reliance and trust in the police. The chief problems can be grouped into three broad categories: structural elements, whereby police reform is part of wider institutional and legal reform; operational elements, which involve trying to integrate different ethnicities into a new style of policing; and practical problems of criminality, which the new forces have to face.

## POLICING AS PART OF THE PROBLEM

In many conflict situations the police are regarded as emblematic of a discord that their actions have deepened and perpetuated. Often overwhelmingly staffed by a particular ethnic or political group, the police have been associated with repression, unaccountability, and militarization, and they have tended to act in the interests of their own group to the exclusion of others. Sizeable communities in both Kosovo and Macedonia were either under-represented in or completely absent from the ranks of the police. Police behaviour was frequently cited as a cause of concern and a factor that further divided the already polarized populations. In each area, when conflict flared, members of the police apparatus engaged in actual combat operations, thereby further cementing their one-sided image. More often than not, their work was carried out with scant regard for human rights, the rule of law, or due legal process.[2]

They were following a deep-rooted trend. Police in divided societies have historically been characterized as interested more in protecting the state than in protecting the citizenry, a state identified as representing one community over the other. They have also been hampered by more prosaic problems, such as antiquated methods and equipment.

In response, communities that are absent or ostracized from the ranks of the police have tended to develop their own mechanisms for policing and regulating their own communities. Informal networks of family or clan, together with policing functions assumed by insurgents or para-military groups, have created a large societal sphere from which the uniformed police are largely missing.

## POLICING AS PART OF THE SOLUTION

Since the police have been such a major part of the problem, it is somewhat ironic that – once reconstituted – they are handed a central role in protecting and safeguarding the implementation of a peace process. Nevertheless, they are absolutely necessary because, without civil order and law enforcement, the chances of wider political, social, and economic progress taking root are reduced almost to nil. A reformed crime-fighting apparatus does much more than guarantee public order. The police are equally important as symbols. For them to be effective in carrying out their functions, and for the new political regime to have any chance of success, they must demonstrate that they can command the trust of all sections of the community. Their being seen as making a clean break from the repressive practices of the past is an important sign of a society's transition from conflict to a more peaceful dispensation. It indicates a community-wide acceptance of the peace settlement and the wider resolution process. Moreover, their character is a defining badge of a new political and ideological outlook.

An important element – both practical and symbolic – of the new era's approach to policing is boosting the representation of communi-ties that were historically under-represented in the force. In Northern Ireland, Catholics have been encouraged to join a reformed and renamed police apparatus, the Police Service of Northern Ireland. In the southern Balkans, Albanians are being encouraged to join new police services in southern Serbia, Kosovo, and Macedonia. Similar processes are currently taking place in Sierra Leone and Afghanistan, among other countries.

The hope is not just that the make-up of the police will change but also that there will be a change in the ethos and attitudes by which policing is carried out. The shared aim of reformers is to create police forces with a softer image. Three critical objectives – the "three Rs" – characterize the reform effort: redefinition of the force's mission; restructuring of its deployment and operations; and re-attunement of its political orientation.

The ethos that underpins police reform has become known as democratic policing. A distillation of ideal practice, democratic policing is systematically respectful of human dignity, civil rights, accountability, and the rule of law, and it has been the guiding principle behind many reform processes throughout the past decade.[3] As part of these processes, existing police organizations have been extensively restructured. Old militaristic structures have been dismantled and replaced by inclusive, slimmed-down institutions that have transparent, clearly defined roles. The aim is that police institutions will henceforth operate in a non-partisan, law-abiding, professional, competent, and democratically accountable fashion. The hope is that the police force will be an institution that only criminals need fear. The intention is also to decentralize decision making and make local communities feel that they are involved in the reform process. But these goals, in many ways, are ideals that are impossible to meet.

## THE MAJOR CHALLENGES OF POLICE REFORM

Post-conflict police forces must surmount seemingly overwhelming challenges if they are to achieve all that is expected of them. Indeed, the challenges are so vast and varied that they would be severe for police forces of much longer lineage and with much higher standards of technology and equipment. An untoward by-product of many peace agreements is a sharp rise in crime – the cumulative consequence of a shattered economy, lawlessness in a traumatized society, a large number of idle former fighters, and numerous weapons in circulation.[4] Also, criminal gangs tend to take advantage of these conditions to create nests for the production or trafficking of illicit weapons, narcotics, and human beings. The perception has taken root that many post-conflict societies (including those in the southern Balkans) are lawless dystopias awash with illegal weaponry, where criminality is allowed to reign supreme. As if this were not enough, new police forces are often hamstrung by equipment that is outmoded or insufficient in quantity. Other factors, such as economic collapse, weak traditions of statehood, and continuing political uncertainty, make these ethnic tinderboxes even more potentially combustible and consequently even more difficult to police. Just one incident has the risk of damaging political fabrics that have been delicately sutured together.

Many factors conspire against effective police reform. Old habits die hard. Police forces everywhere tend to be distrustful of outsiders and resistant to change.⁵ Thus, changes in philosophy and approach at the top are often slow to percolate throughout the organization. While some officers will be amenable to change, all will not be. Also, although reforms may redress the issues of numerical under-representation, new recruits begin as beat-patrol officers and have little influence. It takes time for them to rise to leadership positions and so be able to affect the institutional culture.

Convincing the general public of the sincerity of police reforms also presents a major challenge. In societies where police uniforms are associated with occupation and repression, non-institutional policing mechanisms such as family and clan have deep roots and long histories. Initiatives to include communities in policing and the mere presence of a newly reformed police force do not erase that tradition. Moreover, there may be benefits to be had by community leaders from a policing vacuum that would not exist if there were an effective policing service. There is also the problem of changing perceptions. In deeply divided societies, one section of the public is apt to perceive the police as protectors of the public good, while the other section will perceive them as instruments of discrimination or repression. These conflicting perceptions, reinforced through generations of interaction, are difficult to change speedily. Many torn societies see political reform as a zero-sum game in which a gain for one community inevitably entails a loss for the other. Accordingly, new police forces in the early stages of reform may actually begin with less firm support than the police enjoyed under the previous regime.

Institutional reform of the police alone has been shown to be ineffective unless there is also reform of other criminal justice institutions, namely, the courts and prison system. If judicial or prison reform is too slow or insufficient to make an impact, the positive effects of whatever policing improvements have been made will be reduced considerably.⁶

The difficulty of policing in difficult circumstances is demonstrated below by an examination of two instances where "power sharing in a police car" is being attempted: Kosovo and Macedonia. While each reform process is being carried out separately, both share interconnected political roots that stem from a rise in Albanian political activism. This has been variously interpreted – as everything from a campaign for civic recognition and equal political rights to an irredentist campaign for separation of the areas where Albanians are a majority and unification with a greater Albanian state – but the peace settlements in both Kosovo and Macedonia accepted the former inter-pretation and emphasized the need for power sharing between the communities. Hence, Serbs share committee places and sit in the min-isterial cabinet with Kosovar Albanians; in Macedonia, a grand coali-tion of Albanian and Macedonian political parties shares power. The power-sharing approach is also reflected in police reform. In Kosovo, since mid-1999, an international force under the United Nations (UN) banner has been carrying out interim policing functions and training a multi-ethnic local service that will eventually inherit this responsibility. In accordance with a key provision of the 2001 Ohrid Agreement, Albanians are being integrated into the Macedonian police in numbers intended to be more reflective of their population size.

## KOSOVO

### Policing the peace

Kosovo's UN administrators faced a complete policing vacuum when they inherited administrative responsibilities for the province following the war in 1999 between the North Atlantic Treaty Organization and Yugoslavia. Policing had previously been the preserve of the Serbian police and paramilitaries, who departed in the aftermath of the war. The Kosovar Albanian police officers had been sacked by Yugoslav authorities in 1989–90 and had not worked in over a decade. High levels of ethnically motivated crime and a glut of car thefts were the most visible signs of an absence of policing and public order. The need to establish some sort of official policing mechanism was urgent.

The United Nations Interim Administrative Mission in Kosovo (UNMIK) took responsibility for policing. Under UN resolution 1244, its mandate had two elements: to enforce civil order and to establish a suc-cessor. This mandate was more robust than anything previously approved for a peacekeeping operation. International civilian police, drawn from over fifty countries, were given primary executive authority for policing, rather than simply having a monitoring function. The second element of their mandate was, in effect, to work themselves out of a job by estab-lishing and developing a professional, impartial, and politically neutral police service that in time would assume policing responsibility.

Like other Kosovo institutions, the Kosovo Police Service (KPS) was envisaged by UNMIK as a multi-ethnic institution, embracing the

Kosovar Albanians and Serbs as well as much smaller Turkish, Goran, Bosniac, Ashkali, and Roma minority groups. Moreover – against regional conventions – applications from women were encouraged. UNMIK's stated aim was that women would comprise 20 per cent of the new service. This service was also to differ from its authoritarian predecessors in organizational ethos, with an emphasis on community policing. The recruits came from a variety of backgrounds. Around 50 per cent had fought with the Kosovo Liberation Army (KLA) during the conflict in 1999. Many of the older recruits had previous experience as officers in the former Yugoslav police.

The new police force, as envisaged, would not be easy to achieve:

It's a combined model of North American and Western European policing traditions – a collective version of those countries that have a history of providing democratic policing, that is, policing where the rights of the citizen are meant to come before protecting the interests of an ethnic group or the state. It's an alien model and one that few of these new officers will have had exposure to. Culturally it means overcoming barriers that we [the international police] are working against all the time: perceptions of the police, perceptions of other groups. There are also the problems of funding and having the time to set aside to ensure that each of these individuals become mature police officers.[7]

Six years on, the transition is well under way. The KPS patrols some areas independently of the UNMIK international police, and the transfer of policing authority from UNMIK to the KPS is making progress. Some new recruits have already begun to fill senior management positions, shadowing international officers whom they are eventually to replace.

Publicity for the force highlights its multi-ethnic nature. In particular, UNMIK is at pains to stress that the KPS is comprised of officers from all the province's ethnic groups who train in fully integrated units and wear the same badge. All who sign up for the service take a pledge of impartiality and are bound by extensive and wide-ranging regulations.[8] But the reality on the ground is different. There are only a few stations where Albanians and Serbs work side by side. Attempts to impose integration have not been successful, partly because of the continuing political uncertainty. So, while officially the KPS is multi-ethnic, in practice there are few instances of genuine cooperation. Although officers from different ethnicities learn together in police school, the situation for the most part remains too delicate away from the classroom for them to share a squad car and policing tasks. Local animosity, coupled with the unwillingness of Kosovo's international administrators to risk inflaming local passions, has meant that actual power sharing remains a distant prospect.

Given the political turmoil surrounding the creation of the force, it would have been unrealistic to expect members of the KPS to insulate themselves from the charged political environment around them. Generally, KPS officers sense that their institution is of importance in leading Kosovo into a new political future. But, while this feeling is common to officers of all ethnic backgrounds, individual preferences regarding the future political direction of the force depend largely on the community to which the officer belongs. The experience in Kosovo indicates the difficulties of instituting real power-sharing mechanisms amidst a turbulent and uncertain political environment.

### Sharing Classrooms but Not Stations

It takes just six months to become a police officer in Kosovo. Recruits of all backgrounds train together in the same classroom for a period of twelve weeks. After graduation, the cadets are sent to police stations for field training and a taste of real policing. Following that, the new officers are deemed sufficiently prepared to undertake independent assignments.

The combination of time constraints and the cadets' unfamiliarity with the core concepts of democratic policing has been a constant challenge to those running the training program. Because of the tight schedule, there is little time to address topics in depth and the trainers are forced to deal quickly with complex concepts. Consequently, it is difficult for recruits to absorb the new information fully. The time available for teaching is reduced further by the need for simultaneous translation from English (the language of instruction) into Albanian and Serbian.[9] Instruction for the course is provided by international police officers, many from Western Europe or North American countries that are supposedly exemplars of democratic policing.

But there is little consensus among them on what democratic policing means in practice. For many international officers, it remains a vague concept that they variously describe as "making sure people were helped out" ... "the difference between the present type of policing and the past" ... "not hitting suspects" ... "taking down thorough notes on a case" ... "doing what you know to be the right thing." Among all the officers interviewed, there was a desire to emphasize their democratic policing credentials, but at the same time they made other remarks that suggest a discordant vision of effective policing. Many officers referred to the "mentality" of the local population, alluding to how locals would take advantage of the situation if they thought that the police showed any sign of weakness or leniency. This is another example of the difficulties encountered in refashioning the very ethos of policing.

The difficulty of reorienting a police force becomes apparent when the cadets leave the classroom. Although members of different ethnic groups study and train together, they attend separate graduation ceremonies, since an occasion incorporating all ethnic groups is considered too inflammatory. It is a telling sign of how far Kosovo still has to go.

When the new officers enter the stations, they encounter another difficult reality of policing. When the first batch of graduates arrived at their stations in late 1999 to join international police officers, more often than not they moved into an empty shell. Many of the buildings were without heating or electricity and few possessed as much as paper and pens, let alone cars or a communications system. No criminal record database existed. More significantly, the institutional pillars of a criminal justice system were absent. There was no correctional service and such prisons as existed had a tiny capacity. The larger facilities had been comprehensively destroyed during the war. There was no functioning court system. During the previous ten years, the courts had been run by the Serb-dominated Yugoslav administration, which had systematically disbarred Albanian judges and lawyers. With the departure of many of Kosovo's Serbian inhabitants in the aftermath of the war, there were not enough trained lawyers, prosecutors, judges, and administrators to allow the system to run effectively.

Many of the institutional problems that UNMIK met on arrival remain.[10] While UNMIK has established a correctional service and some existing facilities have been expanded and refurbished, Kosovo's prisons are still chronically short of cell space.[11] The judicial system is equally ill equipped.[12] Lacking infrastructure, money, equipment, and personnel, it remains unable to cope with the volume of cases brought before it.[13]

The challenges of instituting true power-sharing policing in Kosovo can be seen in their most intractable form in the northern city of Mitrovica, which has the reputation of being the most disorderly of Kosovo's cities.[14] Lying twenty-five miles north of Pristina and containing just over 100,000 inhabitants, the city has been described by Richard Holbrooke, a former u.s. envoy to Yugoslavia, as "the most dangerous place in Europe."[15] Split down the middle into Albanian and Serb neighbourhoods, it is a tragic symbol of Kosovo's ethnic division. The Albanian population, numbering about 95,000, lives mostly south of the river Ibar, which runs through the centre of the city, while 15,000 Serbs – local residents and internally displaced persons driven from other parts of Kosovo – live in the northern part of the city and its hinterland. The city had a mixed population before the war, and some Albanians continue to live in tower blocks on the northern bank of the river. The bridge connecting the two halves of the city is heavily fortified and guarded by military peacekeepers. It is often a focal point for communal disturbances.

There is no power sharing in terms of political administration in Mitrovica. The city has, in effect, been divided into two administrations. In the southern part, UNMIK runs local services in conjunction with the elected municipality. In the north, however, service provision is often disrupted owing to local resistance. The atmosphere is so tense that the international police are largely unable to carry out their day-to-day duties. No members of the KPS are stationed on the northern side. Albanian cadets were not posted there for fear of inflaming tensions, and all the Serb KPS officers were withdrawn after suffering physical attacks. Nor do Serb officers deploy with their Albanian counterparts in the southern stations. It is deemed too dangerous, and too likely to antagonize local Albanians. Faced with a tense political situation and pressing security problems, the international officers do not have time to oversee the delicate process of integration.

A further major problem affecting the police is that so much policing continues to go on without them. Customary laws governing dispute resolution among the Albanian population means that problems are resolved through forms of communal law and tradition, without recourse to the formal justice system. The police are frequently called to take witness statements when someone is hurt or injured, fully aware of the likelihood that the victim will take action independently and not through the court system. Moreover, before the war, there had been little general reporting of crime to the Yugoslav police by the Albanian population, and the habit of non-reporting has not changed.

Mitrovica and its surrounding villages are important transit points in the trafficking of women and illegal goods. Yet it has proved impossible for the international police to penetrate local smuggling rings, even though the identity of the rings' members is often an open secret. In addition to a language barrier, the hybrid force faces intelligence short-comings, particularly a lack of informants, and a paucity of investigative resources. The police in Mitrovica, like those throughout Kosovo, lack a central identity or vehicular licence database. There is also a lack of institutional support. The inadequacy of the court and penal systems in Mitrovica is particularly felt. Both the court and the correctional facility are located on the north side of the river, and consequently it is often more practical to transport prisoners to court eighty miles away in Pristina rather than run the gauntlet of crossing the bridge. Moreover, there are only three holding cells in the entire police station and no facilities for segregating prisoners. (Suspects from different ethnicities cannot be housed in the same cell for fear of the consequences.)

Wider political uncertainty has raised troubling questions about about whether the KPS will manage to preserve the democratic policing model that – in theory at least – is now in place. Kosovo's long-term status remains in limbo, which serves to exacerbate the continuing problem of time and financial constraints placed on the training pro-grams. In most communities, police forces mature over long periods, with supervisory responsibility being awarded only after years of ser-vice; the most senior leadership positions often take decades to achieve. The abbreviated start-up period in Kosovo has meant that those appointed to supervisory and leadership positions have much less experience. In addition, the problem of funding is expected to grow ever more acute as increasing responsibility is handed from UNMIK to the KPS. Behind such obvious "front-end" needs as uniforms, weapons, and vehicles, there appears little prospect that Kosovo will be able to shoulder by itself all of the financial burdens associated with running a modern police service. Even the annual international budgetary sup-port of just under 40 million Euros is deemed insufficient to meet the basic equipment and overhead needs of the force, and certainly is not enough to achieve the democratic policing ideals of its founders.[16] There is a concern also about how much political influence outside parties will wield over the force. For those orchestrating the transition, the question of how well the elaborate system of administration will be upheld and maintained once UNMIK hands over control to the KPS remains very much in doubt. As an UNMIK officer in charge of designing the transition observed: "The whole idea behind establishing a KPS is to hand policing over, for the first time, to local control. However, that also means loosening and possibly losing the controls we have over recruitment criteria, quotas for women officers, multi-ethnicity et cetera. There's no way of knowing how 'democratic' the KPS will be as it settles down and takes shape."[17]

## MACEDONIA

Whereas in Kosovo power-sharing policing is being attempted within the context of a fledgling force, in Macedonia it is being tried with an existing police force. That force, however, is strongly identified with – and has the reputation of favouring – one part of the country's population, the Macedonian Slavs, over the other main group, the Albanians.

The changes since 2001 in Macedonia's political architecture and the way in which the country is policed are considerable. The country has seen an Albanian insurgency, followed by a peace agreement, and now the leaders of the insurgency occupy ministerial office as leaders of the country's largest Albanian political party. Reforms to policing are central to the agreement and to the government's response to the insurgency, and they are a key institutional benchmark for how much real and effective change there has in fact been. Police reform has consequently received extensive international support in its first phase, primarily from the Organization for Security and Cooperation in Europe (OSCE). However, the processes of institutional change have not been simple, nor has it been easy to persuade Macedonia's Albanian community to put their faith in the reformed police force. Indeed, in many ways the task has only just begun. Although there are now greater numbers of Albanians in the force and they are deployed throughout the country, safeguarding this achievement requires deep institutional and management reform.

In the first few months of 2001, things were looking extremely bleak for Macedonia, the only country that had seceded from former Yugoslavia without bloodshed. An ethnic Albanian force that called itself the National Liberation Army (NLA), and had close organizational links to the Kosovo Liberation Army, began an insurgency. While the NLA's public demands were for equal civil and political rights and economic opportunity for the country's Albanian minority, there was a widespread fear among the Macedonian majority that the NLA's unspoken aim was partition of the country. Their insurgency, which began with the killing of a Macedonian police officer, soon gathered pace. Macedonian police and military officers were expelled from towns and villages from the north and west of the country. Declared liberated zones, these areas soon came under sustained attack from the Macedonian army and special police units. During the fighting, more than 200 were killed, including 60 members of the Macedonian security and police forces. Around 100,000 – one-twentieth of the entire population – fled or were ejected from their homes. There were allegations of ethnically motivated violence committed by members of one community against the other. A number of human rights organizations cited the Macedonian police for their role in the fighting.

## Ceasefire and the Ohrid Agreement

Considerable international pressure was brought to bear to stem the fighting and prevent the situation spiralling further out of control. In talks brokered by the European Union (EU), a ceasefire plan was arranged. Although not perfectly observed, it provided a platform to allow negotiations to begin, and parliamentarians from the most electorally significant Macedonian and Albanian parties met at the resort city of Ohrid during the summer of 2001 in an effort to come up with a new form of political compact for the country.

An issue at the heart of the negotiations was policing. Albanian representatives demanded that their community be proportionately represented on the force. At the time, the police force was overwhelmingly Macedonian Slav (95 per cent) and was perceived as favouring the interests of that community over those of the large Albanian minority (around one-quarter of the population). For the accord to take hold, the police as an institution would need to enjoy broad rather than purely sectional support.

The Ohrid Agreement, reached on 13 August 2001, accordingly contained the following key features addressing police reform:

- making the force better reflect the ethnic composition of the country by boosting the numbers of minority officers (who would be mostly Albanians) by 1,000 by mid-2003, through fast hiring and quick-start police training programs;
- redeploying, as a confidence-building measure, the ethnically mixed police patrols to the "crisis areas" they had been ejected from during the conflict;

- retraining the police force in the principles of best-practice and community policing; and
- restructuring the police as an organization.

The component of the Ohrid Agreement that needed to be implemented most urgently was the commitment to increase the number of Albanian officers in the force. In a country of high unemployment, there was an enthusiastic clamour to sign up for the police: a total of nearly 6,000 (from all ethnic groups) applied for the first batch of 500 berths. Applicants had to be aged 18–25, have completed secondary school education, and have a clean criminal record. Sixty per cent of the new cadets were to be selected from the Albanian applicants, and 15 per cent were to be women – a first for a country where policing was traditionally a male-dominated preserve.

The model adopted for the accelerated training of new recruits closely followed the fast-track officer-training program pioneered for Kosovo. Turning successful applicants into officers would take nine months: an initial three at the police academy, followed by six months in the field to acquire some practical experience and develop community policing skills. Only after completion of the nine-month course were the new recruits vested with their weapons and given authority to carry out independent policing tasks.

As the head of the police school has admitted, the abbreviated training course is just about enough to teach the new recruits the bare essentials of policing but not much more than that: "Having fulfilled the basic course, the student is still not a fully trained police officer; he/she should be a safe officer both in relation to himself/herself and the working environment when working with an experienced colleague."[18] Thus, there is a trade-off inherent in putting police officers onto the streets as quickly as possible. Not being fully trained, they require further training on the job as well as support from colleagues, mentors, station commanders, and international police monitors in order to develop into effective police officers.

In Macedonia, the concept of community policing is at the forefront of the government's attempts to reclaim, reintegrate, and stabilize the northern portions of the country where effective control was lost during the NLA insurgency. Joint patrols of equal numbers of ethnic Albanian and Macedonian Slav police officers, usually accompanied by international police monitors, were the first representatives of the state to

return to the north following the Ohrid Agreement.[19] Travelling by
jeep, the officers called in on remote villages that were strongholds of
the NLA during the insurgency. Their daily assignments would not be
found on many Western European police rosters: for instance, arrang-
ing transport to take sick villagers to hospital in nearby towns, and,
more generally, listening, arbitrating, and negotiating. In many ways
they were social workers and representatives of the state as much as
police officers. Albanian officers have tended to take the lead in encoun-
ters with Albanian villagers while their Macedonian Slav colleagues
hang back. It is a doubly difficult task for these patrols, many of whose
officers are just out of training school. As well as trying to engender a
first-time trust from the local Albanian communities, they also have to
help foster trust among fellow officers of different ethnicities.

An extended lunch with the headman in one village to which the
police have returned provides an example of community policing,
Macedonian style. Though the talk did not directly cover policing
issues, creating a trust in the police was its intention. The delicate
process of winning the elder's trust was undertaken by using deference
(taking off one's holster belt when entering his house) and by the sheer
act of stopping by to engage in extended conversation with him in his
house. After a few hours, by the time the lunch was winding to a close,
a valuable relationship had been woven and a small step taken towards
building trust in the police as an institution.

While confidence in the police as an institution may be built by such
informal means, a trade-off is that the law may not be as rigorously
enforced as it could be and large policing challenges may be given
reduced priority. The porous Macedonia-Kosovo frontier has been a
long-standing conduit for smugglers and traffickers, and organized
criminal networks took advantage of the policing vacuum during the
conflict to further strengthen their cross-border links. In an effort to
ingratiate themselves with the residents of the border areas, the police
are liable to ignore existing problems or defer tackling them. As a
result, they find themselves in something of a "damned if they do and
damned if they don't" situation: strong action in an effort to improve
security and choke off criminal networks risks alienating the community, but a "softly-softly" approach leads to charges of ineffectiveness.

Yet no policing can be effective without the consent of those being
policed. The uneven history of policing in Macedonia, together with
the advantages of having a sphere that the police cannot penetrate, has
meant that many people continue to put their trust in traditional,

familial solutions rather than in the police. Nor can the police alone re-establish governmental control and legitimacy. Only when their efforts are allied with equally long-term local government reform and economic development projects can the police hope to be successful in building lasting legitimacy and trust.

## Longer-term Challenges: Changing the Ethos, Changing the Structure

It would have been whistling in the wind to concentrate only on training new officers without also trying to reform the police structure they will join, and without changing the principles and attitudes to policing that are integrally linked to that structure. In many ways, the two initial objectives of training minority candidates and police re-entry into the northern areas have been achieved. Now the challenge is to address the more difficult task of instilling a new community-minded ethos for policing within Macedonia, while at the same time restructuring the organization in such a way that it will be able to embody and promote this new ethos. That will involve changing attitudes within the police regarding their role as a reactive, state-centred agency, continued retraining, and structural, management, and leadership changes. For the communities that are the intended beneficiaries of this new approach, it will involve participation in a range of workshops, seminars, and outreach programs in an effort to unlearn old attitudes and inculcate new ones. Like most strategies, these are easier to formulate than they are to implement. There is still a long way to go.[20]

## The Difficulty of Effecting Structural Change

Community policing needs to be backed up by structural change to the force so that it will personify the new approach. If the structure does not support and help inculcate the new approach, then community policing cannot succeed. This, the last but probably the most telling and important part of the reform effort, is thus about issues of management and leadership as much as about policing issues. There is international support for structural change. The lead agency that in late 2002 began working on structural reform issues is the EU's Justice and Home Affairs Agency. So far, however, progress has been slow.

There are four key issues that still need to be addressed. One of the most important structural changes required to make community policing effective is decentralization. Before reform, Macedonia had one of the most highly centralized police structures in Europe. The police cannot adopt strategies tailored to the particular needs of the community, or be accountable to it, if decision making on the smallest operational matter rests with officers at police headquarters and the Ministry of Interior in Skopje. Creating regional, local, and community-based commands would allow policies to be tailored to the specific requirements of the locale.

The second most pressing need is the development of codes of conduct and a mechanism for reporting public complaints about the police. A citizenry that feels that it is worth reporting police misconduct is indicative, paradoxically, of trust in the service and confidence that one's complaints will be dealt with fairly. This still remains an objective rather than a reality.[21] There is still no agency to which complaints about officers can be reported.

A third issue is clarity in career recruitment and promotion structures. At present, both remain opaque, and the perception is still strong that career development in the police has more to do with political and familial affiliation than with workplace endeavour and merit. This is obviously a delicate matter, given the commitment under the Ohrid Agreement to make the force more inclusive of minorities, but the principle of deserved advancement nevertheless needs to be more clearly enshrined.

The fourth point – which should be considered in light of the third – involves redressing the ethnic imbalance at all stages and levels of the force. In their first few years of deployment, the Albanians who came into the force as part of the accelerated training package were still learning the ropes and for the most part remained at low-level positions. For the police to be a truly inclusive force, however, the path must be open for Albanian and other minority officers to be integrated at all levels, including the more senior. Of course, ascending to positions of authority does not take place overnight. Full integration cannot be expected in so short a period, but the advancement of the more able Albanian and other minority officers must nevertheless take place with sufficient speed for change to be felt.

## CONCLUSION

To preserve domestic tranquillity and increase confidence in the political process, policing has come to be seen as one of the most crucial elements of peacemaking. Experience has shown that without robust policing structures, fragile new political institutions find it difficult to survive and take root. However, despite being the recipient of considerable international support and goodwill, reformed police forces face daunting political, financial, logistical, and historical obstacles.

The experience in Kosovo and Macedonia indicates that reforming a police force is as formidably complex and fraught with uncertainty as attempting to solve the disputes themselves. Policing, it bears repeating, is a tough nut to crack. In both Kosovo and Macedonia, newly constituted police forces have been made responsible for policing territories where there had never before been a legitimate local force. They do not have the luxury of a settling-in period. They must establish their authority immediately, often without adequate funding, equipment, training, or personnel. Frequently, too, the long absence of legitimate law enforcement and justice systems has encouraged the development of alternative systems of conflict management and dispute resolution. To the extent that the new police are seen as threatening these mechanisms without offering a viable alternative, the task of embedding the legitimacy of the police is all the more difficult. In all of this there is the danger that, if the new police forces are not funded and equipped well enough to make an immediate show of their authority, the already fragile public confidence will shatter, endangering the entire process.

Meanwhile, there are major obstacles blocking attempts to make the police institutionally embody power sharing as a matter of routine – in other words, to practise power sharing in a police car. Perhaps this is asking too much, or asking too much too soon. These are forces without much experience, operating in the most challenging of contexts. Yet, because police forces are among the most visible symbols of the new regime, they are burdened with high expectations. It is hardly surprising that they find such expectations difficult to fulfil. That they often seem as inept and unloved as the forces they replaced is perhaps a reflection less of their own failings than of the multiplicity of demands that are placed on them. A period of two or three years is therefore not long enough to judge their effectiveness. It is worth remembering that even long-established Western police forces – those they are meant to imitate – don't always get it right. These new forces, operating as they must while undergoing major structural changes and in the midst of incomplete peace processes, should realistically be judged over a much longer time, say at least a generation.

## NOTES

1 Fen Osler Hampson, *Nurturing Peace: Why Peace Settlements Succeed or Fail* (Washington D.C.: United States Institute of Peace 1996); Tor Tanke Holm and Espen Bath Eide, ed., *Peacebuilding and Police Reform* (London: Frank Cass 2000); Otwin Marenin, *Policing Change, Changing Police: International Perspectives* (New York: Garland 1996); Jane Chanaa, *Security Sector Reform: Issues, Challenges and Prospects* (Oxford, U.K.: Oxford University Press 2002).

2 For a more comprehensive typology of the characteristics, see John D. Brewer, "Policing in Divided Societies: Theorising a Type of Policing," *Policing and Society* (1991): 183–5.

3 Robert Trojanowicz, Victor E. Kappelar, Larry. K Gaines, and Bonnie Bucqueroux, *Community Policing: A Contemporary Perspective* (Cincinnati, Ohio: Anderson Books 1998); Errol P. Mendes, Joaquin Zuckenberg, Susan Lecorre, Anne Gabriel, and Jeffrey A Clark, *Democratic Policing and Accountability: Global Perspectives* (Aldershot, U.K.: Ashgate 1999).

4 Mats R. Berdal, *Disarmament and Demobilisation after Civil Wars* (Oxford, U.K.: Oxford University Press 1996).

5 David H. Bayley, *Patterns of Policing: A Comparative International Analysis* (New Brunswick N.J.: Rutgers University Press 1985).

6 Rama Mani, "The Rule of Law or the Rule of Might? Restoring Legal Justice in the Aftermath of Conflict," in Michael Pugh, ed., *Regeneration of War-Torn Societies* (Basingstoke, U.K.: Macmillan 2000).

7 Interview, deputy commissioner for planning and development, Kosovo Police Service, Pristina, 11 April 2001.

8 Among the pledges made in the oath sworn by new officers is that "I will never act officially or permit personal feelings, prejudices, animosities, or friendships to influence my decisions." Kosovo Police Service, *Policy and Procedures Manual* (1999).

9 Kosovo Police Service School, *Annual Report 2000; Annual Report 2001; Kosovo: A Review of the Criminal Justice System 1 September 2000–28 September 2001* (Pristina, OSCE/LSMS 2001).

10 Jeffrey Smith, "With Few Police to Stop It, Crime Flourishes in Kosovo," Washington *Post*, 23 October 1999; Associated Press, "UN Lacks Funding to Protect Kosovo," 1 January 2000; Steven Erlanger, "UN Chief in Kosovo Says Lack of Money Imperils Mission," New York *Times*, 4 March 2000.

11 Interview, head of planning, Kosovo Correctional Service, 19 August 2000; Kosovo Correctional Service, *Strategic Plan 2000–01*.

12 Lawyers Committee for Human Rights, *A Fragile Peace: Laying the Foundations for Justice in Kosovo* (New York: LCHR 1999); Alexandros Yannis, "Kosovo under International Administration," *Survival*, 43 (2001): 38.

13 Bota Sot, "Kosovo Police Refuse to Enforce 'Yugoslav' Traffic Laws," *Summary of World Broadcasts*, EE/D3979/C (2000).

14 Observations based on participant observation at Mitrovica South police station, April 2001.

15 Andrew Purvis, "A Bridge Too Far in Kosovo: Is Mitrovica the Most Dangerous Place in Europe?" *Time* (6 March 2000): 47.

16 Three-quarters of that figure goes to wages. See also Kosovo Consolidated Budget 2000, 2001.

17 Interview, head of downtown patrol unit, Pristina, 19 April 2001.

18 Interview, chief of police training, 3 October 2002.

19 Observations based on time spent with joint police patrols, Blace, Macedonia, 4–5 October 2002.

20 International Crisis Group, *Macedonia: Towards Self-Sufficiency: A New Security Approach for NATO and the EU*, 5.

21 Report to the Government of the Former Yugoslav Republic of Macedonia on the Visit Carried out by the European Committee for the Prevention of Torture and Inhuman or Degrading Treatment or Punishment (CPT) from 15–19 July 2002 (Strasbourg: Council of Europe); Amnesty International, *Former Yugoslav Republic of Macedonia: Police Allegedly Ill-Treat Members of Ethnic Minorities* (January 2003).

# 7

# Power Sharing and Rights Protection in the Prevention and Management of Ethnic Conflict: The Case of Post-apartheid South Africa

KRISTIN HENRARD

Power sharing is often drawn upon as a means of preventing and managing ethnic conflict in an ethnically divided plural state, such as South Africa, and tends to be understood in terms of political arrangements for government structures that guarantee a voice for the distinctive population groups involved, thus creating and maintaining a political balance among the groups concerned and giving them a stake in the country.[1] Rights protection can arguably be seen as a different but supplementary means of preventing and managing ethnic conflict.

This chapter uses the case of post-apartheid South Africa to evaluate to what extent rights protection can indeed be an alternative or, better, a supplementary way, often closely interrelated with power-sharing mechanisms, of addressing ethnic divisions in a society.[2] When talking about rights protection in this context, I refer mainly to minority rights protection or the protection of rights aimed at the accommodation of population diversity in multinational societies. Strains in inter-ethnic relations and particularly tensions between majority and minority groups have often been a prelude to conflict and violence. This is why, in international instruments (conventions, declarations, and so on) concerning minorities, it is emphasized time and again that minority rights protection contributes to the prevention and regulation of ethnic conflict.

In this respect it can already be seen that both power sharing and minority rights protection lead to or entail measures that can be considered as limitations to strict majority rule[3] though they are not necessarily problematic from a democracy viewpoint. Indeed, it can be argued that pure majority rule in a plural society is not only inadequate but can actually be incompatible with democracy.[4]

South Africa's democratic transformation process itself reveals power-sharing features, for the constitution to govern the new democratic state was made in the following two steps: an interim constitution formulated in 1993 by the negotiating parties, including the former apartheid government, prior to the first multiracial elections; and a so-called "final" constitution adopted by the elected Constitutional Assembly in 1996. The 1996 constitution had to comply with thirty-four Constitutional Principles, which formed part of the 1993 constitution, thus giving the previously ruling white minority an important say in the foundations of the first fully democratic constitution of South Africa. Another facet of power sharing was achieved by an agreement (and a constitutional provision) establishing a Government of National Unity, a kind of coalition government, for a five-year period after the election of the Constitutional Assembly (27 April 1994).[5] The Government of National Unity meant that each party with at least eighty seats in the National Assembly (one of the two legislative chambers of parliament) was entitled to designate a deputy president, while every party that had at least twenty seats in the assembly and had decided to take part in the government was entitled to representation in the national cabinet on a proportional basis.[6] In this way, some of the minority political parties had an ensured participation in decision making [7] – a factor that is especially appropriate in terms of managing ethnic conflict, because South Africa's voting pattern is (to some extent) racially determined.

In addition to the provisions aimed at the participation of minority political parties in the legislative process, two related power-sharing issues are present in the South African constitution, namely, a state structure that included some federal elements and the inclusion of traditional leaders in government structures. These will be discussed below in terms of the 1996 constitution.

Whereas the obligation to have a Government of National Unity was abandoned in the 1996 constitution, several of its provisions are arguably focused on accommodating the needs of specific communities. Some of these provisions can be understood largely in terms of power sharing, others largely in terms of rights protection. Regarding the former, one could cite the possibility of giving traditional leaders a legislative role in (especially local) government. Furthermore, the semi-federal structure created by the establishment of provinces provides a certain measure of autonomy for those population groups that are relatively concentrated in one province, and this also can be understood in terms of power sharing. The provisions of the 1996 constitution that can be considered as measures of rights protection aimed at accommodating population diversity include the "minority rights" provision in Section 31, the related Section 185 (Commission for the Protection and Promotion of the Rights of Cultural, Religious and Linguistic Communities), and the legislature's circumscribed constitutional capacity to (1) incorporate Muslim personal law in the national legal system, (2) regulate the extent to which customary law is recognized, and (3) enable a community with a common cultural heritage to obtain a measure of self-determination.[8] Several of these measures can be related to the right of internal self-determination for the related communities. As the latter right arguably has certain power-sharing dimensions, this reveals the close interrelation between power-sharing measures and measures of rights protection. Whereas external forms of self-determination would clearly fall outside the purview of power sharing, internal self-determination tends to have more affinity with power-sharing ideas. Indeed, internal self-determination can be seen to realize a degree of self-government for the population groups concerned, analogously to the semi-federal structures referred to above.

In the following pages I intend to show, in each instance, the ways in which the respective constitutional provisions have the potential to accommodate the specific needs of the population groups concerned, thus contributing to the inclusivity of the South African legal order and hence also to nation building. From the outset, I want to acknowledge that a crucial distinction needs to be made between full-blown rights and the constitutional possibility for the national legislature to make certain regulations that can enhance the accommodation of South Africa's population diversity. The discretion of the legislature in the latter case (and the legitimate constitutional constraints on that discretion) obviously reduces the conflict management/conflict prevention potential of the measures concerned. Nevertheless, the mere constitutional opening for these inclusive measures is highly meaningful for conflict management and prevention in a country still haunted by its apartheid legacy.

## BACKGROUND INFORMATION ON SOUTH AFRICA
## AND THE APARTHEID REGIME

By way of background, it seems appropriate to provide a few facts about the demographic structure of South Africa[9] and outline the most striking features of the apartheid era that are relevant to the issues focused upon in this chapter. Several authors writing on South Africa emphasize that the state is characterized by a high degree of ethnic, linguistic, and religious diversity.[10] Regarding racial divisions, reference could be made to the classifications used during apartheid, namely, white, African, Indian, and coloured (the latter category referring to the people of mixed race). Nationally, the racial breakdown is more or less as follows: African, 77 per cent; white, 10 per cent; coloured, 9 per cent; and Indian, 3 per cent. The African population group in turn is subdivided into nine groups along ethnic lines, which coincide with linguistic ones. The current constitutional provision on the status of languages recognizes eleven official languages, nine of which are indigenous, while acknowledging that there are many more languages spoken in South Africa.[11] Significantly, there are concentrations of linguistic groups in the provinces, with such striking examples as the Eastern Cape (now Mpumalanga), where 84 per cent are Xhosa, and Kwazulu Natal, where 80 per cent are Zulu.

While it is generally known that the great majority of South Africans are Christian,[12] it is less known that during the apartheid era the state recognized 3,000 religious groups and another 6,000 were in fact represented in South Africa. The Muslim minority constitutes a mere 1.2 per cent of the national population, but it is strongly concentrated in the province of Kwazulu Natal.

There have been signs of a resurgence of racial and ethnic identification among the South African population since the 1994 elections, even though various surveys have yielded divergent results. It has been argued in this respect that the coloured and Indian populations are increasingly alienated from the African population and that ethnic identification lines within the African population are becoming stronger and more noticeable.[13] Even though changes in the scale of political parties may mitigate this, there appears to be a significant degree of correspondence between race group and political preference, which points to the existence of ethnic/racial voting patterns.

## APARTHEID STRATEGIES OF SPECIAL RELEVANCE

Apartheid is typically characterized by its central policy of "divide and rule," which was aimed at ensuring white survival and hegemony by dividing the non-white population along racial and, for the African group, ethnic lines.[14] Apartheid, with its labyrinth of regulations, was indeed based on an imposed group membership, primarily on the basis of race and also, for the black population, on ethnicity.[15] Moreover, it imposed a pervasive system of segregation, not only residentially but also in relation to education, public amenities, and labour.[16] Ultimately, the strategy of "Grand Apartheid" (or Separate Development) was devised, which attempted to concentrate and limit African political rights to the ethnically defined Bantustans, or "homelands."[17] The forced resettlement (and resulting misery) for millions of Africans[18] further underscored the apartheid regime's aim of dividing the African population on ethnic grounds in an attempt to entrench white supremacy. Hence, because the "Grand Apartheid" strategy was justified in terms of self-determination on ethnic grounds, both that concept and the concept of federalism based on ethnic grounds are burdened with negative connotations and thus looked upon with suspicion in contemporary South Africa.

It should also be pointed out that, from early colonial times, starting around 1652, until the post-apartheid era, unequal status was accorded to the different belief systems.[19] Since public policy was characterized by Protestant hegemony and a concomitant restrictive attitude towards other religions, it can be said that nearly 350 years of religious apartheid closely matched socio-political apartheid.[20]

Two other distinct but closely related issues that are greatly influenced by the apartheid policies are the recognition of customary law and the status of traditional leaders. During apartheid, a segregated system of justice was installed, with a separate system of courts for civil disputes between Africans, while the recognition of customary law was subject to a repugnancy proviso. These special courts increasingly became an agency of the apartheid regime and were abolished in 1986.[21] The 1988 Law of Evidence Amendment Act subsequently extended the possibility of applying customary law in all courts, but this was still a matter for the courts' discretion. The Amendment Act maintained the repugnancy proviso (with the exception of bride wealth), a matter that is currently being revisited. Furthermore, certain codes of customary law were made during the apartheid era, and it is now claimed that this codification process often entailed a distortion and redefinition of customary law. The main issue regarding traditional leaders is that, during apartheid, there had been a clear and partially successful attempt to co-opt them and interfere with the leadership structures. Consequently, the legitimacy of several leaders under customary law is being questioned.[22]

In the following section I shall focus on the 1996 constitution, the negotiations preceding it, and its ongoing implementation. The interim constitution will be discussed only to the extent that it adds to our understanding of the 1996 document.

## POWER-SHARING CONSTITUTIONAL PROVISIONS AND THEIR IMPLEMENTATION

### Traditional Authorities' Role in the Democratic Dispensation

The fact that customary law still governs *de facto* (if not always *de jure*) in domestic affairs for about half of the South African population (mainly the African population living in the rural areas)[23] underlines the ongoing importance of traditional leaders, since they and their functions are part and parcel of this body of law. Thus, the status of these traditional leaders in South Africa's democratic dispensation influences the degree of power sharing allotted to the traditional African communities.

The patriarchal, authoritarian, and hereditary foundations of the institution of traditional leadership obviously sit uneasily with democratic values. Nevertheless, all the players in the constitutional negotiations realized that it was not possible simply to abolish the institution of traditional leadership. The ambivalent attitude towards traditional leadership meant that, although the role of traditional leadership according to customary law is still recognized, subject to the constitution, there is no longer a constitutional obligation to establish a national council or provincial houses made up of traditional leaders, nor is there a guarantee of an *ex officio* membership for traditional leaders at the local government level.[24] Consequently, the extent to which the institution of traditional leadership and its role in matters of governance will be recognized in the future will depend on the goodwill of the national and provincial legislatures.

Thus far, constitutional developments have presented an ambivalent picture. Three national bodies were established soon after the 1996 constitution took effect (on 4 February 1997): a Chief Directorate on Traditional Affairs in the Department of Constitutional Development, meeting of the minister and members of the provincial executive councils (MINMEC) on traditional affairs, and a National Council of Traditional Leaders. This extensive degree of institutional support arguably reveals a genuine attempt to integrate traditional leadership into the democratic state structure. However, while the Chief Directorate immediately began work on a white paper on traditional leaders as a basis for legislation, this document was not ready until August 2002. The slow, painstaking process reflects a low level of consensus on the appropriate degree of power sharing for traditional leaders.

Similarly, the MINMEC (consisting of the national and provincial ministers responsible for traditional leaders), which is meant to be a political discussion forum to coordinate policy and action in the field of traditional affairs, has so far not contributed much. Finally, the Council of Traditional Leaders, later renamed the National House of Traditional Leaders, has a significant symbolic value, but its functions are mainly advisory.[25] Obviously, only future practice will reveal the actual degree of power sharing accorded to traditional authorities.

Recognition of the status and powers of traditional leaders would, to the extent that it materializes, amount to a measure of self-governance for the various indigenous communities involved, while also qualifying as a measure of internal self-determination. The actual degree of power sharing realized will depend on ongoing policy and legislative developments, as well as the actual implementation of the latter.

### State Structures

The extent to which semi-federal features in South Africa can contribute to the accommodation of population diversity is linked to the relative concentrations of most ethnic and racial population groups in the provinces. It is also linked to the theory that the devolution of powers to lower levels of government, in combination with a degree of autonomy for these levels, tends to contribute to the accommodation of population diversity and minority protection.[26]

During the constitutional negotiations preceding both constitutions, the debates on the form of the South African state – and more specifically on the division of powers between the national and the provincial spheres of government – revealed that it was a highly contentious issue.

The overall assessment of South Africa's state structures is ambivalent. Descriptions range from "a federal state with unitary features"[27] to "a unitary but strongly decentralized state."[28] The focus here will be partly on the degree of autonomy given to the provinces to regulate matters that are relevant to the separate identities of the provincial population, and partly on similar issues pertaining to local government.[29] In this connection, it needs to be emphasized at the outset that the negotiating parties in 1996 made the conscious choice to use the term "spheres of government" instead of "levels of government," in order to avoid the impression of a hierarchical structure with the national level being at the top.

In addition to several concurrent competencies of the provincial and national spheres of government (for instance, cultural matters, education, language policy, and the regulation of official languages), there are two exclusive provincial competencies that can be used to accommodate intra-provincial cultural diversity, namely, "provincial cultural matters" and "museums other than national museums."[30] Finally, the possibility to adopt a provincial constitution should be underscored, since it would seem to allow for a more comprehensive accommodation of population diversity at the provincial level, as long as the provisions of the provincial constitutions are not inconsistent with the national constitution and comply with the latter's central values, such as equality, human dignity, non-racialism, and democracy.[31]

Only very late during the 1996 negotiations was the framework of the powers, functions, and structures of provincial and local spheres of government focused upon, even though this was required by one of the Constitutional Principles. In the first certification judgment by the Constitutional Court, the court decided that there were eight areas of non-compliance with the Constitutional Principles, resulting in a non-certification. Two of these areas of non-compliance are especially relevant here: (1) there was not enough detail regarding local government in the constitution; and (2) the provinces' powers and functions were substantially weaker than and inferior to those under the interim constitution. Obviously, in the court's view, the distinctive spheres of local and provincial government and their respective competencies and functions – and thus regionalism – had a central place and needed to be addressed in the constitutional scheme.[32] The Constitutional Assembly amended these flaws, and the Constitutional Court duly certified the second version of the 1996 constitution on 4 December 1996.

In terms of actual practice, the overall perception is that the provinces are not functioning well because there is a lack of capacity in the administrations and also because the three-tier system is too expensive.[33] At some point it was even suggested that the African National Congress (ANC) would *de facto* work towards a two-tier system, namely, national and local government, converting the provincial level into an executive arm of the central level. In this respect and regarding the autonomy principle of federalism, it should be underlined that the seven ANC-dominated provinces chose not to have their own constitutions and that the national level of the ANC attempts to control the composition and functioning of the provincial governments.[34] Certain national initiatives could, furthermore, be construed as attempts to curtail provincial autonomy.[35] Still, the two non-ANC provinces – Kwazulu-Natal and the Western Cape – demonstrate that it is constitutionally possible to have a certain, albeit limited, degree of provincial autonomy regarding identity-related matters, as is reflected in their provincial constitutions and confirmed by the related certification judgments of the Constitutional Court.

Finally, local government is in the process of being restructured and transformed in order to counter at the local level the racial segregation resulting from apartheid and to give local government a more developmental role. It seems, though, that the local government powers envisaged by the constitution deal mainly with infrastructure and not so much with identity-related matters. The 1998 white paper on local government as well as the act implementing its principles, the 1999 Local Government Municipal Structures Act, do not give any indication that this will be altered. Consequently, it is still unclear to what extent local government powers can and do contribute to the accommodation of local population diversity.

By way of an interim conclusion, it seems that the provisions in the constitution related to power sharing do have potential to contribute to the management and prevention of ethnic conflict. However, the actual implementation is still taking shape and remains ambiguous.

## CONSTITUTIONAL PROVISIONS ENSHRINING RIGHTS PROTECTION AND THEIR IMPLEMENTATION

### Minority Rights

A crucial issue for the constitutional negotiations preceding the enactment of both the 1993 and the 1996 constitutions was how to accommodate and protect ethnic, religious, and linguistic minorities in a democratic state. During these negotiations, the focus was mainly on how to persuade the ruling white minority to give up power, but gradually other dimensions of minority protection were included. In 1993 the National Party (NP) was concerned mainly with issues of power sharing, since it felt that minority interests could best be protected through certain measures affecting the distribution of governmental power. It made modest demands regarding the Bill of Rights, concentrating mainly on protecting the right of an individual to speak a language and participate in the cultural life of his or her choice. However, this position changed in the course of the negotiations for the 1996 constitution, in which the most pressing issues for the NP became the right to education and, more specifically, the guarantee for mother-tongue education in single-language institutions, as well as minority-protection guarantees in general.

Throughout the negotiations, the Freedom Front (FF) strongly advocated the recognition of a right to self-determination for a community sharing a common cultural or language heritage, as was revealed in bilateral negotiations between the FF and the ANC. During several of these bilateral negotiations, the ANC formulated promises of cultural councils and rights analogous to Article 27 of the International Covenant on Civil and Political Rights (ICCPR), and consequently the NP joined the discussion in order to further its new goal of including minority rights in the constitution. The result was a three-dimensional agreement to establish a Commission for the Protection and Promotion of the Rights of Cultural, Religious and Linguistic Communities (Section 185), to protect cultural rights under Article 27 ICCPR (Section 31), and to include a provision on self-determination for communities sharing a common cultural or linguistic heritage (Section 235, see below).

First of all, agreement was reached on the inclusion in the Bill of Rights of Section 31, which protects additional "cultural rights" and was meant to reflect the spirit of Article 27 ICCPR, the most basic international law provision on minority rights. Section 31 is close in formulation and intent to Article 27 ICCPR and can thus be identified as a minority rights provision. In view of the past – and, more specifically, abuse of minority rights discourse in the apartheid era – it is definitely remarkable to have such a constitutional provision so soon after the official abolition of apartheid. There are, however, differences in formulation, which can be related to the sensitivities resulting from apartheid's legacy in this regard.[36]

The Commission for the Protection and Promotion of the Rights of Cultural, Religious and Linguistic Communities is to be broadly representative of the several communities in South Africa and is empowered to monitor, investigate, research, educate, advise, and report on issues concerning the rights of these communities.[37] Section 185(1) enumerates the following primary objectives of the commission, which reveal that it is meant to contribute to the accommodation of South Africa's population diversity: "(a) to promote respect for the rights of cultural, religious and linguistic communities;(b) to promote and develop peace, friendship, humanity, tolerance and national unity among cultural, religious and linguistic communities, on the basis of equality, non-discrimination and free association; and (c) to recommend the establishment or recognition, in accordance with national legislation, of a cultural or other council or councils for a community or communities in South Africa."

The commission's task to recommend the establishment or recognition of cultural councils – and these councils themselves – can be related to the internal dimension of the right to self-determination, which has obvious power-sharing aspects. The two avenues of accommodation of population diversity identified here are closely interrelated and in many respects supplementary.

The 2002 act establishing the commission does not clarify in any way the content of the Section 31 rights, or the extent to which the group dimension is recognized therein. Part 5 of the act, concerning the functions and powers of the commission, remains vague and open-ended, which can be explained by the sensitivity of the topic. It is indeed not easy to strike the right balance between unity and diversity in South Africa, characterized as it is by deep divisions, high population diversity, and the legacy of apartheid. The commission can (a) "monitor, investigate, research, educate, lobby, advise and report on any issue concerning the rights of ... communities," (b) "facilitate the resolution of conflicts or friction between ... communities," and (c) "receive and deal with complaints and requests by ... communities."[38] Furthermore, the commission must annually convene a national consultative conference, which is meant to provide a forum for consideration of the commission's recommendations and for the evaluation of progress in South Africa regarding the promotion of respect for the rights of communities and the furthering of national unity and tolerance among communities. The commission can also recommend that a cultural community initiate and establish a cultural or other council for itself, which it will subsequently recommend for recognition to a national consultative conference. However, no further criteria are stipulated regarding the establishment and recognition of such cultural councils and their functions are left to be decided by further legislation. Overall, the formulation of the act is so cautious and open-ended that it does not significantly clarify the potential impact of the commission or the rights envisaged by Section 31 of the 1996 constitution.

### Self-determination for a Community Sharing a Common Cultural or Language Heritage

Certain Afrikaners immediately relate claims of self-determination in South Africa to the demands for a *Volksstaat*. The origins of such ideas can be found in the 1980s, when opposition to any kind of reform in the direction of more inclusive political participation and majority rule was manifested. This opposition was subsequently transformed into a claim for an Afrikaner homeland when the end of apartheid loomed. A group of right-wing parties, which united in May 1993 as the Afrikaner Volksfront, demanded self-determination for the Afrikaner people. They set out to establish an independent Afrikaner state, the *Volksstaat*.

There was, however, another political group pressing for self-determination – the Inkatha Freedom Party (IFP), because it felt that its aspirations for a federal system with extensive autonomy for the provinces were not being met. The more the IFP was convinced that the ANC was not going to agree to give more powers to the provinces, the more it felt drawn to the language of self-determination, and more specifically to secession.[39]

During the negotiations for the 1993 constitution, both sensitive matters – stronger powers and more autonomy for the provinces, and the *Volksstaat* issue – remained outstanding until the last moment. Although the interim constitution was passed overwhelmingly on 18 November 1993, the Afrikaner Volksfront and IFP both rejected it and consequently refused to participate in the elections. After several intense discussions, a set of constitutional amendments was agreed to as a last bid to undermine their objections. The Constitution of South Africa Second Amendment Act, 2, passed in 1994, provided not only for more extensive provincial legislative and revenue-raising powers but also for a Volksstaat Council, and it included as well another constitutional principle dealing with the right to self-determination for a community sharing a common "cultural or language heritage."[40]

Constitutional Principle 34 embodies a qualified recognition of a right to self-determination and states that the following would not be precluded: "constitutional recognition of a notion of the right to self-determination by any community sharing a common cultural and language heritage, whether in a territorial entity within the Republic or in any other recognized way."[41] The Volksstaat Council was meant to "enable the proponents of the idea of a Volksstaat to constitutionally pursue the establishment of such a Volksstaat."[42] It should nevertheless be pointed out that the council's powers were not that far-reaching, for it was envisaged as an advisory body that would have powers to gather information and make representations on the *Volksstaat* issue to the Constitutional Assembly.[43]

Before we turn to the negotiations preceding the 1996 constitution, it should be pointed out that since the 1994 elections the FF has been the political party that is most strongly connected to the quest for a *Volksstaat* for Afrikaners. The eventual agreement on a provision on self-determination for a community sharing a common cultural or language heritage during the trilateral negotiations between the ANC, the FF, and the NP has already been referred to. Section 235 was intended to enshrine the content of Constitutional Principle 34 in the 1996 constitution. This provision, which was eventually acceptable to the parties, is as vague in its formulation as the Constitutional Principle and is so open-ended that it cannot be said to enshrine a right at all: "The right of the South African people as whole to self-determination, as manifested in this Constitution, does not preclude, within the framework of this right, the recognition of the notion of the right to self-determination of any community sharing a common cultural or language heritage, within a territorial entity in the Republic or in any other way recognized by national legislation."

The fact that national legislation will determine the acceptable ways of implementing self-determination underscores the fact that Section 235 does not actually grant a right to self-determination to communities but leaves this to the discretion of the national legislature. Nevertheless, it may be argued, Section 235 "requires that the phrase 'self-determination' is interpreted "as not excluding the possibility of vindication of the right of self-determination by external or by internal political means" and also that the expression "community sharing a common cultural or language heritage" refers to an ethnic minority.[44] Consequently, Section 235 would at least leave the door ajar for forms of both external and internal (even with a territorial dimension) self-determination for minorities, thus securing the possible emergence of a *Volksstaat*, however tenuous that possibility might seem. Considering its weak formulation, Section 235 does not seem to be a strong basis for actual rights protection. At the same time, it should be pointed out that self-determination has in some respects power-sharing dimensions.

Overall, the 1996 constitution seems to move away from recognition of a right to self-determination that might result in a *Volksstaat*. The wording of Section 235 already gives significant indications in this regard, in that it clearly does not enshrine a right but merely mentions that the recognition of the notion of the right to self-determination is not precluded. Furthermore, the way it will be exercised will be determined by "national legislation," which amounts to another safety valve for the ANC government to prevent the actual realization of a *Volksstaat*.[45]

Since the 1996 constitution came into force, negotiations between the ANC and the FF have been ongoing, without, however, any significant breakthrough. In any event, it should be emphasized that the Volksstaat Council (in the past) as well as the FF have exhibited an understanding of most if not all of the ideological and practical problems stemming from the legacy of apartheid. Consequently, an incremental approach has been favoured, along with efforts to realize corporate or cultural self-determination for Afrikaners living (and staying) outside the *Volksstaat*. Furthermore, it is stressed that there can be no forced removals and that the rights of non-Afrikaners in the area will be fully respected.[46] The FF also takes an incremental approach towards matters in the northwestern Cape region, where it pursues measures of corporate self-determination by means of short- and medium-term plans.[47] The party fully realizes that the degree of self-determination actually reached will depend to a great extent on the agreement of the people already living in the area and of the relevant authorities.[48]

In contrast to the other questions related to the accommodation of population diversity, the question of self-determination for a community with a common cultural or language heritage seems to be fundamentally opposed by the ruling party. The lack of a genuine attempt to go down this path at all thus seriously questions the potential for the realization of a *Volksstaat*.

## Customary Law

The question of the way in which customary law would be recognized in view of the potential clashes between that body of law and certain provisions of the Bill of Rights was also hotly debated during the negotiations leading up to both the 1993 and 1996 constitutions.[49] Since customary law, in its great diversity, is still so important for a substantial group of South Africans, arguably it should not be done away with in one stroke. Such an action would probably have a severely destabilizing effect on South African society, affecting the lifestyles of about three-quarters of the South African population.[50]

The future of customary law in post-apartheid South Africa will to a large extent be influenced by the relationship between customary law and the Bill of Rights. The debates in this area focus mainly on the applicability of the equality principle and its impact on the intrinsically and all-pervasive patriarchal structure of customary law.[51]

It became apparent during the negotiations for the 1993 constitution that a complete exemption of customary law was not acceptable to the negotiating parties, and the debate then conflated partially with the issue of the horizontal applicability of the Bill of Rights.[52] The issue of horizontal applicability concerned the question whether the Bill of Rights would be directly enforceable against only the state and its organs or also against private social institutions and persons. Since in the latter option the Bill of Rights, including the equality principle, would extend to customary relationships, the two matters do overlap. Eventually, "it was agreed that the chapter should operate vertically only, but that provision be made for seepage to horizontal relationships," which was realized via the interpretation clause of the Bill of Rights.[53]

Throughout the 1996 negotiations and discussions, it was obvious that the negotiating parties were strongly inclined to acknowledge the supremacy of the Bill of Rights in general, while being aware of the sensitivities surrounding the debate about the place of customary law in a democratic state that was respectful of fundamental rights and freedoms. Ultimately, customary law has been recognized but in a qualified way, in that it is subject to the entire Bill of Rights, including the equality clause, which points to the supervisory role of the legislature and the courts in this respect.[54]

Furthermore, the ANC made abundantly clear from the beginning of this set of negotiations that it wanted the Bill of Rights to apply both vertically and horizontally, while the Democratic Party and the NP urged caution. The main "problem" provision regarding horizontal application was the equality clause. After intense discussions, the non-discrimination provision was divided in two, one part dealing with discrimination by the state, the other with discrimination by private persons (sections 9[3] and 9[4], respectively). Furthermore, the general application provision (Section 8) also contains several indications about a more general possibility of the horizontal application of the Bill of Rights. Unlike in the 1993 constitution, the judiciary is now explicitly enumerated as being bound by the Bill of Rights, and Section 8(2) explicitly mentions the qualified possibility of horizontal applicability of the provisions of the Bill of Rights.[55] Consequently, the 1996 Bill of Rights has a qualified horizontal application. The ANC's strong stance in favour of horizontal applicability can be explained by the party's wish to be able to get to the roots of the legacy of apartheid's pervasive discrimination policies, but it has obvious repercussions not only for customary law but also for Muslim personal law, as described below.

Since the adoption of the 1996 constitution, the South African Law Commission has been involved in several projects concerning customary law and its qualified recognition in the national legal system. While the commission's projects on the administration of estates and the conflicts of law have been proceeding slowly and are still ongoing, the one on the recognition of customary marriages has been concluded and has resulted in The Recognition of Customary Marriages Act, no. 120, of 1998. The act effectively recognizes existing customary marriages, including polygamous ones, and also future customary marriages, as long as they comply with the requirements of the act. It should be underscored that the "rules of customary law determine the validity of a customary marriage between persons related to each other by blood or affinity" (Section 3[6]), which is apparently an example of a culturally inspired rule that is acceptable in the new constitutional regime.

The act is, however, quite firm about the equal status of spouses in customary marriages, "thus introducing measures which bring customary law in line with the provisions of the Constitution of the Republic of South Africa, 1996 and South Africa's international obligations."[56] The act apparently demonstrates a willingness to recognize and respect certain culturally specific features of marriages according to customary law, such as polygamy, while holding onto the equality principle within the marital relationship.

Although there has not been a Constitutional Court judgment dealing with customary law and its validity under the new constitution, the case law of the lower courts since 1994 has indicated that the courts are convinced that they should apply customary law, but only to the extent that it complies with the Bill of Rights. In the latter respect, there seems to be a tendency to take the complete picture of customary obligations into account when judging compliance with the equality clause of the Bill of Rights, where certain rules favouring males can be balanced by duties of support with respect to the females.

Overall, there seems to be a genuine attempt by the South African post-apartheid regime to accommodate indigenous communities and their divergent cultural values and identities while protecting the fundamental rights and freedoms enshrined in the Bill of Rights. However, with the exception of the recognition of customary marriages, the actual harmonization process of common law and customary law is developing extremely slowly and thus leaves much to be desired.

## Muslim Personal Law

The potential recognition of "systems of personal and family law adhered to by persons professing a particular religion," as provided for by Article 14(3)a of the 1993 constitution, and of the "validity of marriages concluded under a system of religious law," under Section 14(3)b, have similarly raised problems concerning compatibility with the Bill of Rights, and especially its equality clause.[57] During the negotiations for the 1993 constitution, there was indeed a strong lobby to obtain this constitutional opening, in view of the systemic religious discrimination that was practised during apartheid, when Christian values completely dominated legislation regulating all relevant spheres of life.[58] Consequently, this provision was clearly aimed at accommodating religious diversity in South Africa and reflected a positive predisposition towards religious minorities.

However, during the 1996 negotiations, the negotiating parties wanted to avoid the impression, created by Section 14(3), that "systems of religious law trumped all provisions of the Bill of Rights."[59] Consequently, it was agreed to add a requirement of consistency with the entire constitution. The Muslim community, however, felt that requiring consistency not only with the entire constitution but also specifically with the section on religious freedom would leave them more scope to regulate family matters according to their religion, given that the courts would have to balance the equality provision with the provision on freedom of religion. In the end, representatives of the Muslim community managed to persuade the ANC to propose an amendment to the effect that the legislation must be consistent with the religious freedom section and all provisions of the constitution. This concession was merely symbolic for the ANC and was also acceptable to the other parties. However, for the Muslim community, it was an important sign that their concerns were being taken into account.

Whereas the recognition of Muslim marriages is at first sight not problematic, the concomitant regulation of these marriages would rely on the broader system of religious law, and it is widely known that Islamic personal law has several features that are contrary to the constitution's non-discrimination provision.[60] On the other hand, the prohibition against discrimination could conceivably be invoked, in combination with the provision on freedom of religion, to argue for the need to recognize Muslim family law.[61] Also in this domain, the appropriate parameters of the recognition of systems of personal law according to a particular religion, as well as the recognition of marriages concluded under a system of religious law, appear to be determined by a difficult balancing act, taking into account both the constraints of the Bill of Rights and the need to accommodate the religious diversity of the South African population.

The issue of the recognition of Muslim marriages – and, related to that, Muslim personal law, which has been a sensitive point for decades – still needs to be addressed. The central question is whether the integrity of Muslim principles can be maintained in a way that does not contravene the dominant legal system and the essential principle of equality in the new constitutional order.[62] Understandably, the Muslim community in South Africa has been highly divided on the appropriate approach. The reason why this question has remained unresolved for so long and why the entire process moves so slowly is its highly sensitive and divisive nature.

## CONCLUSION

The preceding analysis suggests that the 1996 constitution makes a positive contribution to the accommodation of South Africa's population diversity and conflict management. The constitution uses two supplementary and closely interrelated avenues for this purpose: one that can be characterized as power sharing and the other as rights protection. Both avenues reveal a considerable degree of potential for the prevention and management of ethnic conflict.

Of course, while enshrining institutions and rights in the constitution is an important first step to reach these goals, the actual implementation of these constitutional provisions is equally if not more important. This stage of the process is problematical in South Africa and is bound to have repercussions for the success of the project of nation building and ultimately for the management of ethnic conflict.[63]

## NOTES

1 Arend Lijphart, "The Power Sharing Approach," in J.V. Montville, ed., *Conflict and Peacemaking in Multiethnic Societies* (Lexington, Mass.: Lexington Books 1990), 491–509.

2 The discussion in this section draws on Kristin Henrard, *Minority Protection in Post-apartheid South Africa: Individual Human Rights, Minority Rights and the Right to Self-determination* (Westport, Conn.: Greenwood Press 2002); and Kristin Henrard, *Devising an Adequate System of Minority Protection* (The Hague: Kluwer 2000).

3 Henrard, *Minority Protection*, 314; see also David Wippman, "Practical and Legal Constraints on Internal Power Sharing," in Wippman, ed., *International Law and Ethnic Conflict* (Ithaca, N.Y.: Cornell University Press 1998), 213, 228.

4 See Lani Guinier, *The Tyranny of the Majority: Fundamental Fairness in Representative Democracy* (New York: Free Press 1995), 6, 17. Forms of power sharing can be understood as modes of the right to self-determination in its internal (as opposed to its external) dimension. It can be argued that, in deeply divided societies, consociationalism is not only compatible with self-determination but may be the only way to give effect to self-determination that is consistent with the rights of minorities to effective political participation. See Arend Lijphart, *Power-sharing in South Africa* (Berkeley: University of California Press 1985).

5 Hugh Corder, "Towards a South African Constitution," *Modern Law Review* (1994): 491–500; A.J.H. Henderson, "Cry the Beloved Constitution? Constitutional Amendment, the Vanished Imperative of the Constitutional Principles and the Controlling Values of Section 1," *South African Law Journal* (1997): 543.

6 Sections 84 and 88 of the 1993 or interim constitution of South Africa.

7 The eventual election results enabled the National Party (previous government) and the Inkatha Freedom Party (ethnic Zulu party) to participate in the Government of National Unity, which they did. However, the National Party pulled out of the government in the course of the negotiations for the 1996 constitution.

8 In my book *Minority Protection in Post-apartheid South Africa,* I analyse, in more detail and more broadly, the various mechanisms that can contribute to the accommodation of the state's population diversity. The additional issues covered there include the equality principle (constitutional provision as well as the legislative and judicial specification), several educational rights (language in education, religion in education), the status of the languages spoken in South Africa, and the protection against hate speech.

9 For a more elaborate description and analysis, see Henrard, *Minority Protection,* 42–6.

10 See, e.g., H. Kotze, *Culture, Ethnicity and Religion: South African Perceptions of Social Identity* (Johannesburg: Konrad Adenauer Stiftung, April 1997), 2.

11 Section 6(5)(b)(i) refers to all languages commonly used by communities in South Africa, including German, Greek, Gujarati, Hindi, Portuguese, Tamil, Telegu, and Urdu.

12 R.B. Nicholson, "Ethnic Nationalism and Religious Exclusivism," *Politikon* (1994): 57; M. Prozesky, "Religious Justice at Last? Believers and the New Constitution in South Africa," *Journal of Theology of South Africa* (1995): 11.

13 Neville Alexander, "The Great Gariep: Metaphors of National Unity in the New South Africa," in W. James et al., ed., *Now That We Are Free: Coloured Communities in a Democratic South Africa* (Johannesburg: Institute for Democracy in South Africa 1996), 107.

14 Nigel Worden, *The Making of Modern South Africa: Conquest, Segregation and Apartheid* (Oxford, U.K.: Blackwell 1994), 95, 110–11; B. Manby, "South Africa: Minority Conflict and the Legacy of Minority Rule," *Fletcher Forum of World Affairs* (1995): 29.

15 Manby, "Minority Conflict," 27.

16 Among the measures imposing segregation were the Group Areas Act, 1950; the Reservation of Separate Amenities Act, 1953; a host of pass laws and labour-control legislation; and the Bantu Education Act, 1953.

17 Manby, "Minority Conflict," 29; Worden, *Making of Modern South Africa,* 110–11.

18 Kristin Henrard, "The Internally Displaced in South Africa: The Strategy of Forced Removals and Apartheid," *Jura Falconis* (1995–96): 498–502, 513–14.

19 N. Moosa, "The Interim and the Final Constitution and Muslim Personal Law: Implications for South African Muslim Women," *Stellenbosch Law Review* (1998): 199.

20 Prozesky, "Religious Justice at Last?" 14.

21 Act no. 34, 1986.

22 C. French, "Functions and Powers of Traditional Leaders," *Konrad Adenauer Stiftung Occasional Papers* (Johannesburg, September 1994): 26.

23 J.C. Bekker, "How Compatible Is African Customary Law with Human Rights? Some Preliminary Observations?" *Tydskrif vir die Hedendaags Romiens Hollandse Reg* (1994): 441.

24 Sections 211–12 of the 1996 constitution. A transitional provision provided for the continuation of *ex officio* membership in local government for traditional leaders until the next general elections, which have since taken place.

25 Council of Traditional Leaders Act, 1997, Section 7.

26 See V. Sacks, "Multiculturalism, Constitutionalism and the South African Constitution," *Public Law* (1997): 679. Sacks stresses the connection between provincial autonomy and multiculturalism.

27 Jonathan Klaaren, "Federalism," in M. Chaskalson et al., ed., *Constitutional Law of South Africa* (Kenwyn, South Africa: Juta, n.d.), 5.1. (looseleaf).

28 H. Coveliers and M. Veys, "De Zuid-Afrikaanse Grondwet van 1996," *Tijdschrift voor Bestuursrecht en Politieke Wetenschappen* (1998): 238–9.

29 A feature of the structure of government that is relevant to the degree to which the provinces are able to accommodate their respective population diversity is the National Council of Provinces, the second chamber of parliament. The scope of this chapter does not allow me to elaborate on the existence and functioning of the National Council, but it should be noted that provision is made in Section 67 of the constitution for the inclusion in the council of representatives of local government, which ensures that local interests are voiced at the national level even though these representatives have no right to vote.

30 Schedules 4 and 5, 1996 constitution.

31 Section 143, 1996 constitution.

32 Jonathan Klaaren, "Structures of Government in the 1996 South African Constitution: Putting Democracy Back into Human Rights," *South African Journal on Human Rights* (1997): 12.

33 J. Wehner, *What Is the Future of South Africa's Provinces?* (Cape Town: AFREC Discussion Paper Series, 1997), 2.

34 For example, the national ANC intervened in the removal of the provincial premiers of the Free State and Gauteng in January and February 1999 and in the appointment of new premiers.

35 For example, there was an abortive attempt by the ANC to remove the power to call provincial elections from the provincial premier and give it to the president.

36 The concept "community" was used in Section 31 instead of "minority" because the latter word was too tainted by apartheid ideologies. "Community" was intended to express ties of affinity rather than ties of blood. Apartheid's abuse of ethnicity also explains the use of the adjective "cultural" instead of "ethnic."

37 Section 185(2), 1996 constitution. See also H.A. Strydom, "Minority Rights Issues in Post Apartheid South Africa," *Loyola of Los Angeles International and Comparative Law Journal* (1998): 901.

38 Act on the Commission for the Protection and Promotion of the Rights of Cultural, Religious and Linguistic Communities (Act no.19, 12 June 2002, 21).

39 See H.A. Strydom, "Self-determination and the South African Interim Constitution," *South African Yearbook on International Law* (1993–94): 48.

40 Corder, *Towards a South African Constitution,* 504–5.

41 Constitutional Principle 34(1), Schedule 4, 1993 constitution.

42 Section 184, 1993 constitution.

43 See D. Van Wyk, "Introduction to the South African Constitution," in D. Van Wyk et al., ed., *Rights and Constitutionalism: The New South African Legal Order* (Kenwyn, South Africa: Juta 1994), 165–8.

44 I. Currie, "Minority Rights: Culture, Education and Language," in Chaskalson, ed., *Constitutional Law of South Africa,* 34–5 (looseleaf).

45 The Volksstaat Council officially disbanded on March 1999, in view of the government's indication that it would introduce legislation abolishing it.

46 Accord on Self-Determination between the FF, the ANC, and the South African Government/National Party, 23 April 1994.

47 In the short term, the FF envisages the countrywide establishment of cultural councils wherever the need exists and where enough people are in favour. Preferential settlement areas should be identified as a step on the way to territorial self-determination. Medium-term actions include the statutory establishment of Afrikaner councils on local and provincial levels

as well as a national Afrikaner Council, the development of regional
autonomy in areas with Afrikaner concentrations, and, finally, the establishment of two nucleus areas that may gradually expand to form a
*Volksstaat* (see Freedom Front website: <www.vryheidsfront.co.za>).

48 It should be mentioned that, in view of the lack of progress at the official
level, and the increasing unlikelihood that an official *Volksstaat* will come
about, there are some private initiatives regarding the development of a
*Volksstaat*, one of which appears to be rather successful, namely, the village
of Orania (Orange Free State), established on land bought by the Afrikaner
Vryheidsstichting. It remains to be seen how this community will develop
and what reaction it will provoke from the wider public and the authorities.
However, it sends a strong signal to the state that certain Afrikaners choose
to separate instead of integrate and take this kind of action because they
feel that their right to identity is not sufficiently protected in the South
African state.

49 Sacks, "Multiculturalism," 678.

50 T.W. Bennett, "The Equality Clause and Customary Law," *South African
Journal on Human Rights* (1994): 122; Bekker, "How Compatible Is
African Customary Law with Human Rights?" 441–3.

51 I. Currie, "The Future of Customary Law: Lessons from the Lobola
Debate," *Acta Juridica* (1994): 147.

52 See T. Nhlapo, "Cultural Diversity: Human Rights and the Family in
Contemporary Africa: Lessons from the South African Constitutional
Debate," *International Journal of Law and the Family* (1995): 209–10.

53 Section 35(3) of the interim constitution required courts interpreting and
developing the common law and customary law to have due regard to the
spirit, purport, and objects of the Bill of Rights.

54 Strydom, "Minority Rights Issues," 905–6.

55 Section 8(2), 1996 constitution. A provision of the Bill of Rights binds a
natural or a juristic person if, and to the extent that, it is applicable, taking
into account the nature of the right and the nature of any duty imposed
by that right.

56 Memorandum on the Objects of the Recognition of Customary Marriages
Bill, 1998, para. 1.

57 F. Cachalia, "Citizenship, Muslim Family Law and a Future South African
Constitution: A Preliminary Inquiry," *Tydskrif vir die Hedendaags Romiens
Hollandse Reg* (1993): 395.

58 See C. Dlamini, "Culture, Education and Religion," in Van Wyk et al., ed.,
*Rights and Constitutionalism*, 587.

59 N. Smith, "Freedom of Religion under the Final Constitution," *South African Law Journal* (1997): 222.

60 E. Bonthuys and L.M. Du Plessis, "Whither the Validity of Marriages Concluded under a System of Religious Law under the Transitional Constitution," *South African Public Law* (1995): 205.

61 F. Cachalia, "Citizenship, Muslim Family Law and a Future South African Constitution," 410.

62 For a discussion of the most important case law, see Kristin Henrard, "The Accommodation of Religious Diversity in South Africa against the Background of the Centrality of the Equality Principle in the New Constitutional Dispensation," *Journal of African Law* (2001): 63–6.

63 There have been legislative and electoral developments since this chapter was written. Legislation may be found at http://www.info.gov.za/documents/index.htm and election results at http://www.elections.org.za/

# 8

# Power Sharing in South Africa: The African National Congress as a Consociational Party?

## MATTHIJS BOGAARDS

Although there is much debate about the extent to which South Africa after apartheid was a consociational democracy, there is little doubt that the interim constitution contained power-sharing arrangements. However, the permanent constitution and the departure of the National Party (NP) from the Government of National Unity (GNU) in 1996 have weakened political accommodation in this plural society. With the African National Congress (ANC) emerging as the dominant party, some observers now put their hope in the ANC becoming more inclusive and participatory. This development can be conceptualized as the transformation of a standard form of consociationalism between (segmental) parties to consociationalism within a single (consociational) party.

The preliminary analysis presented here examines the prospects of the ANC becoming a consociational party. It looks at party organization, internal representation, and internal accommodation of social cleavages within the context of the dominant position of the ANC in the wider political system. The analysis will draw on the comparative experience of such parties as the Congress Party in India, the Alliance and National Front in Malaysia, and the Kenya African National Union (KANU) in Kenya. The conclusion will be that the ANC appears even more negatively disposed to internal consociationalism than it has been to inter-party consociationalism, pointing at the possibility of a long-lasting political marginalization of minority interests.

## POWER-SHARING IN THE NEW SOUTH AFRICA

South Africa's first experience with consociationalism dates from 1977, when the National Party introduced constitutional proposals, later incorporated in the 1983 constitution, that included separate parliaments for the previously disenfranchised coloureds and Indians. Blacks remained excluded and white supremacy within the overall political system was maintained. Although the debate surrounding the new constitution made frequent reference to consociationalism, the reality was different.[1] The 1983 constitution violated consociational principles in four major ways: by denying political presentation to the black majority; by denying coloureds and Asians effective veto power; by predetermining racial categories rather than allowing for self-determination of social groups; and by preserving white and more specifically NP or Afrikaner dominance. In addition, there were four minor weaknesses: a strong executive presidency; lack of negotiations; no over-representation of non-white minorities; and a fixed ratio of communal representation. All this made the 1983 constitution at best "quasi-consociational"[2] or, less kindly, a case of "sham consociationalism."[3]

The second experience with consociationalism was during and after the transition to inclusive democracy. It was the NP that promoted consociationalism in an attempt to entrench minority rights and to give itself a durable place in a democracy based on majority rule. The ANC, in contrast, insisted on a post-apartheid polity that was non-racial in character. The ANC as well as many academics were concerned that consociationalism "elevates ethnicity to the status of the primary organising principle of political life for a society."[4] The experience of the 1983 constitution had further tainted consociationalism. The interim constitution, adopted in 1993, reflected the compromise between the outgoing NP of President F.W. De Klerk and the ANC as the leader of the extra-parliamentary opposition. In the words of Vincent Maphai, "at the beginning of South Africa's transition to democracy, there was no viable alternative to power-sharing. It was the only system acceptable to all sides."[5]

According to Arend Lijphart, the 1993 constitution embodied all four principles of consociational democracy – a grand coalition of segmental elites, proportionality, segmental autonomy, and a mutual veto – making it a "perfectly consociational constitution."[6] With respect to the "grand coalition" principle, the 1993 constitution provided for a Government of National Unity in which all parties with a minimum of 5 per cent of the seats in the National Assembly could participate. Each party with more than one-fifth of the seats was entitled to a deputy president. The 1994 elections resulted in a three-party government led by the ANC under President Nelson Mandela. The NP garnered 20.4 per cent of the vote, thereby securing a deputy presidency (filled by former president De Klerk) and six cabinet portfolios. The Inkatha Freedom Party (IFP) won 10.5 per cent of the national vote and obtained three cabinet positions. The nine new provinces were similarly governed by broadly constituted executive councils.

As for the other three principles of consociational democracy – proportionality, segmented autonomy, and a mutual veto – Lijphart found the evidence equally clear-cut. Proportionality was the leading principle of election and representation: election by proportional representation was prescribed for both the National Assembly and the provincial legislatures, and the composition of the GNU was also based on proportionality. Group (i.e., segmental) autonomy was granted in the realm of education, through the provision that every person should have the right to establish, where practicable, educational institutions based on a common culture, language, or religion, provided there was no discrimination on the ground of race. The minority veto appeared in the form of the two-thirds majority requirement for amending the constitution and for adopting the permanent constitutional text by the Constitutional Assembly. A number of fundamental principles, such as proportional representation and collective rights of self-determination in forming, joining, and maintaining organs of civil society, including linguistic, cultural, and religious associations, could not be infringed even by a two-thirds majority. Still other qualities of the 1993 constitution praised by Lijphart include a parliamentary instead of presidential form of government and self-determination rather than predetermination of politically relevant groups. The one weakness was the absence of federalism.

The high point of South African consociationalism occurred in the five months preceding the first democratic elections, from December 1993 to April 1994, when a Transitional Executive Council in which all parties participated on equal footing ruled the country. The 1994–96 GNU, Lijphart acknowledges, "already represented a slight decline in consociationalism because of the predominant power of the ANC in this power-sharing cabinet."[7]

In 1996 two important developments took place: the permanent constitution that was adopted that year and took effect in 1999 no longer prescribed a GNU; and the NP left the cabinet. These changes notwithstanding, Lijphart advances five reasons why South Africa is still much closer to a consociational democracy than to a majoritarian democracy. First, the continued presence of the IFP means that the government remains a broad and oversized coalition. Second, even without the constitutional obligation to form a GNU, the ANC may still decide at any moment to invite opposition parties to join the government, as indeed has happened. Third, "the ANC is a strongly multi-racial and multi-ethnic party."[8] This crucial claim will be at the heart of the examination below. Fourth, even if black parties were to dominate the government and white parties were relegated to the opposition, black political power would be counterbalanced by white economic power – like the situation in Malaysia, where the Malays are politically dominant but the Chinese possess countervailing economic power. Fifth, a shift to a pure type of majoritarian democracy as can, or rather could be, found in the United Kingdom – with plurality elections, an unwritten constitution, the absence of constitutional review, and centralized government – is simply not on the agenda. To this list, one could add the introduction of two clauses into the 1996 constitution aimed at securing the cooperation of the Afrikaner conservatives: Article 185, which envisages the establishment of a Commission for the Protection and Promotion of the Rights of Cultural, Religious and Linguistic Communities; and Article 235, which underwrites the right of self-determination of any community sharing a common cultural and language heritage. However, the commission can only monitor and make recommendations, and the *Volkstaat* Council investigating the feasibility of an Afrikaner state lasted only three years, feeding suspicions that "the ANC was probably never serious about either of these two clauses."[9]

The outcome of the 1999 elections – in which the ANC strengthened its lead, the Democratic Party (DP) replaced the New National Party (NNP) as the official opposition party, and the IFP consolidated its support – did not significantly change this picture. Even though the ANC obtained an enlarged majority of votes and seats in the 1999 parliamentary elections, falling only one seat short of the two-thirds required to amend the constitution, the IFP was again invited to join the cabinet, with its leader Chief Gatsha Mangosuthu Buthelezi returning to the department of Home Affairs. The IFP was not necessary to achieve a qualified majority, since the ANC had already obtained the support of a small party.

Lijphart's consociational interpretation of South African politics under the interim constitution, and even more so after adoption of the final constitution, is contested.[10] Criticism focuses on the absence of real segmental autonomy and a mutual veto for minorities. Segmental autonomy in the form of freedom of education is not necessarily consociational, since it is perfectly compatible with the liberal-democratic desire to maximize individual rights and minimize collective rights. To exercise a veto on constitutional amendments, the opposition needs to secure one-third of the seats in parliament. Given South Africa's demography, this means that minorities can always be outvoted. As predicted, the recent allowance of floor-crossing has benefited the ANC, which can now unilaterally change the constitution and boasts legislative majorities in all nine provinces. In a dominant party system, a qualified majority does not constitute a minority veto. Although South Africa has some of the political institutions of a consensus democracy, its consensual functioning is contingent on the behavior of the ANC as the dominant party.[11] Likewise, advocates of majoritarian democracy have to face the fact that effective opposition and alternation in government, characteristic of this type of democracy, are unlikely in a dominant party system.[12]

Increasingly, alternative forms or interpretations of power sharing are advanced, most prominently corporatism. A common argument is that consociationalism was an adequate transitional arrangement but that, in the long run, South Africa needs different institutions. Consociationalism, critics argue, promotes political stability to the detriment of other goals, such as equality and social transformation. Corporatism is seen both as a countervailing force and as a way for the dominant party to extend its control over civil society.[13] In any case, even apart from the claim that globalization limits the policy space,[14] corporatist institutions such as the National Economic Development and Labour Advisory Council (NEDLAC) cannot substitute for power sharing between communal groups, because the reach of such institutions is naturally limited to social and economic issues debated by labour and business.[15] Therefore, corporatism cannot be a functional equivalent of consociationalism.

In sum, the elements of power sharing in the GNU under the interim constitution are best viewed as a temporary arrangement, "designed to smoothen the path to majority rule, not to be an alternative to it."[16] With the exception of Lijphart and Andrew Reynolds, the latter recommending a return to the GNU through what he calls "integrative consensual power-sharing," few see a future for consociationalism in South Africa under the 1996 permanent constitution.[17] By now, "consociationalism has disappeared from public discussion."[18]

## THE EMERGING DOMINANT PARTY SYSTEM

Any understanding of the present state of South African democracy and its future development has to start with the dominant electoral position of the ANC. The lively scholarly debate about institutional choices for post-apartheid South Africa was premised on the expectation that, in free, fair, and competitive elections, ethnic divisions would split racial blocs. Yet both Donald Horowitz's recommendation of an electoral system promoting vote pooling and Lijphart's advocacy of consociational democracy were doomed by a black majority mobilizing behind a single party.[19] If "the presence of a majority segment constitutes a problem for consociational democracy, and it is the constitutional engineer's task to neutralize this element as much as possible," the drafters of the interim, and even more so, of the final constitution failed from a consociational point of view.[20] It would appear that constitutional engineers, rather than facing up to the prospect of a black majority, interpreted the situation in such a way that it allowed them to promote their favourite institutions.[21] This left them and South Africa ill-prepared for the emergence of a dominant party system and the challenges it poses.

In striking contrast to the expectations of ethnic-party fragmentation in the 1980s, a decade later the view is widespread that "although formal constitutional provisions and formalities appear to guarantee a multiparty system, the racial polarisation of the electorate decrees South Africa to be, potentially, a one-party 'dominant' state for the foreseeable future."[22] Following the 1999 elections, J.E. Spence concluded that "by and large, voting behaviour conformed to racial identity, with blacks voting overwhelmingly for the ANC and the majority of whites for either the DP or the NNP ... This pattern of political preferences is likely to persist."[23]

Given the dominant position of the ANC, "it is hard to see the formal democratic system playing any significant role in constraining the power of the majority party and, therefore, ensuring accountable government."[24] This lends credence to the prediction that "political pluralism in the state will not exist without internal democracy in the dominant party."[25] In view of the ANC's dominance, "its internal politics is likely to provide more important clues to the state of democracy than any contest between the government and the opposition, at least for the next five years."[26] There are sources of countervailing power within the ANC itself, for example, the distinction between those who fought apartheid from exile, such as the current president, Thabo Mbeki, and those who did so inside the country in the trade union movement and the United Democratic Front (UDF). The former are said to be substantially less enthusiastic about internal democracy than the latter.

In a dominant party system, the prospects for democracy are directly related to the degree of inclusiveness within the dominant party. Inclusiveness is neither a given nor an electoral imperative in a post-apartheid society with a racial majority. The finding that 71 per cent of voters in 1998 (and 77 per cent in 1994) thought that the ANC represented all South Africans – far outdistancing the other parties – may simply reflect the belief of the majority that their preferred party represents the whole country while opposition parties look after only their own minority constituencies.[27] The ANC is inclusive in the sense that it is an "all-class black party" that succeeds in attracting support from black voters irrespective of their socio-economic status.[28] Given that the overwhelming majority of black South Africans are poor, however, this fact has less political relevance than the close link between race and wealth. The race/wealth connection provides fertile ground for an appeal based on "race populism," reinforcing a distinction between poor blacks and rich whites, as in the "two nations speech" made by president Mbeki.[29] During and after the ANC's 50th National Conference in Mafikeng in 1997, these ideas were worked out in a project of "transformation" which has been translated into policies of positive discrimination in the public and private sectors, accompanied by a further extension of party control and democratic centralism.[30]

If there is any trend, it is towards increased centralism.[31] Closed-list proportional representation (PR) and internal reliance on appointments or elections without choice strengthens the hand of the ANC leadership. The ANC's national party structures have extended their powers at the provincial and local levels. A central party committee now nominates candidates for provincial premierships and local mayoralties. Several provincial party structures have been dissolved and reformed and more than one provincial premier has been removed by the national party leadership.[32] Party discipline in parliament is strongly enforced. The interval between party conferences was extended from three to five years, further limiting opportunities for the rank and file to elect senior party organs. The ministerial and parliamentary wings of the ANC overshadow the extra-parliamentary wing. The ANC party organization "suffers from a declining number of paid-up members, a dwindling number of branches and several financial problems."[33] The decision to lift periodically the prohibition on floor-crossing has strengthened the ANC at all levels. The initial reason for the move was the break-up of the Democratic Alliance between the DP and NNP, formed prior to the local government elections of December 2000, and the signing of a cooperation agreement in November 2001 between the ANC and NNP. This agreement gave the ANC shared control over many of the areas it did not yet rule, including Cape Town and the Western Cape.

## THE CONSOCIATIONAL PARTY

There is a tendency to perceive only two options for South Africa: a consociation of communal parties or long-standing dominance of a black majority party.[34] Power sharing was limited to the transition period and the constituent assembly under the interim constitution. Even before the coming into force of the new constitution, the departure of the NP from the GNU in 1996 marked the end of power sharing. The weak and divided white and coloured opposition, so far unable to make significant inroads into the black vote, and the marginal black opposition do not present a threat to continued ANC dominance. Post-apartheid political history could well be summed up as "from power sharing to a dominant party system." The continued coalition between the ANC and IFP at the national level and the recent cooperation between the ANC and NNP do not alter this picture. Classic consociational democracy involving segmental parties is not an option. The appointment of two NNP members as deputy ministers in November 2002 falls far short of the formation of a new grand coalition, not to mention the absence of veto rights or extensive segmental autonomy.

Nonetheless, the juxtaposition of power sharing and one-party dominance ignores the possibility of forms of power sharing *within* the dominant party. Power sharing within a party, as compared to power sharing between parties, can be analysed with the help of the concept of the "consociational party." Recent advances in consociational theory have elaborated on the crucial role of segmental parties in consociational democracy in systems where political accommodation is achieved by cooperation among the elites of parties that represent a single segment of society.[35] However, Spain, Canada, Fiji, Malaysia, India, the Gambia, and Kenya have all been described as consociational democracies on the basis of political accommodation that takes place not *among* political parties but *within* the main political party. The Union de Centro Democratico (UCD) (Spain), the Liberal Party (Canada), the Fijian Alliance (Fiji), the Alliance and National Front (Malaysia), the Congress Party (India), the People's Progressive Party (PPP) (Gambia), and the Kenya African National Union (KANU) (Kenya) are not segmental political parties but what I call "consociational parties."

Three types of consociational party can be distinguished, depending on the nature of the party system (multi-party or party state) and the composition and internal organization of the party. The Alliance type of consociational party is made up of separate organizational entities that function as a unity in the context of competitive multi-party elections. Although first used to describe the short-lived Spanish UCD, this type of consociational party is best represented by the Malaysian Alliance, later the National Front, which was originally composed of three ethnic parties: the United Malays National Organization (UMNO), the Malayan Chinese Association (MCA), and the Malayan Indian Congress (MIC). The Alliance has ruled Malaysia since independence. Operating under an electoral system of plurality elections in single-member districts, the Alliance has been highly effective in organizing the exchange of votes across ethnic lines among the constituent parties, making it a prime example of Horowitz's model of "vote pooling." Within the Alliance, there is proportional power sharing, as reflected in the relative symmetry of party representation in the Alliance councils, in the distribution of electoral seats, cabinet positions, and patronage appointments, and "in the general perception that despite UMNO dominance, the MCA and MIC leaders were efficacious representatives of non-Malay interests because of the moral linkages between the senior Alliance leaders."[36] The party organization has always been highly centralized, with party nominations decided by the central body. A mutual veto is absent, segmental autonomy is conditional on approval of the dominant party in the Alliance, and proportionality and participation in the grand coalition are very much on the terms of the dominant segment. Even more important than internal tensions is the external threat presented by outbidding from ethnic flank parties. The success of radical opposition parties led to a temporary breakdown of democracy in 1969, and, when democracy was restored in 1974, it was under the guidance of an enlarged Alliance, now operating as the National Front. The ever more prominent role of the Malay component and the forceful advancement of Malay interests has resulted in claims of "coercive consociationalism."[37]

The second type of consociational party is the Congress model. A defining characteristic of the Congress type of consociational party is that it consists of factions and/or subnational party organizations representing socio-cultural constituencies and operates in the context of a multi-party system. The Congress Party in India and the Liberal Party in Canada exhibit these features. Previously considered a deviant case, if not a refutation of the consociational prediction that majoritarian democracy in plural societies is not sustainable, India has recently been reconsidered as a case of consociationalism, at least in the period from independence in 1947 until 1967.[38] The main vehicle for the grand coalition was the cabinet in the days that the Congress Party was the dominant party and governed alone. The Congress Party was then broadly representative and inclusive, manifested by an internally federal organization, a high degree of intra-party democracy, and a strong penchant for consensus. In the view of Lijphart, "the combination of the Congress Party's inclusive nature and political dominance has generated grand coalition cabinets with ministers belonging to all the main religious, linguistic, and regional groups."[39] Segmental autonomy was present in linguistic federalism, educational autonomy for religious and linguistic minorities, and separate personal laws for Hindus, Muslims, and smaller religious minorities. Congress cabinets accorded proportional shares of ministerships to the Muslim and Sikh minority, as well as to the different linguistic groups, states, and regions of the country.

The electoral law reserved a large proportion of parliamentary seats to designated disadvantaged social groups and minority rights were protected by an informal minority veto.

Lijphart's analysis draws heavily on Rajni Kothari's description of the Congress Party as a system, characterized by a party of consensus that has assumed electoral and governmental dominance within a competitive multi-party system.[40] The centralization of the party under Indira Gandhi and the loss of dominance, first temporarily in 1977 and then more durably since the late 1980s, weakened consociationalism within the Congress Party and the position of the party within the broader system. In any case, there were always limitations to the degree of consociationalism achieved within the Congress Party. Segmental autonomy and the mutual veto were weak and it was difficult to identify segmental leaders and to determine the representativeness of group representatives within the party. In India as well as in Canada, it would seem that federal structures provide a crucial additional site of representation and accommodation supplementing – and in India ultimately substituting for – processes within the consociational party.

The third type of consociational party is the single party. From the outset it should be clear that the single party, whatever its internal degree of representation and accommodation, can never be part of a consociational *democracy* and that the absence of multi-party competition and the lack of freedom of organization contradict the very idea of power sharing. Dirk Berg-Schlosser, who classified Kenya under the rule of KANU as a consociational democracy, "although a special and somewhat limited version," writes that "all cabinets have consisted of an (admittedly somewhat lopsided) 'grand coalition' of representatives of all ethnic groups."[41] Representation extended to the district level, through an elaborate system of "assistant ministers." This kind of "ethnic arithmetic" has also been seen in other African single-party states.[42] However, it is not sufficient to share power with any representative of a particular ethnic group. In Lijphart's definition of a grand coalition, the key players are "the political leaders of all significant segments."[43] The link between leader and segment is crucial in consociational theory because leaders count on the control over and support of their constituencies when they engage in nation-saving compromises. In Kenya, cabinet members were not segmental leaders, in the absence of ethnic organization and political autonomy. It is even doubtful whether some of them were representatives, since "not all members of the government are necessarily those which would have been put forward by the majority of their ethnic groups."[44] Therefore, cabinet formation in Kenya is better regarded as a case of "hegemonic exchange"[45] than of grand coalition.

Berg-Schlosser also identified the other three consociational elements in Kenya. Proportionality was achieved through plurality elections in single-member districts that followed settlement patterns of the geographically concentrated ethnic groups. The allocation of finances and public sector jobs was roughly proportional. There was no formal mutual veto, but, according to Berg-Schlosser, the government protected each group's rights. Segmental autonomy was absent. Many administrative boundaries followed ethnic and other traditional social lines, but subnational government was tightly controlled by the central government.

Consociational parties of the single-party type exhibit certain peculiarities. First, more than anything else, they stand out by their emphasis on proportionality for the composition of parliament and/or government. Second, broad proportionality in the government of a hegemonic or single party does not imply a grand coalition of segmental leaders. Group representation tends to be more symbolic than effective. Political recruitment is top-down, not bottom-up, and "representatives" normally lack an independent power base in their purported constituencies. Instead of power sharing, we find a strong concentration of power. There is no mutual veto, and, if there is a limited form of segmental autonomy at all, this is conditional on the continuing support of the party elite. In sum, consociational parties in a single-party state such as Kenya are not consociational.

## THE ANC AS A CONSOCIATIONAL PARTY

After this brief introduction of the concept of the consociational party and an overview of its three types, the question is to what extent we can recognize elements of the consociational party in the ANC and, if so, which type of consociational party the ANC approximates most closely. Lijphart hints at the ANC's nature as a consociational party when he observes how "the ANC is a strongly multi-racial and multi-ethnic party; in particular, its members of parliament and its cabinet ministers have been broadly representative of all of the major racial and ethnic groups in South Africa." Even if the ANC governs alone, Lijphart predicts, "it is quite possible that its rule will be similar to that of the

Indian National Congress, which has been so inclusive of all religious, linguistic, and regional groups in India that it has embodied the essence of a grand coalition *within* the party and within the long succession of Congress cabinets."[46] Clearly, Lijphart refers here to a possible change in the nature and place of consociationalism in South Africa: from classic consociationalism between segmental parties in the GNU to consociationalism within the dominant (consociational) party. Yet, if we take a closer look at the ANC as an organization to determine how and where representation and accommodation are supposed to take place, the picture changes with the nature of the cleavage under examination.

In light of its history as a national liberation movement, an exile movement, and a domestic mass movement, it is remarkable how quickly and successfully the ANC has made the transition to a political party.[47] The formation of the United Democratic Front (UDF) in 1983 united a wide range of anti-apartheid organizations under the leadership of the ANC. In 1985 the Congress of South African Trade Unions (COSATU) was formed. Together with the South African Communist Party (SACP), it is part of the so-called Tripartite Alliance with the ANC. The Tripartite Alliance had the objective to maximize opposition against the apartheid regime and to ensure a working-class bias in the policies and programs of the national liberation movement.[48] While the first objective has been achieved, the second is found to be floundering, especially after the government's adoption in 1996 of the Growth, Employment and Redistribution Strategy (GEAR), which puts the emphasis on growth. Some commentators therefore put their hope of a viable, non-racial opposition to the ANC on COSATU and the SACP breaking away from the ANC.[49] So far, however, the ANC leadership has shown great skill in "quashing genuine opposition and controlling the boundaries of debate" within the Tripartite Alliance "through a combination of outright political intimidation, ideological mysticism and the cooption ... of key ANC 'trouble-makers' and COSATU/SACP leaders."[50]

COSATU and the SACP represent left-wing ideological and socioeconomic positions within the Tripartite Alliance. Its members are elected on ANC slates, sit in parliament for the ANC, and take up cabinet positions as ANC officeholders. The fact that the component parts also exist as autonomous organizations indicates an Alliance model. As with the Malaysian Alliance/National Front, the right of nomination and appointment is reserved for the central party office.

The picture is different for the racial and ethnic cleavage. Non-blacks are over-represented in the ANC caucus. Thirty per cent of its deputies come from the coloured, Indian, and white communities despite the fact that these communities contributed only six per cent to the overall ANC vote. A slightly higher percentage of its caucus consists of women. However, unlike communal groups, women in the ANC have secure representation through a quota guaranteeing that at least 30 per cent of the party's candidates are women.[51] The other main parties have multi-ethnic lists too, but, as Herman Giliomee and Charles Simkins warn, these "multi-ethnic lists may only create a dangerous illusion of representation."[52] Under South Africa's electoral system of closed-list PR, the central party determines the candidate lists. The candidates preferred by the central party may not be the same as those preferred by their communities and it is alleged that in the ANC "most of its white, coloured, and Indian candidates would have great trouble winning a seat in their respective ethnic communities under the first-past-the-post plurality system."[53] Additionally, there are no indications that minority candidates on the ANC's list and in the ANC's caucus consider themselves representatives of their respective communities or that they are perceived as such by voters. The political identity of most white ANC politicians is, in the first place, left-wing and non-racial. When in the last elections the ANC reached out to minority electorates, this was not done by deploying ANC minority candidates to appeal to their respective constituencies but by inviting non-ANC voters to, in the words of ANC leader Mbeki, "become part of the mainstream."[54] This implies that, if the ANC succeeds in attracting a greater share of the non-black vote, the representation of these minorities as minorities inside the ANC does not necessarily increase.

There are no organizations or even factions representing communal or ethnic constituencies within the ANC. There could not be, since the ANC has a strong commitment to non-racialism and has always refused to accept the legitimacy of the idea of multiracialism, with its implications of durable and politically significant social divisions based on ascriptive traits.[55] The policy of non-racialism itself is relatively recent. Only since 1969 have non-Africans become members of the ANC and only since 1985 have they been allowed to participate in the decision-making process of the organization.[56] Also, because of strong party discipline and the taboo on factionalism, if there is any representation of minorities within the ANC, it is not organized and not explicit. There are no indications that the ANC is modelling itself on the Indian Congress Party or the Malaysian Alliance/National Front, despite Lijphart's comparison. On the contrary, minority members in the ANC's caucus are closer to their colleagues in a party such as KANU in Kenya, since they lack an autonomous basis of organization, have no control over their recruitment, and are not necessarily recognized by their respective social groups as representatives. In other words, if the ANC is consociational at all, it comes closest to the single-party type, at least with respect to what arguably remains the most important cleavage in South African politics and society: race. The resemblance between the ANC and KANU is based not on the position of these parties in the political system, for dominance should never be confused with hegemony, but on the internal structure and process of communal representation and accommodation. If anything, consociationalism within the ANC is on an even weaker footing because the official ideology of non-racialism negates the legitimacy of communal representation within the party, closed-list PR weakens the link between constituencies and deputies, and minority officers in the ANC do not see themselves as delegates of their respective communities. In sum, there is every reason to believe that the ANC is even more negatively disposed to consociationalism within its organization than it was to the idea of consociationalism between parties.

## CONCLUSION

Most observers would welcome an end to ANC dominance although few see any signs of this happening soon. The opposition seems largely confined to minorities, with the small left-wing African parties unable to capitalize on dissatisfaction with government delivery. The recent wave of floor-crossing has further weakened opposition parties and consolidated and extended ANC dominance throughout the country.

From the perspective of consociational theory, the dominant party system is worrying. A plural society without political accommodation is prone to social conflict and democratic breakdown or erosion. Lijphart was too sanguine about the ANC internalizing communal representation and accommodation. The prospects of the ANC transforming itself into a consociational party are minimal because of the official ideology of non-racialism, the policy of "transformation," and the organizational culture of democratic centralism. The question remains whether South African democrats should focus their hopes on the ANC as a multiracial, consociational party. The experience of consociational parties elsewhere suggests that representation and accommodation are less extensive, effective, and durable within a dominant party than in a classic consociational democracy with power sharing between segmental parties. Although consociational democracy in any form has its critics, the classic type of consociationalism between segmental parties is preferable to consociationalism within a party.

The ANC has always strongly supported the building of a unitary non-racial South Africa safeguarding individual rights. Could non-racialism be a substitute for consociationalism? Is there a need for consociationalism when "there is majority support for an inclusive non-racial democratic position concerned with breaking down ethnic divisions?"[57] The answer would be that minorities may not share these goals but on the contrary may well perceive such policies as a threat to their identity. For minorities, a majoritarian system in which there is a numerical majority group spells permanent exclusion from power and no effective correction to the dominant policy vision. Such lack of influence becomes all the more urgent if the dominant party deviates from its self-professed doctrine of non-racialism. This implies that South Africans may have to think again about how to represent and accommodate racial and cultural minority groups in a plural society with a dominant party representing a racial majority.[58]

## NOTES

1 L.J. Boulle, *Constitutional Reform and the Apartheid State: Legitimacy, Consociationalism and Control in South Africa* (New York: St Martin's Press 1984).

2 Arend Lijphart, *Power-Sharing in South Africa* (Berkeley, Calif.: Institute of International Studies 1985), 61.

3 Sammy Smooha and Theodor Hanf, "The Diverse Modes of Conflict Regulation in Deeply Divided Societies," *International Journal of Comparative Sociology* 33, nos.1–2 (1992): 26–46.

4 Mark Simpson, "The Experience of Nation-Building: Some Lessons for South Africa," *Journal of Southern African Studies* 20, no.3 (1994): 463–74; see also Rupert Taylor, "South Africa: Consociation or Democracy?" *Telos* 85 (1990): 17–32.

5 Vincent Maphai, "A Season for Power-sharing?," *Journal of Democracy* 7, no.1 (1996): 79; see also Timothy Sisk, *Democratization in South Africa: The Elusive Social Contract* (Princeton, N.J.: Princeton University Press 1995).

6 Arend Lijphart, "South African Democracy: Majoritarian or Consociational?" *Democratization* 5, no.4 (1998): 146.

7 Ibid., 147.

8 Ibid., 148.

9 Hermann Giliomee, James Myburgh, and Lawrence Schlemmer, "Dominant Party Rule, Opposition Parties and Minorities in South Africa," in Roger Southall, ed., *Opposition and Democracy in South Africa* (London: Frank Cass 2001), 166; see also Kristin Henrard, *Minority Protection in Post-apartheid South Africa: Human Rights, Minority Rights and Self-Determination* (New York: Praeger 2002).

10 Michael Kelly Connors, "The Eclipse of Consociationalism in South Africa's Democratic Transition," *Democratization* 3, no.4 (1996): 420–34; Thomas Koelble and Andrew Reynolds "Power-sharing Democracy in the New South Africa," *Politics and Society* 24, no.3 (1996), 221–36; Adrian Guelke, *South Africa in Transition: The Misunderstood Miracle* (London: I.B. Tauris 1999).

11 See Thomas Koelble, "The New South African Constitution: A Case of Consensus Democracy?" in Markus Crepaz, Thomas Koelble, and David Wilsford, ed., *Democracy and Institutions: The Life and Work of Arend Lijphart* (Ann Arbor: University of Michigan Press 2000), 129–53.

12 See the debate between Courtney Jung and Ian Shapiro on the one hand and Thomas Koelble and Andrew Reynolds on the other in the journal *Politics and Society* in 1995/96.

13 Steven Friedman, "No Easy Stroll to Dominance: Party Dominance, Opposition and Civil Society in South Africa," in Hermann Giliomee and Charles Simkins, ed., *The Awkward Embrace: One-Party Domination and Democracy* (Amsterdam: Harwood Academic Publishers 1999), 97–126; Heribert Adam, "Corporatism as a Minority Veto under ANC Hegemony in South Africa," in ibid., 261–80.

14 Kidane Mengisteab, "Globalization and South Africa's Transition through a Consociational Arrangement," in Francis Adams, Satya Dev Gupta, and Kidane Mengisteab, ed., *Globalization and the Dilemmas of the State in the South* (Basingstoke, U.K.: Macmillan 1999), 133–51.

15 Hermann Giliomee and Charles Simkins, "The Dominant Party Regimes of South Africa, Mexico, Taiwan and Malaysia: A Comparative Assessment," in Giliomee and Simkins, ed., *The Awkward Embrace*, 1–45.

16 Adrian Guelke, *South Africa in Transition*, 188.

17 Andrew Reynolds, *Electoral Systems and Democratization in Southern Africa* (Oxford, U.K.: Oxford University Press 1999).

18 Hermann Giliomee, "South Africa's Emerging Dominant-Party Regime," *Journal of Democracy* 9, no.4 (1998): 131.

19 Donald Horowitz, *A Democratic South Africa? Constitutional Engineering in a Divided Society* (Berkeley: University of California Press 1991; Arend Lijphart, *Power-Sharing in South Africa*; see also Michael Macdonald, "The Siren's Song: The Political Logic of Power-Sharing in South Africa," *Journal of Southern African Studies* 18, no.4 (1992): 709–25.

20 Arend Lijphart, "Federal, Confederal, and Consociational Options for the South African Plural Society," in Robert Rotberg and John Barratt, ed., *Conflict and Compromise in South Africa* (Lexington, Mass.: Lexington Books 1980), 67.

21 By looking at ethnicity rather than race, Lijphart saw a multitude of small ethnic groups instead of a black majority. Many scholars have criticized Lijphart's overly optimistic assessment of favourable factors in South Africa. See, for example, John McGarry and S.J.R. Noel, "The Prospects for Consociational Democracy in South Africa," *Journal of Commonwealth and Comparative Politics* 27, no.1 (1989): 3–22.

22 Lawrence Schlemmer, "Democracy or Democratic Hegemony: The Future of Political Pluralism in South Africa," in Giliomee and Simkins, ed., *The Awkward Embrace*, 282.

23 J.E. Spence, "Second Chance for the ANC: The 1999 South African General Election," *Government and Opposition* 34, no.4 (1999): 469.

24 Steven Friedman, "South Africa: Entering the Post-Mandela Era," *Journal of Democracy* 10, no.4 (1999): 10.

25 Hermann Giliomee and Charles Simkins, "Conclusion," in Giliomee and Simkins, ed., *The Awkward Embrace*, 350.

26 Friedman, "Entering the Post-Mandela Era," 12.

27 Robert Mattes, Helen Taylor, and Cherrel Africa, "Hegemonism, Dominance or Weak Opposition? The Partisan Situation on the Eve of South Africa's Second Election Campaign," *Transformation* 38 (1999): 14, graph 8.

28 Giliomee and Simkins, "Dominant Party Regimes," in Giliomee and Simkins, ed., *The Awkward Embrace*, 24.

29 Gerhard Maré, "Race, Democracy and Opposition in South African Politics: As Other a Way as Possible," in Southall, ed., *Opposition and Democracy*, 85–102.

30 Giliomee, Myburgh, and Schlemmer, "Dominant Party Rule," 161–82.

31 Kenneth Good, "Accountable to Themselves: Predominance in Southern Africa," *Journal of Modern African Studies* 35, no.4 (1997): 547–73;

Robert Mattes, "South Africa: Democracy without the People?" *Journal of Democracy* 13, no.1 (2002) 22–36.

32  Geoffrey Hawker, "Political Leadership in the ANC: The South African Provinces 1994–1999," *Journal of Modern African Studies* 38, no.4 (2000) 631–58.

33  Giliomee and Simkins, "Dominant Party Regimes," 43.

34  See, for example, Schlemmer, "Democracy or Democratic Hegemony," 297–300.

35  Kurt Richard Luther and Kris Deschouwer, ed., *Party Elites in Divided Societies: Political Parties in Consociational Democracy* (London: Routledge 1999).

36  Stephen Chee, "Consociational Political Leadership and Conflict Regulation in Malaysia," in Stephen Chee, ed., *Leadership and Security in South East Asia: Institutional Aspects* (Singapore: Institute of Southeast Asian Studies 1991), 65.

37  Diane Mauzy, "Malaysia: Malay Political Hegemony and "Coercive Consociationalism," in John McGarry and Brendan O'Leary, ed., *The Politics of Ethnic Conflict Regulation: Case Studies of Protracted Ethnic Conflict* (London: Routledge 1993), 106–27.

38  Arend Lijphart, "The Puzzle of Indian Democracy: A Consociational Reinterpretation," *American Political Science Review* 90, no.2 (1996): 258–68. For a different view, see Steven Wilkinson, "India, Consociational Theory, and Ethnic Violence," *Asian Survey* 40, no.5 (2000): 767–91.

39  Lijphart, "The Puzzle of Indian Democracy," 260.

40  Rajni Kothari, "The Congress System in India," *Asian Survey* 4, no.12 (1964): 1162–73, and "The Congress System Revisited: A Decennial View," *Asian Survey*, 14, no.12 (1974): 1035–54.

41  Dirk Berg-Schlosser, "Elements of Consociational Democracy in Kenya," *European Journal of Political Research* 13, no.1 (1985): 107, 97.

42  Donald Rothchild, *Managing Ethnic Conflict in Africa: Pressures and Incentives for Cooperation* (Washington, D.C.: Brookings Institution Press 1997).

43  Arend Lijphart, *Democracy in Plural Societies: A Comparative Exploration* (New Haven, Conn.: Yale University Press 1977), 25.

44  Berg-Schlosser, "Elements of Consociational Democracy in Kenya," 100.

45  Rothchild, *Managing Ethnic Conflict in Africa*.

46  "South African Democracy," 148 (emphasis in original).

47  Philip Nel, "The Three 'Faces' of the ANC," in Willie Esterhuyse and Philip Nel, ed., *The ANC and Its Leaders* (Capetown, South Africa: Tafelberg

Publishers 1990), 25–41; Marina Ottaway, "The ANC: From Symbol to Political Party," in Helen Kitchen and J. Coleman Kitchen, ed., *South Africa: Twelve Perspectives on the Transition* (Westport, Conn.: Praeger 1994), 28–48.

48 Adam Habib and Rupert Taylor, "Parliamentary Opposition and Democratic Consolidation in Southern Africa," *Review of African Political Economy* 80 (1999): 261–7.

49 See the debate between Roger Southall and Geoff Wood on the one hand and Adam Habib and Rupert Taylor on the other in the journal *Transformation* in 1999; also, J. Maree, "The COSATU Participatory Democratic Tradition and South Africa's New Parliament: Are They Reconcilable?" *African Affairs* 386 (1998): 29–51.

50 Dale McKinley, "Democracy, Power and Patronage: Debate and Opposition within the African National Congress and the Tripartite Alliance since 1994," in Southall, ed., *Opposition and Democracy*, 200.

51 Gisela Geisler, "'Parliament Is Another Terrain of Struggle': Women, Men and Politics in South Africa," *Journal of Modern African Studies* 38, no.4: 605–30.

52 Giliomee and Simkins, "Dominant Party Regimes," 15.

53 Ibid.

54 Quoted in Tom Lodge, "The African National Congress," in Andrew Reynolds, ed., *Election '99 South Africa* (New York: St Martin's Press 1999), 80.

55 See Horowitz, *A Democratic South Africa?*

56 Nhlanhla Ndebele, "The African National Congress and the Policy of Non-Racialism: A Study of the Membership Issue," *Politikon* 29, no.2 (2002): 133–46.

57 Taylor, "South Africa: Consociation or Democracy?" 27.

58 This chapter was completed before the elections of April 2004 in which the ANC enlarged its majority to 70 per cent of the seats in parliament and won control over all nine provinces. The new government included the NNP, which was reduced to a marginal presence in parliament with 7 out of 400 seats, but excluded, for the first time since 1994, the IFP.

# 9

# Anarchy and the Problems of Power Sharing in Africa

IAN S. SPEARS

Power sharing has been repeatedly advocated as a method of post-conflict governance in Africa. In virtually all cases, however, the results have been the same: inclusive power-sharing agreements have been resisted by local leaders or, if accepted, have rarely been fully implemented or adhered to over the long term. Given this unimpressive record, it is remarkable that power sharing nevertheless continues to be the centrepiece of so many African peace initiatives. To expect power sharing to work in Africa is to expect it to work under the most difficult conditions, and this, in fact, is part of the problem. For the conditions of anarchy[1] that accompany civil war and state collapse often require solutions that are prior to, or in addition to, power sharing – or ones that exclude power sharing altogether.

Power sharing is admittedly a broad term and can involve a number of different approaches and models. As used here, following Timothy D. Sisk, it refers to "practices and institutions that result in broad-based governing coalitions generally inclusive of all major ethnic groups in society."[2] In Africa, however, in many cases, the allocation of power to representatives of broadly defined ethnic groups has led to the exclusion of the specific parties, movements, or "liberation fronts" that were involved in the conflict – and whose continued existence poses a direct threat to the peace process.[3] Providing political voice to disenfranchised ethnic groups, in other words, does not necessarily mean the end of violent conflict. In cases where power sharing is determined to be the best political route forward, at some point the leaders of *all* warring factions must meet directly and agree to enter into some sort of cooperative relationship. Not surprisingly, these agreements are the most difficult to forge and the least likely to last. This is because, among other reasons, conditions of anarchy effectively force local factions to look after their own security interests before they consider options that entail cooperation and risk. Instead of power sharing, local disputants often prefer other more self-interested and, in their view, more durable approaches to peace – such as complete victory over their opponents. This chapter will examine the problems of power sharing in the context of Africa's recent civil wars and explain why lasting power-sharing agreements have been so rare.

## AFRICAN EXPERIMENTS IN POWER SHARING

Some scholars have lamented the fact that peace processes are not always as inclusive as they should be, implying that the lack of inclusiveness is the critical missing element responsible for the resumption of violent conflict. Fen Osler Hampson, for example, suggests that, if only there had been power sharing at the time of the 1991 Bicesse Accords in Angola, the peace process would not have fallen apart.[4] On other occasions and in other locations in Africa, there have been expectations among observers on the ground that power-sharing agreements would placate the central disputants in the conflict. David Rieff, for example, writes that "foreigners in Burundi, notably aid workers and U.N. [United Nations] officials as well as, of course, the conflict resolution specialists who descend on the place intermittently, remain attached to the idea" of an integrated polity.[5] In Sierra Leone, Abiodun Alao and Comfort Ero note, the expectation among UN personnel was that the July 1999 Lomé Accord would hold. They write that the UN force "appeared to have banked on the assumption that the peace agreement would work, and seemed prepared to only focus on the tasks of demobilisation and disarmament."[6] On occasion, even the disputants themselves, when they feel they have no choice other than submission, place their faith in power sharing. The president of Sierra Leone, Dr Ahmed Tejan Kabbah, told John Hirsch, the former American ambassador to Sierra Leone, that he believed that Revolutionary United Front (RUF) leader Foday Sankoh "truly wanted to end the war and that the time for peace and reconciliation had arrived."[7]

In each of these cases, the assumption was made that all the belligerents actually wanted to share power, and that a slice of power would satisfy the disputants and end the conflict. In each case, however, the agreement either collapsed outright or remains on shaky ground. In Angola, when a subsequent power-sharing arrangement was agreed to in 1994, the promise of inclusion was not a sufficient incentive to induce the leader of the União Nacional para a Indepencia Total de Angola (UNITA), Jonas Savimbi, to travel to Angola's capital, Luanda, and join the government. Impatient with his intransigence, the government in Luanda finally re-engaged Savimbi and UNITA in battle in 1998 and killed him in a February 2002 firefight.

In the case of Sierra Leone, the provisions of the Lomé Agreement were extremely favourable to Sankoh. In addition to four ministerial and four deputy ministerial posts for the RUF, Sankoh himself was made chairman of the Commission for the Management of Strategic Resources, National Reconstruction and Development, a position from which the president could not remove him. By placing him in a position to protect Sierra Leone's vast natural resources, Sankoh gained control over the country's lucrative diamond mines. The agreement did not, however, end the fighting or satisfy Sankoh; on the contrary, it whetted his appetite. When it was clear that he was not abiding by the agreement's terms, Sankoh was finally captured and imprisoned.

Finally, in Burundi, the peace process has continued to stumble despite the intervention of Nelson Mandela, the most famous participant in South Africa's power-sharing experiment. According to David Rieff, "that Mandela would immerse himself in the Burundian negotiations was certainly to his credit, but in fact the power-sharing deal he finally brokered in the summer of 2001 was utterly fanciful. Neither of the main rebel groups signed on, which made the agreement "for all intents and purposes an arrangement between Bujumbura politicians ... the situation in Burundi is not better today; if anything, it is worse."[8]

Clearly, power sharing has had a difficult time in Africa's brutal conflicts. But what of the cases where it has been an effective path to peace? René Lemarchand elaborates on the conditions that made South Africa's transition to democracy so successful. He argues that structural factors may be crucial "in restricting or enlarging the range of opportunities available to social actors," but that "in the last analysis their choices, if any, are what made a difference." His analysis leads him to warn of the "dangers of overly deterministic explanations."[9] In other words, peaceful outcomes to civil wars are open to those who choose them. Indeed, in South Africa the respective movements were led by exceptionally credible leaders who, against all odds, were willing to accept a power-sharing deal and were able to persuade their compatriots to follow their lead.

That the principal leaders both wanted an agreement and recognized that peace required that they deal directly with each other was certainly admirable and would confirm Arend Lijphart's contention that the success of power sharing is contingent on it being a deliberate and desired act by the disputants.[10] But what happens when, as is more often the case, belligerents do not want to share power? Can an agreement that requires cooperation ever be imposed?

African leaders have not shied away from lecturing outsiders on why power sharing is an unacceptable form of democracy for African states. Following the collapse of the Bicesse Accords, Margaret Anstee, the UN's special representative to Angola, was upbraided by the Namibian prime minister for suggesting that power sharing might have helped bring an end to Angola's ongoing violence. According to Anstee, he said: "Then you want second-class democracy for Africa! In the UK one party wins and governs, the others lose and don't and that is the way it should be. That is the way it is here."[11] Other states have also resisted outside efforts to impose power-sharing agreements. In Mozambique, where the conditions for power sharing appeared to UN observers to be reasonably favourable, both parties preferred to contest the 1994 elections than to cut a power-sharing deal. As Richard Synge observed in a follow-up report on the peace process, "the proposal to establish a government of national unity at the end of the peace process was favored by many in the international community as a way to restore the state's authority, but all attempts to pressure Frelimo [the ruling policial party] to accept the idea backfired. Frelimo was quick to interpret any form of pressure as an attempt to lever Renamo [the main opposition party] into power." Other diplomats cited by Synge emphasize the manner in which Frelimo resented the UN's efforts as an infringement on the country's sovereignty. In a comment that echoes that of the Namibian prime minister, one Zimbabwean official stated, "once there was pressure from the outside, there was a tendency to resist. The government detested being patronized and wanted to be treated as a government."[12]

To be sure, local leaders do recognize the need to be inclusive. Most regimes in Africa are built on delicate coalitions of different ethnic groups. But leaders are also selective about whom they are willing to share power with. The end of apartheid in South Africa is exceptional precisely because the African National Congress (ANC) and the National Party (NP), the two central players in the conflict, deliberately and willingly focused their attention on each other. As Nelson Mandela later noted when he advised politicians in Northern Ireland: "You don't make peace by talking to your friends; you have to make peace with your enemies."[13] But agreements such as those established in South Africa are rare because the kind of power-sharing deal that is necessary for peace is also the most unpalatable to disputants. Even if political leaders are willing to share power, they do not want to share it with their principal enemy. More often, groups will seek out more acceptable alternative partners for the power-sharing coalition. During the 1990s, for example, the Rwandan president, Juvenal Habyarimana, a Hutu, was willing to share power with minority Tutsi living in Rwanda. But he refused to provide political space to the returning Tutsi diaspora who made up the Rwandan Patriotic Front (RPF), because he regarded them as non-indigenous and therefore unwelcome. Yet it was the RPF that posed the greatest threat to his regime. While Habyarimana finally relented – largely as a result of foreign pressures and failures on the battlefield – other hardliners did not and they eventually killed the president and brought down the entire peace process. For Habyarimana, it was fatal to be accused of "selling out" to the enemy – and "selling out" is precisely how many power-sharing agreements in Africa are perceived.

More critically, while Lemarchand takes pains to emphasize that South Africa's remarkable transition was a demonstration of choice where outcomes were not predetermined, many of the other factors he uses to explain South Africa's successful transition, and the failures in Rwanda and Burundi, in fact point to a structural explanation. Consider, for example, the measures that groups take to protect themselves during times of transition. Realist analysis of civil conflicts has emphasized that disarmament creates vulnerabilities that local disputants find intolerable.[14] However, as Lemarchand and others have also noted, President F.W. De Klerk shrewdly kept many of his own hardline officers in, and the ANC's armed wing Umkonto we Sizwe out, of the South African Defence Force until it was clear that ordinary white South Africans were willing participants in the peace process. This had the effect of reassuring whites that their interests would be secure during the transition, and it was critical in persuading them to support reforms in the 1992 referendum that ultimately led to the end of apartheid.[15] This approach has also helped smooth the way in other power-sharing transitions. In Rhodesia/Zimbabwe, a decade earlier, Robert Mugabe included the white commander of the Rhodesian army as head of the armed forces and another white as head of the Central Intelligence Office.[16] Zimbabwe also benefited from a substantial international presence in the form of a British-led Commonwealth Monitoring Force, which went a long way towards reassuring the disputants that their interests would be protected, even in the aftermath of a particularly bitter civil war.[17] Significantly, neither party in Zimbabwe was required to disarm – a fact that ultimately allowed each party to control its own security.

The peace processes in both South Africa and Zimbabwe also benefited from a domestic environment that compared favourably to the relative upheaval and uncertainty that has existed in Rwanda, Burundi, and elsewhere. Lemarchand notes, for example, that "South Africa's 'fragility' seems by comparison to have a rock-like stability" in part because of the "Republic's historic legacy of 'stateness' and political competitiveness, so strikingly at odds with the patrimonial syndrome encountered in virtually every other state in the continent ..."[18] Jeremy Ginifer makes a similar characterization of the situation in Rhodesia/Zimbabwe during the late 1970s. There, he observes, "the fact that a coherent state structure existed during the operation with a functioning bureaucracy enabled decisions to be centrally implemented and avoided the administrative chaos inherent in a number of current 'failed-state' peacekeeping operations." Ginifer concludes, "The existence of strong state structures onto which peacekeeping operations can be 'bolted' appears to be a major contributor to the success of a peace process and demilitarization."[19]

Together, these factors – the provisions that allowed disputants to ensure their own security, the relative "stateness" of the two countries, and a constructive and substantial international presence (particularly for Rhodesia/Zimbabwe) – went a long way towards preventing anarchy and reducing the vulnerabilities that anarchy creates, and these factors in turn conditioned subsequent choices. Consequently, while one would not want to underestimate the uncertainty that inevitably characterized these transitions, in both South Africa and Rhodesia/Zimbabwe the conditions were comparatively favourable for power sharing and a smooth peace process. In short, the remarkable and exceptional transitions in these two countries should be regarded as just that: remarkable and exceptional.[20]

More often, these favourable conditions have not existed. Indeed, a discussion of the utility of power sharing requires an understanding of the difficult circumstances in which it has been expected to work. Governments in Africa have always had difficulty consolidating their rule, but the end of the Cold War has further exacerbated these problems of state building and nation building. States such as Angola and Somalia, which received the largest amounts of military aid from their Cold War patrons, have been among the most troubled states in Africa. Deep ethnic cleavages and the aggressive exploitation of valuable resources have also meant that even non-client states such as Rwanda, Burundi, and Sierra Leone have experienced profound state collapse, and their reconstruction has proved to be extremely difficult.[21]

Added to these problems is the general reluctance on the part of the international community, particularly the United States and the UN, to intervene in African conflicts in a substantial way. Even when resources and personnel have been committed, as in Somalia in 1992–93 and Sierra Leone in 2001 (at which time, the UN mission in Sierra Leone was the largest peacekeeping operation in the world), they have been geographically limited in scope and have thus been incapable of imposing order across the country. Moreover, they have tended to come after the processes of state collapse were well under way, and to be hampered by limited or uncertain mandates regarding the use of force. In some cases, local belligerents were well aware of the UN force's unwillingness to tolerate casualties, and so they committed violent acts in an effort to force them to withdraw.[22] As Terrence Lyons has observed, in reference to peacemaking efforts in Liberia, "because the international community cannot in any real sense 'guarantee' peace agreements in internal conflicts, the agreements must be largely self reinforcing."[23] Power sharing is an intuitively appealing response to this problem because it promises to give all belligerents what they claim to be fighting for and thus relieves the international community of having to make a meaningful commitment. In many African cases, however, power sharing requires a demonstration of cooperation in the midst of almost complete anarchy – an environment that is the least hospitable to cooperation. In such circumstances, while local decision makers conceivably do have some choice, their choice is heavily constrained by the situation.

The theory of "structural realism,"[24] while generally applied to international relations, contains elements that may usefully be adapted to local situations where human beings must seek to survive in the midst of anarchy. When central authority is critically weakened or nonexistent, structural realists argue, actors feel tremendous uncertainty and this forces them to take actions to defend their security. Hence, Edward D. Mansfield and Jack Snyder state, groups threatened by social change are often compelled to take an inflexible and short-term view, and "compromises that may lead down the slippery slope to social extinction or irrelevance have little appeal to such groups."[25] More fundamentally, structural realists claim that proponents of cooperative approaches to conflict resolution misunderstand why conflicts occur. Richard Betts challenges the view, often assumed, that the parties actually want peace, that "war is not a rational act ... that outsiders can pull the scales from the eyes of fighting factions, making them realize that resort to violence was a blunder, and substituting peaceful negotiation for force." Wars, he argues, "are rarely accidents."[26] Instead, disputants go to war when conflicts cannot be solved by other means or when incentives to violence vastly outweigh the costs. Under these circumstances, the assumption that disputants have an interest in any sort of cooperative compromise – particularly one that requires a sharing of power or resources – is misguided.

Critics of structural realism reject the claim that there are so few possibilities for peace. Even in seemingly unfavourable circumstances, they suggest, there are confidence building measures that can be implemented and that will make peace more likely; and they point to the value of gestures of reconciliation, which are most credible when they expose vulnerabilities or come at potentially high cost.[27] Structural realists, however, respond that decisions made in environments where security is in jeopardy often differ from decisions made in environments where survival is not in question. Anarchy forces risk-averse groups to make choices they might not otherwise make, so even those who are genuinely interested in peace cannot afford to make risky gestures of reconciliation if vulnerabilities are exposed which their adversary can then exploit. Anarchy also means that it is difficult to distinguish nervous belligerents who would nonetheless prefer peace from aggressors who prefer war. Consequently, it was difficult for some to tell if UNITA's Jonas Savimbi was a predatory warmonger or a reformed though paranoid belligerent when he refused to take up his power-sharing post in Angola in 1994. Those who desire peace as well as those who are predators tend to behave the same way under conditions of anarchy, insofar as they may prefer conflict to cooperation if this is believed to be the best way to ensure survival.[28]

In either case, local actors want security more than a share of power. And in the zero-sum game that has come to characterize the collapsed state, belligerents feel that they have the greatest security when they have total control over the political system rather than the partial control offered by power sharing. As Mahmood Mamdani has argued in his analysis of the peace process that followed the RPF's invasion of Rwanda in 1990: "For Hutu Power propagandists, the Tutsi question was not one of rights, but of power. The growing appeal of Hutu Power propaganda among the Hutu masses was in direct proportion to the spreading conviction that the real aim of the RPF was not rights for all Rwandans, but power for the Tutsi. This is why one needs to recognize that it was not greed – not even hatred – but *fear* which was the reason why the multitude responded to the call of Hutu Power the closer the war came to home."[29] Even in apparently non-threatening situations, political leaders insist on total control. Following Liberia's brutal civil war in the early 1990s, the warlord Charles Taylor clearly was unwilling to share power or allow the international community to interfere with his presidential aspirations. As Terrence Lyons has noted in his report on the Liberian peace process, "post election power sharing or the need to negotiate the composition of the new Armed Forces of Liberia, for example, received little attention ... Charles Taylor in particular objected to any process that might limit his powers following the electoral victory he anticipated."[30]

Many Liberians also indicated that the weak interim governments that had been in place since 1990 had been ineffective and had done little to end the war. Lyons states that Liberians "worried that a power sharing pact and broad-based government might result in another weak regime like the series of flawed interim governments that they had suffered under since 1990." Liberians claimed that they preferred a strong government if it provided safety from the random violence and the militias that terrorized Liberia's countryside. As Lyons concludes, "seven years of weak interim governments convinced many Liberians that only a unified government could keep the peace, and Taylor was perceived as the candidate most likely to bring strong government. Many voters said they did not care who won so long as a single president ruled the country again and the period of interim government ended."[31] Of course, anyone familiar with Charles Taylor's rule knows that the president did not change his ways, and he continued to plunder Liberia's resources for his own benefit even after the 1997 election. As long as the international community refuses to enforce the more equitable alternatives that it proposes, no one should be surprised that ordinary citizens will seek solutions that that they hope will pacify the most dangerous threats.

Anarchy is particularly problematic when there is a history of non-cooperation or betrayal. Confidence is built among disputants when they have the opportunity to defect but still choose to cooperate. On the other hand, an adversary's defection is a sure sign that it cannot be trusted. Hence, even if one party is initially willing to make efforts at reconciliation, once it feels that it has been betrayed it tends not to make the same "mistake" twice. The 1991 peace process in Angola, which led to the Bicesse Accords and a competitive election, was a sign that the disputants were willing to reconcile, despite the long-standing civil war that had preceded it. Confident that it would win any election, UNITA spoke little about power sharing but promised to respect the decision of the people in the event of a loss. "If I lose the election, this is my country and I am an ordinary citizen," declared Jonas Savimbi. "No one will push me to go back to the bush anymore."[32] But Savimbi's failure to keep his word when he in fact lost the election undermined subsequent efforts at power sharing. In effect, a power-sharing deal had been made a virtual impossibility by UNITA's apparent defection. From that point on, the government's central preoccupation was to dominate and eventually decapitate UNITA as a viable fighting force.

Recent history has also played a role in undermining the prospects of any sort of cooperative relationship in Burundi and Rwanda. Efforts to construct a new power-sharing agreement in Burundi, for example, have taken place in the shadow of a previous betrayal. In 1993 the Tutsi-dominated army assassinated the newly elected Hutu president, Melchior Ndadaye, a Hutu, before launching killings that left an estimated 50,000 to 100,000 Hutu dead. After these events, any hope for an integrated polity is, according to David Rieff, "now utterly irrelevant to Burundian realities."[33] Significantly, the assassination and killings were also seized upon by hardliners in neighbouring Rwanda to show that Tutsis could never be trusted and that any agreement was really an effort to restore their previous domination over the Hutu. Tragically, what is clear from all of these cases is that previous violence does not induce ethnic groups to find cooperative solutions to conflict. Rather, it crystallizes hatred and reinforces the perception that reconciliation and cooperation are impossible.

## CONCLUSIONS

There is an obvious need to provide solutions to Africa's post-civil war difficulties. If not power sharing, what else is there? The problem is not that there is anything undesirable about power sharing, but that effective power sharing requires a certain combination of conditions that are almost never found in African post-conflict situations. Therefore, it cannot be assumed that power-sharing ideas that are intuitively self-evident to outsiders will also be self-evident to disputants, or that disputants will translate these ideas into successful long-term or even short-term agreements. For power sharing to be a workable approach in Africa, additional measures may be required. For example, as the cases described above suggest, allowing groups to maintain control over their own security resources, including weapons, may be a step in the right direction. To date, however, the international community has emphasized the disarmament of combatants.

Are these problems of power sharing unique to Africa? Clearly they are not, as similar problems have existed in other conflict zones, such as Yugoslavia. But in no other region has the problem of anarchy been as pervasive as in Africa, and nowhere has it been more difficult for outsiders to impose order, which might make power sharing more likely.

Decision makers in contemporary African peace processes, then, must often choose among extremely unpleasant options. Even when power sharing is considered an option, there can be difficult choices. In Rwanda, the peace process was criticized for leaving out the most dangerous Hutu hardliners, who then derailed the peace process and launched a massacre of hundreds of thousands of Tutsi and moderate Hutu. In Sierra Leone, by contrast, Foday Sankoh was included in a power-sharing pact – but this only provided him with an opportunity to continue his self-enriching and destructive ways. In short, peace processes are not simply about the choice of whether to include in the peace process, or exclude from it, a particular individual or movement. Rather, in the absence of the restoration of authority, peace requires the effective neutralization or removal of, or escape from, the most dangerous and threatening adversaries. No wonder groups more often see options other than power sharing, such as political independence or the outright military defeat of their opponents, as the preferred path to security.

## NOTES

1 Borrowing from Waltz, the term "anarchy" refers to an environment "with no system of law enforceable among [the principal actors and], with each [actor] judging its grievances and ambitions according to the dictates of its own reason or desire." See Kenneth N. Waltz, *Man, the State and War: A Theoretical Analysis* (New York: Columbia University Press 1959), 159.

2 Timothy D. Sisk, *Power Sharing and International Mediation in Ethnic Conflicts* (Washington, D.C.: United States Institute of Peace 1996), vii.

3 In some cases, disputants have avoided engaging their most threatening opponents. In Ethiopia, for example, the ruling Ethiopian People's Revolutionary Democratic Front (EPRDF) created a series of ethnically based People's Democratic Organizations (PDOs) while refusing to work with others such as the Oromo Liberation Front (OLF). In Rwanda, the extremist Committee for the Defence of the Republic (CDR) was excluded from the 1993 Arusha peace process. And in Angola, following the failed peace process of the early 1990s, the ruling Movimento Popular da Libertação de Angola (MPLA) refused to meet with UNITA but agreed to work with UNITA dissidents in a separate organization called UNITA-*Renovada*.

4 Fen Osler Hampson, "Parent, Midwife, or Accidental Executioner: The Role of Third Parties in Ending Violent Conflict," in Chester A. Crocker, Fen Osler Hampson, and Pamela Aall, ed., *Turbulent Peace: The Challenges of Managing International Conflict* (Washington, D.C.: United States Institute of Peace 2001), 395.

5 David Rieff, "Suffering and Cynicism in Burundi," *World Policy Journal* 18, no.3 (2001): 63.

6 Abiodun Alao and Comfort Ero, "Cut Short for Taking Short Cuts: The Lomé Peace Agreement on Sierra Leone," *Civil Wars* 4, no.3 (2001): 152.

7 John Hirsch, "War in Sierra Leone," *Survival* 43, no.3 (2001): 152.

8 Rieff, "Suffering and Cynicism," 65.

9 René Lemarchand, "Managing Transition Anarchies: Rwanda, Burundi, and South Africa in Comparative Perspective," *Journal of Modern African Studies* 32, no.4 (1994): 591, 603.

10 See Arend Lijphart, "Consociational Democracy," *World Politics* 21, no.2 (1969): 212–13.

11 Quoted in Margaret Joan Anstee, *Orphan of the Cold War: The Inside Story of the Collapse of the Angolan Peace Process, 1992–3* (New York: St Martin's Press 1996), 519.

12 Richard Synge, *Mozambique: UN Peacekeeping in Action, 1992–94* (Washington, D.C.: United States Institute of Peace 1997), 149.

13 Quoted in David Bloomfield, Charles Nupen, and Peter Harris, "Negotiation Processes," in Peter Harris and Ben Reilly, ed., *Democracy and Deep-Rooted Conflict: Options for Negotiators* (International Institute for Democracy and Electoral Assistance 1998), 69.

14 Barbara F. Walter, "The Critical Barrier to Civil War Settlement," *International Organization* 51, no.3 (1997), 335–64.

15 Lemarchand, "Managing Transition Anarchies," 598–9. To make this case, Lemarchand cites Herbert M. Howe, "The South African Defence Force and Political Reform," *Journal of Modern African Studies* 32, no.1 (1994), 29–51.

16 See Hevina S. Dashwood and Cranford Pratt, "Leadership, Participation, and Conflict Management: Zimbabwe and Tanzania," in Taisier M. Ali and Robert O. Matthews, ed., *Civil Wars in Africa: Roots and Resolution* (Montreal and Kingston: McGill-Queen's University Press 1999), 223–54.

17 See Jeremy Ginifer, *Managing Arms in Peace Processes: Rhodesia/Zimbabwe* (New York: Disarmament and Conflict Resolution Project, United Nations Institute for Disarmament Research 1995), 29–31. Ginifer notes that the Commonwealth Monitoring Force and the guerrillas' own liaison officers were effective in persuading reluctant fighters that a genuine peace agreement had been forged and that they were safe to come out of the bush. Many of these fighters had previously been tricked into coming out by phony peace agreements.

18 Lemarchand, "Managing Transition Anarchies," 585.

19 Ginifer, *Managing Arms,* 55.

20 One might also add, short-lived. The political process in Zimbabwe under Rober Mugabe's regime became increasingly intolerant of dissent either from within or without the ruling ZANU-PF. For a critical view of Zimbabwe, see Martin Meredith, *Our Votes, Our Guns: Robert Mugabe and the Tragedy of Zimbabwe* (New York: Public Affairs 2002). In South Africa, the National Party pulled out of the Government of National Unity in 1996.

21 See I. William Zartman, ed., *Collapsed States: The Disintegration and Restoration of Legitimate Authority* (Boulder, Colo.: Lynne Rienner 1995).

22 In October 1993 rebels associated with the United Somali Congress killed eighteen U.S. Army Rangers in a firefight in Mogadishu. In April 1994 Hutu extremists in Rwanda killed ten Belgian peacekeepers, inducing the withdrawal of the Belgian and some other peacekeepers. In May 2000 in Sierra Leone, rebels associated with the RUF surrounded UN peacekeepers and took them hostage.

23 Terrence Lyons, *Voting for Peace: Postconflict Elections in Liberia* (Washington, D.C.: Brookings Institution 1999), 8.

24 See Kenneth N. Waltz, *Theory of International Politics* (New York: McGraw Hill 1979).

25 Edward D. Mansfield and Jack Snyder, "Democratization and War," *Foreign Affairs* 74, no.3 (1995): 91.

26 Richard K. Betts, "The Delusion of Impartial Intervention," *Foreign Affairs*, 73, no.6 (1994): 21–2.

27 For example, Egyptian President Anwar Sadat's 1977 trip to Jerusalem was effective in the establishment of peaceful relations between Egypt and Israel because it came at such high personal risk. See Janice Gross Stein, "Confidence Building and Dilemmas of Cooperation: The Egyptian-Israeli Experiment," in Gabriel Ben-Dor and David B. Dewit, ed., *Confidence Building Measures in the Middle East* (Boulder, Colo.: Westview 1994): 210.

28 See Jack Snyder and Robert Jervis, "Civil War and the Security Dilemma," in Barbara F. Walter and Jack Snyder, ed., *Insecurity and Intervention Civil War* (New York: Columbia University Press 1999), 15–37.

29 Mahmood Mamdani, *When Victims Become Killers: Colonialism, Nativism, and the Genocide in Rwanda* (Princeton, N.J.: Princeton University Press, 2001), 191.

30 Lyons, *Voting for Peace*, 48.

31 Ibid., 59.

32 John Battersby, "Angolans Begin to Disarm under Successful Cease-Fire," *Christian Science Monitor*, 3 July 1991, 6.

33 Rieff, "Suffering and Cynicism," 63.

# 10

# Afghanistan: Multicultural Federalism as a Means to Achieve Democracy, Representation, and Stability

REETA CHOWDHARI TREMBLAY

Following the United States-led invasion of Afghanistan in October 2001 and the overthrow of the Taliban regime, an interim Afghan government was put in place pending negotiations on the country's political future. Those negotiations, which involved delegates representing a wide array of Afghan parties and interests, took place in Bonn, Germany, under United Nations (UN) auspices and concluded with the signing, on 5 December 2001, of the Bonn Agreement – which sets out a comprehensive blueprint for democracy, peace, and stability in Afghanistan.[1]

In June 2002, in conformity with one of the terms of the agreement, a specially convened and ethnically broad-based Loya Jirga (traditional grand council) elected as president of Afghanistan Hamid Karzai, the chairman of the previous interim administration and an ethnic Pashtun. In an attempt to achieve a degree of power sharing among different ethnic groups, Karzai appointed thirty-five ministers from Afghanistan's major communities – Pashtuns, Tajiks, Hazaras, and Uzbeks – and some members from smaller minorities. This administration, however, was meant to be transitional. The Bonn Agreement also set out a procedure and timetable for the replacement of these temporary and provisional structures of governance by a democratic constitution and popularly elected representative government. Accordingly, in April 2003 Karzai appointed an ethnically balanced thirty-three-member commission to help prepare a new constitution and to oversee a process of public consultation. At the end of this process, the resulting draft constitution was to be submitted for approval to a constitutional Loya Jirga.

In short, the process initiated by the Bonn Agreement was an exercise in introducing consociational practices and norms for an ethnically divided society. The transitional Karzai government was the product of the conscious and careful balancing and accommodation of the divergent interests of several ethnic and tribal segments, and the constitution-making process was aimed towards getting the political leaders of all segments to accept consociational norms for achieving both integration and self-government for Afghanistan society. Within that framework, it was left largely to the indigenous leaders themselves to establish the specific guidelines and democratic mechanisms for meaningful cross-community, joint decision making at the national level. Essentially, they were given the task of defining the Afghan polity in a way that, on the one hand, makes possible a successful national integration of the diverse segments of Afghan society, and, on the other hand, establishes power-sharing mechanisms which promote self-government or segmental autonomy for distinct ethnic and tribal groups.

The key questions that need to be asked are: How can a stable form of power sharing be implemented in post-conflict Afghanistan? What kinds of institutions will facilitate democracy and the goal of creating a single citizenship with the maintenance of minority identities? What are the best power-sharing arrangements to create stability within a democratic framework?

The new constitution that was approved by the Loya Jirga in January 2004 provides for the establishment of a unitary, highly centralized presidential system of government. The concentration of power at the centre is only slightly mitigated by provisions dealing with subnational levels of government. The constitution calls for the creation of local administrative units (or "provinces") to which the central government may delegate certain unspecified administrative powers and which are to be governed by "provincial councils" whose purpose is "to take part in securing the developmental targets of the state." Similarly, the constitution provides for the establishment of municipalities, but neither they nor the provinces have any independent constitutional powers.[2]

The aim of this chapter is to explore the idea that some form of federalism – a political formula designed to reconcile diverse regional and other interests with those of a single, larger political community – would be a more appropriate system of government for Afghanistan.

The present constitution is more an attempt to create a stable centre of authority than a fundamental social compact,[3] and for that reason there is a strong possibility that the process of constitution making has not yet been completed and will require future adjustments in light of Afghanistan's strongly entrenched cultural pluralism. President Karzai did admit to the limitations of the centralized constitution and suggested to the constitutional Loya Jirga that, once the security and stability of the country had improved, there might be reason to reconvene that body to adopt a different system of government.

Federalism remains a viable future option for Afghanistan if it wants to reconcile the requirements of a nation-state with the recognition of cultural pluralism. But federalism in Afghanistan would have to take a particular form; it would not do simply to emulate the traditions, institutions, and conventions of Western federal systems. In the case of Afghanistan, I propose to argue, federalism would have to be viewed as both a territorial and a non-territorial project, the latter directed to the issues of cultural representation and identity within the concept of a multicultural society. Moreover, given Afghanistan's reliance on the Western alliance, and particularly the United States, for security and economic aid, it is essential that external actors provide incentives for Afghanistan's diverse ethnic constituencies to accept power-sharing arrangements within a new democratic constitutional framework.

## AFGHANISTAN'S CULTURAL DIVERSITY

Afghanistan is one of the poorest countries in the world and its population is divided, often sharply, along ethnic, linguistic, and even religious lines. The population (including more than three million refugees still living in neighbouring countries, primarily Pakistan and Iran) is roughly twenty-five million, occupying a landlocked territory slightly smaller than Texas. The largest group are the Pashtuns, who make up about 40 per cent of the population. They speak Pushto, which is related to but quite distinct from Persian; they live in eastern and southern Afghanistan; and they are are further divided into a patchwork of tribes and clans. The second largest group (about one-third of the population) are the Tajiks, who speak Dari (Persian). They are native to the valleys and mountains north and northeast of Kabul and are ethnically akin to the Tadzhiks of Central Asia. The remote massif of central Afghanistan is home to the Hazaras, who constitute

8–9 per cent of the population and who speak a version of Persian called Hazaragi. The last major group, of about the same size, are the Uzbek, who speak Uzbeki. In addition to these major groups, there are over a dozen smaller ethnic and linguistic minorities.

Socio-economic differences between the majority Pashtuns and other tribal groups have been less significant than the ethnic, cultural, and political distinctions between them. Pashtun relations with non-Pashtuns are defined by rules proscribing intermarriage, by differences of language, sometimes by religion, and by economic exchanges that usually mark the Pashtun's superior status. Pashtuns have also been the dominant political community. During King Mohammad Zahir Shah's regime (1933–73), the top governmental positions remained the monopoly of the elite of the upper class, who were mostly of Pashtun nationality.

The name of Afghanistan was given to it by the British and other Western powers and has come to replace the indigenous terms (the northern half was once known as Khurasan, Zabulistan, or Turkistan and the southern part as Kabul or Kabulistan). Nevertheless, the oral history and traditions of different tribal communities have survived over several generations. Language has remained a divisive and a contentious issue. In an official attempt to make Pushto a viable national language, in 1937 a Pushto Academy was created to produce a standard Pushto language, invent a new vocabulary, and replace Persian and other foreign words. Also, Persian-language newspapers were forced to publish in Pushto. These measures were unsuccessful, however, and the 1964 constitution recognized two official languages: Dari (Persian) and Pushto. And it is Dari that has remained the working language of the country. Anthony Hyman suggests that the failure to adopt a standardized national language was not only because of the difficulty involved in learning Pushto (Dari has a much simpler grammar) but also because of "a general animosity felt against the Pashtun dominance."[4] Similarly, Radio Kabul, which was officially opened in 1940 to help construct a national, pan-Afghan identity, was used by the ethnic minorities to create a sense of pride in their traditions and cultures. Particularly during the 1970s, the "new left" regimes encouraged and promoted the use of Uzbek and other minority languages through radio broadcasts and print publications.

Islam in Afghanistan embraces a wide range of beliefs. While a large majority of the population are Sunni Muslims, 15 per cent of the population are Shi'a Muslims. The Hazara group is predominantly

Shi'a. There are also small numbers of Ismaili Shi'as living in the central
and northern parts of Afghanistan. The Ismailis consider the Aga
Khan their spiritual leader. Even within the Sunni majority, there are
those who follow the Deoband school of India, implementing orthodox
and pure Islamic practices (many of the Taliban belong to this group),
and there are those who subscribe to a mystical version of Islam known
as Sufism, emphasizing tolerance and peaceful coexistence with other
religious traditions. The Wahabi tradition has only recently been
imported from Saudi Arabia, via Pakistan (among the Taliban, who
received their Islamic training in the refugee camps of Pakistan, there
are some Wahabi followers). In this almost entirely Muslim state, there
can also be found a few thousand Hindus and Sikhs, as well as some
Jews and Armenian Christians.[5]

### POLITICAL BACKGROUND

Karzai's government inherited a country that had been ravaged by war
for the previous twenty-two years and that could best be described as
a humanitarian disaster zone. The catalogue of its problems was
lengthy: extreme poverty, a population highly vulnerable to communi-
cable diseases, deplorable sanitation systems, a 25 per cent child mor-
tality rate, one physician for every 50,000 people, 17 maternal deaths
per 1,000 women (the second highest in the world), a life expectancy
for both men and women of less than 46 years, a literacy rate of 15 per
cent for women and 31 per cent for men, and a massive emigration of
a significant part of the population into the neighbouring territories of
Pakistan and Iran. Years of drought had cruelly worsened Afghanistan's
already poor economy, dependent as it was upon farming and livestock
raising. Moreover, a whole generation had grown up amidst this great
poverty, with a pervasive gun culture and under the religious oppression
of the Taliban.

To encourage the de-weaponizing of its population and the integration
of its armed chieftains into the regular army, the interim administration
accepted the peacekeeping operations led by the UN-mandated International Security Assistance Force (ISAF), numbering 4,500 military personnel drawn from sixteen nations. Armed men were no longer allowed
to walk the streets of Kabul, and all armed factions were asked to join
the Afghan army and agree to be trained by the ISAF. International
agencies were also active in areas of public health, education, and famine
relief. International donors pledged $15 billion (U.S.) for economic

rehabilitation and development, but the needs were (and are) immense and aid is only slowly trickling in.

Though Afghanistan is poor by any standard, the Afghan state is not as primitive and archaic as it is portrayed in the Western media, though it suffered tremendous shocks during the Soviet occupation and under the Taliban regime. King Amanullah Khan laid the foundations of a modern nation-state in 1919. The first constitution was promulgated in 1923; it provided freedom for the practice of religious rituals by the Shiite minority and enshrined other minority rights. Amanullah Khan's government also undertook various social and economic reforms, including land reform and the restructuring of the tax system. After a period of turbulence that included a coup d'état in 1930, halting progress resumed. In 1933, under King Mohammad Zahir Shah, the state modernized its bureaucracy (which was significantly expanded), its army, and its police force. Education was vigorously promoted. In 1963 King Zahir democratized the constitution, barring the members of the royal family from participation in the government. The new constitution also allowed the establishment of political parties. One result was political instability, with a series of short-lived ministries, and in 1973 the monarchy was abolished and Afghanistan proclaimed a republic. The new government included women and minorities. In order to respond to the demands of the minorities, the state appointed two members of the Hazara community and one from the Uzbek community to ministerial portfolios.

Education in Afghanistan is also not as backward as it is sometimes painted, or as it became under the rule of the Taliban. From the early 1950s, Koranic education had been complemented by government-sponsored Western-style education; and by the late 1960s, education accounted for some 20 per cent of total government spending. The university was coeducational. Both women and minorities took advantage of the educational system, and this became a factor in furthering their demands for inclusion in the government. Although religion was a compulsory subject in all schools (and, in the religious schools, Sufism was widely studied), most of the reading material emphasized modern aspects of life.

## THEORETICAL CONSIDERATIONS

Before exploring the utility of a multicultural federal structure, I would like to elaborate briefly on three theoretical considerations that are at

the basis of my analysis. First, I would like to point out that the success
of any institutional arrangements regarding power sharing must occur
within the context of the overriding constitutional values that create
the basis for a normative ordering between the state and the civil
society. The success of the new Afghan constitution will depend upon
the extent to which its makers construct a new polity based on both
similarities (the values commonly shared) and differences (the distinct
identities of its various fragments). I suggest that the notion of constructing a multicultural political community with the joint goals of a
single nation and individual citizenship, on the one hand, and the
representation of cultural pluralism, on the other, can be realized – and
therefore needs to be analysed – only within the context of the intervening role of the state in determining the content of nationalism. A
state, through its legal and constitutional apparatus, along with the
ideological role of the political leadership, has significant input in
constructing, shaping, modifying, maintaining, and containing ethnic
identities. Through its legal and constitutional apparatus, the state
arrogates to itself the power of naming an identity and in turn "profoundly affects the process by which individual and collectivized identities
are constructed and maintained."[6] Thus, the success of any democratic
constitutional formula for the new polity in Afghanistan will depend
largely upon the constitution makers' ability to articulate a new identity.

Second, the simultaneous pursuit of the goals of a homogeneous and
heterogeneous nation – creating a single Afghan nation and equal
citizenship, based on similarities, and ensuring the maintenance of the
distinct cultural identities of its population, based on differences – can
effectively take place only in a system whose goals are defined as
multicultural rather than multinational. It is interesting to note that
Western discourse has only recently begun to explore the issues of
multicultural citizenship, cultural pluralism, and a multicultural political community. A major theoretical concern of liberal scholars has
been to show how the politics of recognition of identity and group
rights can be reconciled within a liberal-democratic and cohesive political community. Bikhu Parekh, for example, argues that existing theories of cultural pluralism give a coherent account of the value of culture
(why human beings need a stable culture) but not of cultural diversity
(the interaction of culturally differentiated groups and their presence
together in public institutions). While a theory of cultural pluralism
argues for the respect of diverse cultures and for public policies and

political structures that allow cultural minorities to prevent their domination by majorities, for Parekh, the multicultural project must go further. He approvingly cites the Indian constitution, whose framers attempted to balance contradictory principles of equal citizenship with collective rights, secularism with religious community rights, fundamental equality for all citizens with preferential privileges for backward castes/classes, and an official language with the protection of minority linguistic rights. Parekh concludes: "The Indian state is thus both an association of individuals and a community of communities, recognizing both individuals and communities as bearers of rights."[7]

Third, in a multicultural society (which affirms the value of cultural diversity in terms of equality between groups and the realization of these values in institutions and policies), the power-sharing arrangements, as articulated in the consociational models for plural democracies and considered by some as useful in federal institutions, must go beyond elite accommodation. While it is essential in a democratic consociation that political elites pursue a politics of active accommodation, it must be recognized that the longevity and stability of a democratic consociation depends also on the normative entrenchment of a societal culture of accommodation of diversity. In other words, elite accommodation must be supplemented by the input of the political community at large.

## FEDERALISM AS A TERRITOTIAL AND NON-TERRITORIAL PROJECT

The Western discourse on federalism has been traditionally formulated within the framework of centre-state relations, thus focusing on centralization and inter-governmental relations. As Will Kymlicka points out, the focus on territorial federalism is due largely to the historical influences of American federalism, which has become the model of a "mature" or "classical" federalism.[8] Nevertheless, federalism is also increasingly recognized as a powerful mechanism for power sharing in multinational societies. The relative success of federations such as Canada and Switzerland in accommodating ethnic minorities has prompted their emulation by other multinational countries, such as India, Malaysia, and Nigeria. In the literature on federalism, the latter type of federation is generally referred to as multinational federalism. However, the non-territorial project discussed in this chapter goes further in its goals than a multinational federation. It is directed additionally towards the issues of cultural representation and identity within the concept of a multicultural society. One of the tasks of a multicultural federalism is to provide cultural recognition and ensure that differences from the dominant group do not result in the power-lessness of minorities or the marginalization of minority identities. In a multinational federalism that recognizes only national minorities, and makes the boundaries of its internal units coterminous with these minorities, there is a danger that smaller minorities may remain unpro-tected. Alternatively, a multicultural federal constitution, through con-stitutional and legal provisions, may provide for the protection of minorities irrespective of their location, through cultural, educational, and linguistic rights. In such a system, the constitution attempts to balance the principle of equal citizenship with collective rights.

## MULTICULTURAL FEDERALISM: A VIABLE OPTION FOR AFGHANISTAN

The Bonn Accord stipulated that the Afghanistan constitution of 1964 was to serve as the legal framework for the organization of the interim Karzai government. While the 1964 constitution enshrined equal polit-ical rights and freedoms for all citizens, it also provided for an admin-istration based upon the principle of centralization. However, for such a pluralistic society, and one so deeply divided along ethnic, linguistic, and tribal lines, a centralized form of government seemed bound to create discontent and increased demands for autonomy. It promotes the unity of the country at the expense of the rich diversity of its citizens' cultural inheritance.

The constitutional commission, therefore, was faced with the need to create simultaneously both a single indivisible nation and a set of sub-national governments that are allowed to maintain their diversity and the plural cultural identities of their populations. One means by which a strong central government could be juxtaposed with strong regional units is through federalism – but this is an option that the commission rejected. Fearing that federalism would lead to disintegration, they opted instead for a centralized unitary state with weak subnational units. Whether such structures can accommodate the diversities of Afghanistan, however, is extremely doubtful.

Federalism, in theory, would have provided an opportunity to the framers of the constitution to mould the structure of the governments, both national and subnational, to the specific pluralistic realities of the country. In practice, however, this would have been no easy task. Constitution makers would have faced the challenge of balancing the territorial with the non-territorial requirements of the multicultural, multi-tribal Afghan nation. Furthermore, given Afghanistan's cultural diversity and social pluralism, they would have had to devise a federal system able to reconcile the claims of equal citizenship with group identities and interests.

Since such a federal project is indeed difficult, it is instructive to look at examples of federations that have tried to address these issues. The case of India, in particular, deserves to be closely studied. Historically, the Indian constitution makers were not only sensitive to group identities but were innovative in generating a difficult and challenging non-traditional discourse on political community.[9]

Article 29 of the Indian constitution recognizes the rights of "any section of the citizens of India" who have a distinct language, script, or culture "to conserve the same." While Article 350 allows any linguistic minority to "submit representation for redress of grievance to any central or state authority," Article 350 A makes it obligatory upon all regional and local governments "to provide adequate facilities for instruction in mother-tongue at the primary stage of education to children belonging to linguistic minority groups."[10] Along with the religious communities, the linguistic groups whose minority status is recognized in the Eighth Schedule of the constitution have the right, under Article 30, to establish and administer their educational institutions and the state is barred from any discrimination against them when it grants financial support to private educational institutions. In conformity with these constitutional rules, two types of denominational schools have been organized in India by the four major religious communities: (a) religious institutions aided by a particular community (for example, Maktabs and Madrasas of Muslims; Gurukhulas, Pathshalas, or Sanskrit schools of Hindus; Gurmukhi schools of the Sikhs; and mission schools of the Christians); and (b) religious schools aided by private or government agencies (for example, Islamia schools or colleges of the Muslims, Arya Samaj or Santan Dharam schools of the Hindus; Khalsa schools of the Sikhs; and convent schools of the Christians). The former category of schools imparts religious education; the latter, while having a limited number of hours for religious instruction in the classroom and during morning assemblies, follows the secular government-prescribed curriculum.

In the spirit of accommodation of religious minorities, the secular Indian constitution allows the religious communities to adhere to their personal laws in the governance of their communities in spheres such as marriage, divorce, and inheritance.[11] In the early 1950s Prime Minister Jawaharlal Nehru tried to secularize the Hindu law, but he faced opposition from both within and outside the Congress Party. However, a series of parliamentary acts were passed, which are collectively known as the Hindu Code.[12]

The democratic egalitarian ideology of the Congress Party guided the constitutional decision to provide guarantees of political representation in parliament and the regional legislative assemblies, and the setting aside of posts in educational and administrative institutions, for "Scheduled Castes and Tribes" (Article 335).[13] For example, of the 543 seats in the national parliament (the Lok Sabha), 78 are reserved for the Scheduled Castes and 41 for the Scheduled Tribes. The legislative assemblies have reserved a similar proportion of seats for these groups.[14] In addition, of all central government jobs, 22.5 per cent are reserved for the same targeted groups. Although these guarantees were supposed to end in 1960, they have instead been renewed and expanded to include those designated as "Other Backward Castes." Members of these castes are generally rural and account for approximately half of India's population. In response to their political power, initially at the regional level and now at the national level, 27 per cent of all central governmental jobs were reserved for members of "Other Backward Castes" in 1990. Thus, in India, although the constitution does not allow dual citizenship – and clearly states that there is equality of opportunity for all citizens in matters of employment and that no discrimination is allowed on the basis of religion, race, sex, caste, descent, place of birth, or residence – in fact common citizenship has come to coexist with regional citizenship, which in many cases is a necessary requirement for government employment.

A constitution that combines territorial and non-territorial federalism is undoubtedly more challenging than one that is based on territorial federalism alone, as the Indian case has proven over the years, but it is arguably a better model than a centralized unitary state for a nation such as Afghanistan that is so sharply divided by religious, linguistic, and tribal loyalties.

## NATIONAL STANDARDS, SOCIAL JUSTICE, AND EQUAL CITIZENSHIP

Afghanistan is an impoverished society where the majority of people are illiterate and suffer from insufficient food, housing, and medical facilities. Not only does Afghanistan need a constitution enshrining the fundamental rights of all citizens, religious freedom, universal suffrage, representative democratic institutions, and a national judicial system, it also is imperative that the country address the issue of poverty and make progress towards the equitable distribution of wealth and the equal participation and representation of women and ethnic and religious minorities in political and economic institutions. In short, the government of Afghanistan – whatever form it takes – faces a threefold challenge: nation building, economic development, and state formation. It will not succeed unless it can provide both strong central government and strong regional governments that encourage local initiative.

Strong central government will be necessary to ensure uniform national standards for education, public health, and regional development. During the past two decades, the nation's education system has been used by each successive set of rulers to socialize the population towards the regime's ideology. After 1996, the Taliban eliminated most of the opportunities for girls' education. A national policy on education will help to ensure proper facilities, equal access to education for boys and girls, and a standard curriculum. And, ideally, national education standards will help to create a better-informed citizenry and consequently a stiffer requirement of accountability for elected representatives.

Strong central government will also be necessary to ensure balanced regional economic development, which is desirable both as a matter of principle and because of potentially explosive regional economic disparities. The majority Pashtuns live in the agricultural drought-devastated south, while the minority Tajik and the Uzbek areas in the north hold significant gas and oil resources. While the major occupation of the Afghans is agriculture, only 12 per cent of the land is arable. It will thus fall to the national government to create a strategy of economic development, for which a massive inflow of foreign aid will be needed for both short-term reconstruction and long-term development.[15]

## STRONG REGIONAL GOVERNMENTS
## AND LOCAL PARTICIPATION

The 1964 constitution of Afghanistan divided the country into provinces and municipalities but endowed them with limited autonomy and insufficient capacity for initiating policy in the economic sphere. That unsatisfactory arrangement appears to be replicated under the new constitution. A federal arrangement would appear to offer a better prospect of meeting local needs. The decentralization of powers to regional and local governments would be more likely to ensure the protection of cultural and collective identities and to further the goals of effective regional governance and equitable political participation. Much, however, would depend on the details of the federal formula. In particular, it would have to include provisions that strengthened local government. In many federal systems the local governments are generally ignored and the division of powers is confined to two levels: the national government and a set of regional governments. The reality of agrarian, developing societies (which also possess strong traditions of local community structures and participation) is such that one needs to reconsider the significance of the local governments in general, their location in the overall democratic society, and, in particular, their role in both initiating and implementing policies. There is increasing recognition that local governments respond to the needs of democratic representation, especially of minorities and women, and that the very legitimacy of a democratic government requires the active participation of the local population in its representative structures. Strategies of poverty alleviation in an agrarian society with strong patriarchal and feudal institutions can best achieve results if the otherwise marginalized populations are involved in a partnership with policy makers relating to issues of local significance. It is also at the local level that women are more likely to have a voice.

Here, once again, India's experience might be useful for Afghanistan. The Indian state has emphasized local self-government and decentralization of power since its inception half a century ago. In a country where the majority of people live in the countryside under inequitable economic and social conditions, the Indian state has linked governance at the local level to the realization of its two fundamental goals: (a) to ensure effective governance and equitable political representation through the institution of federalism; and (b) to promote economic growth and social justice. This agenda is not new and can be traced back to the Panchayat, the traditional Indian system of local self-government – essentially a village council of elders – which was strongly advocated by Mohandas Gandhi and Nehru. What is new is the constitutional recognition of the local government as the third tier of Indian federalism.

Persistent poverty and the inability of governmental programs to reach the poorest of the poor at the rural level have persuaded Indian policy makers to reaffirm the relationship between representation of the poor and the socially disadvantaged, on the one hand, and the governing institutions which both set and implement the equity agenda, on the other. According to one estimate, while the proportion of rural households in India had declined from 54 per cent in 1973 to 39 per cent in 1991, the least advantaged sections of society – such as agricultural labour households, which constitute half of the rural poor, as well as scheduled castes and tribes, backward regions, and female-headed households – had simply not benefited from programs aimed either at economic growth or at poverty alleviation.

In light of these disappointing results, in 1992 the Indian parliament passed the seventy-third amendment of the Indian constitution. It formally recognized the Panchayats as the third tier of government and stipulated: "There shall be constituted in every State, Panchayats at the village, intermediate and district levels, duly elected ... reserving seats for the Scheduled Castes and Tribes ... ensuring that one-third of the total number of seats and offices of chairpersons at all levels of the local government are to be filled by women." In addition, the state governments were required to delegate to the local bodies those powers necessary for them to function as institutions of self-government and to fulfil two fundamental objectives: to prepare and to implement schemes for economic development and social justice. Depending on the state legislation, the Panchayats' powers can be quite extensive, including input into the policy process and active participation in areas such as agriculture, education, social welfare, and poverty-alleviation programs. Almost all the Indian states have enacted Panchayati Raj acts, defining the devolution of power to the Panchayats in their regions.[16]

This is a model that Afghanistan might well wish to adopt. Afghanistan's social and political realities have much in common with those of India. Rural poverty, combined with feudal and patriarchal structures, abounds in the countryside. However, as in India, there are also strong traditions of community participation and these traditional structures could be revived, reformed, and rehabilitated in order to maintain continuity with the country's cultural and political heritage. As with the Indian case of the traditional Panchayats, the local Jirgas could acquire a new meaning, a new identity. In Afghanistan, where there are strong traditions of local autonomy, a federal structure will thus have to envision three layers of government – central, regional, and local – each with its areas of autonomous jurisdiction.

In summary, I have argued for a multicultural federalism in Afghanistan. State building in Afghanistan needs to be accompanied by nation building in which the goal of democratic representation cannot deny the collective identities that are defined within a traditional ethnic framework. Multicultural federalism – a political formula to reconcile diverse cultural, regional, and other interests with those of a single, larger political community – appears to be more suited to this ethnically divided plural society than a centralized system. But, to be viable, multicultural federalism for Afghanistan would need to take a distinctive shape; it could not simply emulate an existing system – not even the Indian federal system, which, I believe, is the most appropriate model. Afghanistan would have to pick and choose carefully from among elements of the Western and non-Western experiences of federalism and liberal democracy and combine them with the traditions of its own several communities and structures.

NOTES

1 United Nations Assistance Mission in Afghanistan, Documents, Agreement on Provisional Arrangements in Afghanistan Pending the Re-establishment of Permanent Government Institutions. Website: <www.unama-afg.org/docs/bonn.html>.

2 Constitution of Afghanistan, Year 1382 (2003), Articles 60–70, 136–9.

3 There is some recognition of social pluralism. The new constitution provides for the compulsory representation of women, recognizes Pushto and

Dari as the official languages (while also guaranteeing for five other minority languages the right to publish or broadcast), and grants equal status to the different sects of Islam. However, these measures remain limited within the context of a strong centralized government.

4 Anthony Hyman, "Nationalism in Afghanistan," *International Journal of Middle Eastern Studies* 34 (2002): 310.

5 For extensive background on the country, see Jerry Laber and Barnett Rubin, *A Nation Is Dying: Afghanistan under the Soviets* (Evanston, Ill.: Northwestern University Press 1988; Barnett R. Rubin, *The Fragmentation of Afghanistan: State Formation and Collapse in the International System* (New Haven, Conn.: Yale University Press 2002); and Hyman "Nationalism in Afghanistan."

6 Patrick Macklem, "Ethnonationalism, Aboriginal Identity and the Law," in Michael D. Levin, ed., *Ethncity and Aboriginality: Case Studies in Ethnonationalism* (Toronto: University of Toronto Press 1993), 13.

7 Bikhu Parekh, "The Cultural Politics of Liberal Democracy," *Political Studies* 40 (1992): 171.

8 Will Kymlicka, *Politics in the Vernacular* (Oxford, U.K.: Oxford University Press 2001), 94–100.

9 Reeta Chowdhari Tremblay, "Nation, Identity and the Intervening Role of the State: A Study of the Secessionist Movement in Kashmir," *Pacific Affairs* 69, no.4 (1996–97): 471–97.

10 Paul R. Brass, *The Politics of India since Independence* (New Delhi: Cambridge University Press 1990), 155.

11 The constitution left "personal, or family, law to adjudication by the various communities unless the individuals concerned opted to place themselves under British law." Granville Austin, *The Indian Constitution: Cornerstone of a Nation* (Bombay: Oxford University Press 1999), 123.

12 Since no such attempt was made to modernize Muslim personal law, this generated resentment against Muslims by the Hindu majority.

13 "Scheduled Castes" and "Scheduled Tribes" are technical/formal terms. By retaining a list complied by the British government in 1935, the constitution placed a large number of "untouchable" castes and tribes on the schedule or list.

14 Robert Hardgrave and Stanley Kocahnek, *India: Government and Politics in a Developing Nation* (Fort Worth, Texas: Harcourt Brace Jovanovich 2000), 190.

15 The planning minister of the interim administration, Haji Mohammad Mohaqiq, has asked for a staggering $45 billion (U.S.) in aid.

16 Reeta Chowdhari Tremblay "Globalization and Indian Federalism," *Indian Journal of Public Administration* 47, no.2 (2001): 208–21; Reeta Chowdhari Tremblay, "Living Multiculturally in a Federal India," in C. Steven La Rue, ed., *Regional Handbooks of Economic Development*, vol. 1, *India: Prospects onto the 21st Century* (Chicago: Fitzroy Dearborn Publishers 1997), 158–69.

# 11

# Power Sharing for Cyprus (Again)? European Union Accession and the Prospects for Reunification

## TOZUN BAHCHELI AND SID NOEL

The idea that Greek and Turkish Cypriots can be peacefully reunited under some system of consociational power sharing is an idea that refuses to die. Their one brief attempt to live under a consociational constitution (1960–63) ended amid violent ethnic conflict, prompting in turn a Greek-inspired coup d'état, Turkish military intervention, forced population transfers, and the *de facto* partition of Cyprus into hostile ethnic zones.[1] Nevertheless, every attempt to formulate a basis for resolving the conflict has come to essentially the same conclusion: namely, that the only possible system of government for a united Cyprus is one based on consociational power sharing, but with the addition of federal or confederal elements. Prior to the division of the island into two parts, the Republic of Cyprus (the Greek Cypriot south) and the Turkish Republic of Northern Cyprus (TRNC), there was no territorial basis for federalism or confederalism, but some such arrangement is now regarded as essential in every proposed scheme of reunification. This view has been endorsed by, *inter alia*, the United Nations (UN) and other international bodies, an array of high-level national and international envoys and mediators, and a variety of academic studies. If nothing else, the case of Cyprus provides impressive evidence of the enduring intellectual appeal of consociational power sharing, even in seemingly discouraging circumstances. As Arend Lijphart observes, "UN Secretary-General Javier Pérez de Cuéllar and his two successors have made several proposals for a unified Cyprus that strikingly resemble the basic power-sharing features of the 1960 constitution. Their efforts demonstrate their recognition of the fact that power sharing, although it may not succeed, represents the best chance for a successful solution."[2]

The UN secretaries general, and Lijphart, are surely right. No one seriously believes that Cyprus can be reunited as a unitary state under a system of majority rule – that is exactly the outcome that the Turkish Cypriot minority fears the most. At the opposite extreme, a "two states" solution that would in effect legitimate and make permanent the division of the island, either along the existing boundary line or along a new negotiated line, is unacceptable to Greek Cypriots and faces insuperable international opposition, for reasons that have nothing to do with Cyprus. That leaves only the continuation of the long-standing *de facto* partition or reunification under a system of power sharing. Although to date no one has been able to devise a power-sharing system that is minimally acceptable to both sides, an acceptable system might yet be found if a change in the international context of the issue forced one or both of the communities to recalculate their long-term interests.

The current hope of those who favour reunification is based on the belief that the international context of the Cyprus stalemate, after remaining static for decades, has been fundamentally changed by the decision of the European Union (EU) to admit Cyprus as a member, notwithstanding its division. As a result, it is claimed, it has become possible to reconstitute Cyprus as a single state within the EU and to equip it with new European-style power-sharing institutions. While there had been no lack of power-sharing proposals in the past, including the elaborate "Set of Ideas" framework agreement negotiated under UN auspices in 1992, such proposals have always failed to come to fruition. According to Michael Emerson and Nathalie Tocci, "what was missing then, both technically in the text and politically, was a sufficiently vivid and powerful incentive of EU accession to overcome the resistance to the agreement."[3]

The revised UN blueprint (hereafter the Annan Plan) that was submitted to the parties in November 2002 – and subsequently resubmitted in various revised versions – was intended to provide that incentive. Essentially, what the Annan Plan prescribed was a loose federation with some consociational power-sharing features similar to those found in Belgium and Switzerland. (Its details are discussed in a later section of this chapter.) However, like all previous such plans, the

Annan Plan failed to secure the necessary agreement of both Greek and Turkish Cypriots – though this time with a novel twist. When put to the voters of both communities in simultaneous referendums on 24 April 2004, the plan was strongly approved by Turkish Cypriots (64.9 per cent voting "yes") and even more strongly rejected by Greek Cypriots (75.8 per cent voting "no").[4] For the Greek Cypriots, there were no negative consequences, or at least none that were immediately apparent, for their accession to the EU went ahead as planned.

The EU leadership responded petulantly at what for them was a deeply disappointing outcome. They had negotiated the terms of Cyprus's EU membership only with the leaders of the Republic of Cyprus, since the TRNC (though a *de facto* state) is not internationally recognized. Moreover, though the whole of Cyprus would nominally become part of the EU if the negotiations were successful, they had not made the island's political reunification a condition of membership. Their belief, evidently, was that the lure of EU membership would be sufficient to prompt a political settlement that the Greek Cypriot leaders would support – or at least not oppose. In this they were mistaken. They were particularly disappointed in the Greek Cypriot president, Tassos Papadopoulos, who in negotiations appeared receptive to the Annan Plan but eventually appealed to his community to vote "no" in the referendum. EU Enlargement Commissioner Gunther Verhuegen complained bitterly: "I feel cheated by the Greek Cypriot government. We had a clear agreement on this point. Mr. Papadopoulos must respect his part of the deal. Under no circumstances was a resolution to the conflict to fall [sic] as a result of opposition from the Greek Cypriot authorities."[5] Thus, instead of the hoped-for triumph of EU diplomacy, the EU leadership now had to contend with a still-divided Cyprus and troubling new issues – such as whether to lift (or at least relax) the EU's Draconian trade embargo against the TRNC, since the Turkish Cypriots had shown good faith and voted as Brussels desired.

## EUROPEANIZING THE CYPRUS QUESTION

There can be little doubt that the initial EU decision to enter into accession negotiations with the Republic of Cyprus in 1998 was a momentous step that had the effect of Europeanizing the Cyprus question. That question had always been one in which the domestic interests of Greek and Turkish Cypriots were inextricably tied to, and largely overshadowed by, the larger forces of regional and international politics. However, for a long time the EU (and its predecessor, the European Economic Community) were able to play only a minor role. After the forced partition of the island in 1974, and the intervention of a UN peacekeeping force, the EU could do little more than acquiesce in various UN- and U.S.-led efforts to resolve the issue, or at least keep Greece and Turkey – both members of the North Atlantic Treaty Organization (NATO) – from going to war with one another. But by opening accession negotiations, the EU suddenly catapulted itself into a leading role, in the process neatly eclipsing both the UN and the United States. The Cyprus issue, for the first time, began to revolve largely, if not exclusively, around decisions that were made in Brussels. The UN remained involved through the continuing presence of its peacekeeping force; the United States continued to have important military and strategic interests in the region; and Britain retained an interest as the former colonial power in Cyprus, where it continued to maintain substantial military bases. But the catalyst was the EU.

In essence, after 1998 an already complicated multidimensional issue was made more complicated and more multidimensional by EU intervention. In effect, by opening accession negotiations with the Republic of Cyprus, the EU raised the stakes in the Cyprus game and expanded the range of possible outcomes, thus compelling all of the players to re-examine their past preferences, reconsider their alliances, and recalculate their future prospects.

For Greek and Turkish Cypriots, the stakes were especially high. The prospect of EU membership held out the promise of major economic benefits, particularly for the poorer Turkish Cypriot community. While this was also a significant consideration for Greek Cypriots, it was not the paramount one. For them, debatably, EU membership promised less tangible but perhaps no less enticing benefits: of being included in the seemingly unstoppable progress of European integration (and avoiding the loss of opportunity and isolation that would result from exclusion), and in general of being less of a hostage to the fortunes of others. But EU membership also meant that any new constitutional arrangement that Greek and Turkish Cypriots entered into with one another would be difficult, and perhaps impossible, to change in any fundamental way in the future, since it would be cemented into place by the weight of EU treaties and institutions. Any miscalculation, in other words, would very likely be uncorrectable.

## NESTED GAMES

In the discussion to follow, the options of Greek and Turkish Cypriots are considered from a perspective derived from the theory of "nested games," as prominently advanced in the work of George Tsebelis and widely and variously applied. While we do not share the rather Hobbesian view of ethnic relations as zero-sum game found in certain game theoretic applications, we believe Tebelis's perspective to be valuable in that it applies specifically to decision making under conditions of multi-dimensionality. As Tsebelis explains, "… if, with adequate information, an actor's choices appear to be suboptimal, it is because the observer's perspective is incomplete. The observer focuses attention on only one game, but the actor is involved in a whole network of games – what I call nested games. What appears suboptimal from the perspective of only one game is in fact optimal when the whole network of games is considered."[6] Tsebelis further distinguishes between two types of nested games – games in multiple arenas and games of institutional design. In games in multiple arenas, the players perceive the game they are playing to be nested inside a bigger game; in games of institutional design, the players are additionally engaged in a game about the rules of the game. "Knowledge of the kinds of outcomes different institutions produce," he writes, "can transform preferences over policies into preferences over institutions."[7] A game-theoretic approach that includes both types of games, we suggest, is a useful approach from which to examine the options of Greek and Turkish Cypriots that opened up as a result of EU accession negotiations and the introduction of the Annan Plan.

## GAMES IN MULTIPLE ARENAS

By 1998, the conflict in Cyprus had been thoroughly internationalized for almost a half-century. Its regional dimension (particularly the threat of the Cyprus dispute provoking a war between Greece and Turkey) had ensured the decades-old involvement of such third parties as the United Nations, the United States, and the United Kingdom. Though successful in preventing a Greek-Turkish war, sustained third-party involvement was unsuccessful in bringing about a Cyprus settlement. It was thus against an inauspicious background that the EU assumed the leading role in Cyprus. It did so, moreover, despite a

conspicuous lack of success in its previous efforts to intervene in the
Cyprus conflict.

Cyprus and the EU (known then as the European Community) first
signed an association agreement in 1972. This agreement was prompted
by economic considerations, namely, the desire to protect Cypriot
agricultural exports to the British market in view of Britain's approaching accession. After the war of 1974 divided the island into two ethnic
zones, despite EU efforts to mediate the conflict, European states
remained wary of involvement in Cypriot affairs for many years.
According to John Redmond, "EU efforts to mediate in 1974 had been
the first real application of its European Political Cooperation (EPC)
procedure and had effectively been a failure. The EU had been reduced
simply to falling in line behind U.S. – and U.N. – led endeavours to
resolve the conflict."[8] In addition, it should be noted that the majority
of EU states had no particularly large stake in Cyprus itself, or indeed
in other issues that divide Greece and Turkey. There was, therefore, a
widespread assumption among EU states that the upgrading of the
association agreement with Cyprus to the level of membership would
have to await the settlement of the island's communal dispute. But the
Cyprus-EU membership issue remained a priority matter for Greece,
which saw Cypriot membership as helping its strategic goal of reducing
(if not removing) Turkey's influence on the island.

By the time the Republic of Cyprus submitted its application for
membership in 1990, European resistance to considering Cyprus's
membership had softened. This was largely due to the influence that
Greece had been able to exercise after becoming an EU member in
1981. The European Commission's 1993 opinion on the republic of
Cyprus's application thus cited the need for a political settlement on
the island before proceeding on accession talks but – in a significant
concession to Greece and Greek Cypriots – agreed to reconsider
Cyprus's membership by January 1995 even if no communal settlement
had been reached.[9] Ultimately, Greece was able to secure a commitment
that Brussels would not merely reconsider but actually *open* negotiations on Cyprus's membership. Greece was able to sway EU policy on
this issue because the EU wanted to proceed with a stalled customs
union agreement with Turkey, which would remain stalled if Greece
exercised its veto as an EU member. The quid pro quo was the opening
of accession negotiations with Cyprus. Thus, step by step, the long-
standing dispute over the future of Cyprus became nested within the
new games of EU expansion and EU-Turkey relations.

## Greek Cypriot Calculations

There existed a remarkable consensus within the Greek Cypriot community that EU membership would provide enormous benefits and carry no significant risks. As already noted, however, political and security considerations, rather than economic benefits, were the overriding factors in the Greek Cypriots' strong desire for EU membership. Above all, Greek Cypriots believed that, as an EU member, they would enjoy greater security vis-à-vis Turkey, since their precarious location in the eastern Mediterranean, practically on Turkey's doorstep, would be offset by their membership in the European family. They also anticipated that Turkey would come under strong EU pressure to withdraw its troops stationed in northern Cyprus, since a Turkish military presence on "EU territory" would be seen as a provocation in Brussels.

In the modern history of Cyprus, the movement by Greek Cypriot nationalists to unite Cyprus with Greece (*enosis*) poisoned intercommunal relations and was instrumental in the island's partition in 1974. Since then, the number of Greek Cypriots who favour the island's political union with Greece has declined to the point where it is no longer an issue. Yet relations with Greece remain close. At least part of the appeal of EU membership to Greek Cypriots may be explained by the prospect of Greek Cypriots and Greeks working together as members of the same EU institutions. In effect, Cyprus would become more closely integrated with Greece through the EU's institutional machinery.

Although the preferred choice of Greek Cypriots was to enter the EU as a unitary state that would operate under a system of majoritarian democracy, their political leaders knew that this option was anathema to Turkish Cypriots. In order to prevent the island's permanent partition, they therefore reluctantly accepted the principle that Cyprus be reconstituted as a bi-zonal federation. In negotiations over future constitutional arrangements, however, the Greek Cypriots consistently favoured a model of federation in which the central government would exercise strong and direct authority over the entire island, in the expectation that their majority community would control such a government. Although they acknowledged the need for sharing power with Turkish Cypriots in any new constitutional arrangement, they also displayed great ambivalence towards Turkish Cypriot demands for political equality, which they regarded as implying equal representation in the central government or a central government with only weak or indirect authority over the component parts.

The possible range of federal options, however, is considerable. Faced with Turkish Cypriot rejection of a centralized form of federation, Greek Cypriots expressed a willingness to consider what from their point of view was a less desirable but perhaps acceptable option: consociational power sharing by the two communities in a decentralized multi-tier federation (as in Belgium) within the EU. The proposition that, as a minority of 20 per cent, the Turkish Cypriots should be able to exercise veto powers that thwart the will of a majority, and even conduct its own foreign relations in certain arenas, was unpalatable for most Greek Cypriots. However, it was a price they at times appeared willing to pay, provided the island was reunited and became an EU member.

For Greek Cypriots, the game of institutional design for Cyprus was clearly nested within the larger and more important game of EU membership. Membership in the EU was so highly prized by most Greek Cypriots that they were content to see their part of the island join alone, in the hope (and even the expectation) that the attractions of EU membership would soon drive the bulk of Turkish Cypriots to petition for reunification and to accept terms less favourable than those on offer in the Annan Plan. In this connection, Greek Cypriot officials cited the analogy of Germany, where East Germany gained EU membership through reunification with West Germany, following many years of division.

### TURKISH CYPRIOT CALCULATIONS

Turkish Cypriot perceptions of what EU membership would do for their community were, initially, almost the exact opposite of those of Greek Cypriots. Above all, they looked forward to the economic benefits that EU membership would bring. But whereas Greek Cypriots saw EU membership as enhancing their security, Turkish Cypriots, who are outnumbered by their Greek counterparts by a ratio of four to one, feared that EU membership would diminish their security – first, by weakening or even removing Turkey's protective military umbrella; and second, by making them subject to Greek Cypriot political domination if as a condition of membership they were forced to give up their own state.

Politically, the *de facto* partition of Cyprus and the creation of the TRNC had suited most Turkish Cypriots very well because they were able to exercise self-government in their own state and to enjoy the security provided by Turkey's substantial military presence. Accordingly, they were sceptical of third-party initiatives that sought to alter the status quo. This proved a difficult challenge for both the UN and the United States, who had sought to be peacemakers in Cyprus for over thirty-five years, and was an even greater challenge for the EU because of the Turkish Cypriot and Turkish perception that Brussels was heavily biased in favour of Greek Cyprus and Greece. As seen in the TRNC and Ankara, the EU had allowed Greece to hamper Turkey's EU ties and membership aspirations. Moreover, by proceeding to negotiate Cyprus's accession with the Republic of Cyprus, without a prior political settlement on the island, the EU had arbitrarily taken important bargaining chips away from the Turkish Cypriots. In other words, from a nested-games perspective, the EU's action in the expansion game altered the rules of the Cyprus reunification game (institutional design) that was nested within it.

Even after accession negotiations had begun, Turkish Cypriots continued to hope that Brussels would be unwilling to admit a divided island and effectively import the Cyprus conflict into the EU. They also hoped that, if the EU nevertheless moved in favour of accession, it would pressure Greek Cypriots to recognize Turkish Cypriot sovereignty as a price for admission. That would have been an ideal outcome for many Turkish Cypriots, who would have perceived it as paving the way for the simultaneous EU accession of the sovereign TRNC and the Republic of Cyprus (and, ideally, Turkey as well). All these hopes, however, were dashed by the EU's Helsinki communiqué of 1999, which declared that "the European Council underlines that a political settlement will facilitate the accession of Cyprus to the European Union. If no settlement has been reached by the completion of the accession negotiations, the Council's decision on accession will be made without the above being a precondition."[10]

As with the most desired Greek Cypriot option, the settlement option most desired by Turkish Cypriots – recognition of the TRNC and EU accession – was unattainable. They had therefore to move to what many regarded as the next best option: a two-state confederation on the island. In order to overcome international and Greek Cypriot resistance to the concept of a separate state in the north, they repeatedly expressed their willingness to create a united Cypriot state with a common international personality. However, they also insisted that the envisaged common state be created through the sovereign will of the Turkish Cypriot and Greek Cypriot states.[11] This, too, proved a nonstarter. Predictably, Greek Cypriots adamantly opposed any arrangement that would require them to acknowledge the sovereignty of the "illegal" TRNC.

In 2001, in a bid to garner support from EU states as well as the UN and the United States, Turkish Cypriot officials moved again, this time to what might be termed a "weak federal option" loosely modelled on Belgium. Certain Belgian constitutional features, they suggested, might be considered for adoption in an envisaged new state in Cyprus, approvingly citing in particular the ability of the Belgian constituent units to negotiate treaties and take positions within international organizations. In response, Greek Cypriots pointedly emphasized the single sovereignty of the Belgian state but otherwise did not raise any serious objections. For more than a year, this raised new hopes in various quarters, international and domestic, that the application of the "Belgian model" to Cyprus might be a way of bridging the gap between Turkish Cypriot and Greek Cypriot positions. However, after months of intense negotiations, no compromise on fundamental issues could be achieved.

For the Turkish Cypriot leadership, the nesting of the game of reunification within the game of EU expansion proved to be deeply problematical. It opened up, for the first time, a sharp cleavage of opinion among Turkish Cypriots over reunification and, inevitably, over their political leadership. Any reunification plan that involved giving up the Turkish Cypriot claim to sovereign statehood was bound to spark wrenching political debates, but the actual effects went far beyond that, to the creation of new party and electoral alignments and, after hard-fought parliamentary elections in December 2003, the installation of a new pro-EU governing coalition. Such was the desire of the Turkish Cypriots to enter the EU that, for the first time, settling for a loose federation – even if it meant abandoning their claim to statehood – had become for many a palatable option.

## GAMES OF INSTITUTIONAL DESIGN (EUROPEAN STYLE)

As in so many deeply divided societies, the broad outline of a possible settlement in Cyprus has never been difficult to imagine. Indeed, since the island's partition in 1974, such an outline has been presented by mediators under UN auspices on three separate occasions in three separate documents: the "Preliminary Draft for Joint High-Level Agreement" of 1985; the "Set of Ideas" framework agreement of 1992; and, most recently, the Annan Plan of 2002–03. All of these plans have sought to reconcile the Greek Cypriot desire for a single Cypriot state with the Turkish Cypriot desire for a two-state solution; all have envisaged creating a bi-communal, bi-zonal federation on the island; and all have affirmed Cyprus's single sovereignty.

The Annan Plan borrows its principles explicitly from the Swiss and Belgian models of federalism.[12] That is to say, it outlines a constitution for a bi-communal and bi-zonal state that in its structure (and, the plan's framers hoped, in its functioning) will be essentially federal and consociational. Hence, the design of institutions is intended to ensure, in so far as it is possible to do so, the practices of executive power sharing, proportionality, mutual veto, and segmental autonomy. For example, the plan calls for a rotating presidency on the basis of two terms for Greek Cypriots and one for Turkish Cypriots. In all institutions, proportionality norms would prevail. For instance, in the six-member presidential council, two members would represent Turkish Cypriots. The lower house would have a 75:25 Greek Cypriot/Turkish Cypriot ratio while the upper house would have a 50:50 ratio. Minority veto provisions would prevail throughout. Any constitutional amendment would require approval by both communities, and federal legislation in all key areas would require dual majorities in the lower house if a majority of representatives of either community so decided. Segmental autonomy would be assured in a bi-zonal federation, since the two constituent states would retain their Greek Cypriot and Turkish Cypriot majorities.

While clear in some respects, the Annan Plan also contains large areas of uncertainty and ambiguity. In the division of powers between the federal and state governments – which is always a critical issue in federations, and often a bone of endless contention – the document extensively lists the powers to be vested in the federal government but not those to be vested in the constituent states, since the latter are assigned all residual powers. The listed federal powers include such standard and relatively non-controversial items as defence, central banking, currency, immigration and citizenship, and postal and telecommunication services. However, the federal list also includes certain items that are potent sources of friction – most notably, "federal budget and federal taxation," "federal police," and undefined powers of "co-ordination" over such matters as industry and commerce, tourism, fisheries and agriculture, and "protection of the environment and use and conservation of energy and natural resources, including water." Moreover, there is considerable potential for competition and friction between the constituent states, and between them and the federal government, over "shared powers" in external relations.

The Annan Plan also wrestles with contentious and vital issues that would be no less important than constitutional arrangements in regulating communal relations in the proposed new federation, including territorial adjustments, Turkey's military presence, and other security arrangements and guarantees. The plan foresees the transfer of about 20 per cent of the TRNC's territory (8 per cent of the island's total) to the Greek Cypriot constituent state. This would enable an estimated 120,000 Greek Cypriots who were displaced in 1974 to return to their former homes under a Greek Cypriot administration. In addition, the plan provides for the gradual return and settlement of up to 100,000 Greek Cypriots to the Turkish Cypriot constituent state. It also affirms the validity of the Treaty of Guarantee (a major Turkish-Cypriot/ Turkish demand) but foresees the drastic reduction of the Turkish troop deployment from over 30,000 to 650, and provides for the stationing on Cyprus of 950 Greek troops. Other security arrangements call for the disbanding of Greek Cypriot and Turkish Cypriot forces, and the continued deployment of the United Nations Peace Force with additional responsibilities to monitor the implementation of the plan's security arrangements.

Almost immediately following the submission of the Annan Plan to the parties, in November 2002, UN mediators were forced to backtrack and begin drafting changes to various sections of the document. The problem, essentially, was that both the Greek and Turkish Cypriot leaders disliked many of the plan's key provisions. The Greek Cypriot leadership, worried that an outright rejection of the plan would jeopardize their imminent accession to EU membership, prudently declared the plan to be negotiable. But its negotiability was obviously not simply a matter of fine-tuning. Most Greek Cypriots shared their leaders' fundamental misgivings regarding specific features of the plan that they believed would undercut the ability of the Greek community to exercise power consistent with its majority status and to reduce "external" (read Turkish) influence. Accordingly, Greek Cypriots decried the plan's provision of political equality between the communities and a rotating presidency, the granting of citizenship to an estimated 45,000 mainland

Turks who have settled on the island since 1974, the limitations on the number of Greek Cypriots who would be allowed to return to their homes in the Turkish Cypriot constituent state, and the long-term stationing of Turkish troops in Cyprus even though their number would be drastically reduced.

Unlike his Greek Cypriot counterpart, Tassos Papadopoulos (and his predecessor, Glafkos Klerides), Turkish Cypriot leader Rauf Denktash condemned the Annan Plan outright. He particularly objected to the extensive territorial adjustments envisaged in the plan, which would require the dislocation of about 45–50,000 Turkish Cypriots (a quarter of the community's population), and the lack of acknowledgment of Turkish Cypriot sovereignty.[13]

Most Turkish Cypriots, however, were ambivalent. On the one hand, they objected to three provisions of the plan which they viewed as particularly problematic: the settlement of tens of thousands of Greek Cypriots in their constituent state, the recognition of Republic of Cyprus title deeds in north Cyprus, and the resettlement of tens of thousands of Turkish Cypriots. On the other hand, being tired of the adversities of years of isolation and faced with poor future prospects, they were attracted by several other provisions, including the constitutionally equal status of the two communities, the wide measure of autonomy envisaged for the constituent states, Turkey's continuing role as a guarantor of their security, and, not the least, EU citizenship. The economic depression that had gripped north Cyprus since late 1999 naturally enhanced the appeal of the latter. Moreover, many Turkish Cypriots had concluded that the Annan Plan represented the best terms that that they were ever likely to get and, if it failed, the Greek Cypriots would likely insist on even tougher terms in any future negotiations over reunification and EU accession.

This is why Denktash's rejection of the plan provoked unprecedented public protests and calls for his resignation as the community's negotiator. In January 2003, in one of the largest demonstrations ever held in the TRNC, an estimated 50–60,000 Turkish Cypriots (about a quarter of the entire community) joined a march calling for negotiations based on the UN plan and Turkish Cypriot accession to the EU.[14]

The demonstrations, however, had no immediate effect. Nor did international diplomacy. Intense diplomatic efforts, including a series of summit meetings headed by the UN Secretary General Kofi Annan himself, during February and March 2003, failed to secure an agreement. Annan's main gambit was to pressure the Cypriot leaders to

conduct separate referendums on the UN plan in their respective communities – in the evident hope that Greek Cypriots would not risk
upsetting their smooth advance to EU membership by voting against it,
and, if a majority of Turkish Cypriots voted for it, Denktash would be
forced to acquiesce.[15]

But Denktash countered with one final gambit of his own: after first
securing the support of the Turkish military and senior ranks of the
bureaucracy in Ankara (and defying the wishes of Turkey's newly
elected AKP (Justice and Development Party) government, which
favoured acceptance of the Annan plan), he rejected the holding of a
referendum in the TRNC. In effect, Denktash had countered Annan's
assumption that the Cyprus reunification issue was nested within the
arena of EU expansion with an older and possibly still valid assumption:
that reunification was also nested within the arena of Turkish politics.
Annan declared that "we have reached the end of the road"[16] and
threatened to close the UN office in Nicosia.

For the AKP government in Ankara, however, it had become obvious
that "Turkey's road to Brussels lies through Cyprus" and they were
therefore unwilling to concede victory to Denktash. For the AKP, the
EU arena trumped the arena of domestic politics. Moreover, even in
the domestic political arena, Dentkash's supporters were undercut by
the fact that within Turkish Cyprus there was continued popular
support for keeping the Annan Plan alive. The pressure on Denktash
to make a positive gesture must have been considerable, but no one
could have anticipated the extraordinary drama of his next move: on
22 April the government of the TRNC suddenly opened the long-closed
Green Line, and within hours thousands of Greek and Turkish Cypriots
were streaming across it, in scenes reminiscent of Germany after the
fall of the Berlin Wall. Symbolically, the meaning was clear: the road
to the political reunification under the Annan Plan was still open. This
was confirmed early in 2004 when the Turkish government effectively
gave Denktash no choice but to continue negotiating with the Greek
Cypriots and to accept the binding arbitration of the UN secretary
general if no agreement could be reached. Thus was the way cleared
for the UN-sponsored referendums on the Annan Plan.

## FEDERALISM AS A PANACEA FOR CYPRUS?

A federal system, by definition, means that the federal government is
able to interact directly with all its citizens, rather than interacting with

them only indirectly through the agency of its constituent states. It is this which principally distinguishes a federation from a confederation. For federalism to work, therefore, direct interaction must be generally accepted. Yet achieving acceptance is no easy matter and is often problematical even in long-established federations. It requires a considerable level of trust in the fairness and efficacy of a federal government for a people to accept its direct taxation of their incomes, property, and purchases, and this is especially true in the case of members of a minority community. In Cyprus, federal powers of inspection, auditing, and enforcement, for example, could prove extremely divisive, as could federal attempts to "co-ordinate" matters which the two communities have long been accustomed to administering on their own.

*Theoretically*, a bi-communal, bi-zonal, and consociational constitution for Cyprus is an obvious solution. *Practically*, such a constitution requires prior agreement on many vital and probably irreversible details. And, even if these can be settled, there must still be a leap of faith. The successful functioning of federal systems is facilitated not only by the constitution but also by the processes of politics, and processes cannot be arranged by treaty. Much depends on the type of party system that evolves (for example, whether the parties are ethnically exclusive or inclusive in their membership). Much also depends on the bonds of personal trust that develop between the political leaders of the different communities, and whether those bonds are strong enough to withstand periodic crises of confidence. In Cyprus, these are matters that are difficult to predict. What is known is that decades of negotiations between Greek and Turkish Cypriots have been conducted in an atmosphere of suspicion and have ended fruitlessly in deadlock and impasse, usually over the details of proposed systems of government.

Despite the professed interest of both sides in the Swiss and Belgian models, negotiations on proposals based on those models have followed an all-too-familiar course; for, when they get down to details, the Greek and Turkish Cypriots are no more agreed on exactly what these models represent than they are on anything else. The basic problem is that they are, in fact, engaged in a one-shot "game of institutional design" (Tsebelis). The stakes are high, information is imperfect, and a powerful outside actor (the EU) sets the key rules, which are variable. Neither side is able to predict with much confidence the outcomes that would result from accepting reunification under any particular set of institutions. The only certainty is that, whatever institutions are adopted, some interests would gain from future outcomes and some would lose;

the best that can be hoped is that the overall mix of future outcomes would be more or less equitable and, equally important, would be so perceived by both sides.

In a reunited Cyprus, the leaders of the two communities would have to deal with one another frequently, within specifically structured contexts and according to specific rules of procedure, with the basic interests of their respective communities at stake. In other words, their initial one-shot game would be followed by "iterated games" under rules that would be difficult, if not impossible, to change. As Tsebelis observes: "When players enter into repeated interaction, they are interested in maximizing the payoff during the entire period of their interaction. Therefore they may choose suboptimal strategies in the one-shot game if such strategies increase their payoffs over repeated play."[17]

For both sides, even though they have (or purport to have) different understandings of what it means, federalism is a suboptimal strategy. It was only put into play, in the Annan Plan, because each side saw in it specific features that would potentially be to their advantage in future series of iterated games. Since the game of institutional design for Cyprus, even post-Annan, is irrevocably nested in the international game of EU accession, the anticipated (or feared) effects on future iterated games is all the more crucial, since the latter games will inevitably be played under EU rules. Therefore, the question of who will be able to influence the making of EU rules (and, most significantly, whether Turkey is included or excluded) becomes a relevant consideration for both Greek and Turkish Cypriots, since it will affect the payoffs in their future iterated games.

### Cyprus through the Belgian Looking Glass
### (or Belgium through the Cypriot Looking Glass)

From the EU perspective, and the perspective of many analysts, a Cyprus settlement based on a framework derived from European experience – especially Belgian-style federalism – is the preferred outcome for a number of reasons that are easy to understand. First, there appears to be a reasonably good fit. As Michael Emerson and Nathalie Tocci explain, "Belgium is a small-to-medium sized state with two main cultural communities, and it has restructured its political system (in fact during the period of Cyprus' division) in several stages from being a centralised state to being a largely decentralised one."[18] Second,

Belgium practices a system of federalism that combines territorial elements (regions) and cultural/linguistic elements (communities) and seems to offer a promising model for Cyprus. Third, Belgium's membership in the EU makes it subject to a dominant supra-national tier of decision making which greatly influences the operation of its political system. The EU, it is argued, provides material incentives to Belgium's communities to cooperate with one another and also constrains their propensity for conflict by placing many potentially divisive issues effectively beyond their grasp. Hence, it is hoped, these salutary effects could be replicated in Cyprus. Finally, from a European perspective, solving the Cyprus problem would be a glittering success for Europe.[19]

The trouble is, however, that the preferred EU solution does not much resemble the preferred solution of Greek or Turkish Cypriot leaders, and the leaders' preferred solutions do not resemble each other. According to Tsebelis, "why would the actor and the observer disagree as to what the optimal course of action is? There are two possibilities: either the actor actually does choose a suboptimal strategy or the observer is mistaken."[20] In their consideration of the Belgian model, the Greek and Turkish Cypriot leaders each prefer versions of the model (in a game of institutional design) which they calculate would, if implemented, maximize the payoffs to their respective communities in future iterated games. The result is two oddly distorted versions of Belgian federalism in which nothing is quite what it appears to be – but their preferences are not suboptimal if considered from a nested-games perspective. It is the observers who are wrong. Hence, for example, the Turkish Cypriot leaders' selective emphasis on Article 167 of the Belgian constitution, which establishes the right of the constituent regions to play an international role that includes even treaty-making power in matters falling under their jurisdiction.[21] Hence also the Greek Cypriot leaders' emphasis on the fact that only the Belgian federal government has legal status in international law and among its exclusive areas of jurisdiction are defence, security, and justice,[22] and that in the councils of the EU, Belgium is required to "speak with one voice."

Belgian federalism is much too complex and elaborate a system to be adequately explained here, and we will not attempt to do so. The following observations are meant to emphasize certain contextual and operative aspects of the Belgian case that seem to us to be germane (but are perhaps not sufficiently appreciated) in discussions of the possible transfer of Belgian political institutions to Cyprus.

First, Belgian federalism evolved under almost ideal conditions. Belgium is bi-communal, but its communities have managed to live together in peace, if not always in harmony. There has been no violent rift in their history of dealing with each other and in fact they share a long tradition of consociational bargaining and conflict management.[23] As Liesbet Hooghe observes, "non-majoritarianism has been the main feature of the Belgian political regime from its independence in 1831."[24] Belgium's two communities, moreover, which were once exclusively linguistic – religion having never been a factor since both Flemings and Waloons are predominantly Roman Catholic – have gradually acquired territorial identities and interests as well. It was this relatively recent trend that made federalism the preferred option of both communities, rather than, for example, the stronger constitutional entrenchment of language rights. Federalism, then, was a move that reflected the gradual federalizing of Belgian society. Moreover, switching to federalism did not threaten the security of either community. Both were securely and affluently ensconced in the midst of a developing European Union – whose capital is their own capital of Brussels. While in theory this might have made the break-up of Belgium relatively painless, it also made it relatively pointless, since separate Flemish and Waloon states would "find themselves restricted by EU membership in ways similar to the Belgian state."[25] For the Belgians, the road to federalism was newly travelled and contained some strange twists and turns, but they drove with caution, there were no blown bridges or land mines to contend with, and they rode in the same car. Wherever else the Belgian model may be tried, it is unlikely that the background circumstances will ever be replicated. And, in the case of Cyprus, it would be difficult to imagine a background more starkly different.

Second, although the formal constitutional transformation of Belgium into a federal state took place in 1993, the ground was well prepared. From at least the early 1970s, there was a growing consensus in both communities, and among their major political parties and interest groups, that federalism was the preferred solution. And, while there was no consensus on exactly the type of federalism they wanted, gradually that too emerged. A series of constitutional reforms in the 1980s, which formalized territorial devolution but stopped short of federalism, proved to be workable and set the stage for further negotiations. The result was a unique multi-tiered variant of federalism that combined territorial and communitarian features. It is noteworthy that Belgium's gradual progress towards federalism was marked by the most thorough and detailed negotiation of transitional fiscal arrangements, since it was understood by both sides that these were essential before a viable federal system could be put in place. By contrast, in the case of Cyprus, fiscal issues have received but perfunctory treatment, no doubt because they are so exceedingly difficult to negotiate. But to proceed as though they are not crucial, or can somehow be settled later, is to invite future trouble. It should be remembered that, in the brief unhappy existence of the original bi-communal Republic of Cyprus (1960–63), fiscal questions that had initially been left in abeyance proved impossible to settle. Tax and tax-related disputes helped to paralyse the nascent state and exerted a corrosive influence upon inter-ethnic political relations.[26]

Third, the social and political purpose of federalizing Belgium was not to bring two long-divided communities into closer interaction with one another, but rather to separate them still further by creating large areas of competency in which they would be politically autonomous. As Nicholas Lagasse observes, "Belgian federalism is federalism by disaggregation and disassociation."[27] For Kris Deschouwer, "the process has gradually emptied the Belgian state, but kept it alive."[28] And in Hooghe's telling phrase, Belgian federalism has built-in centrifugal tendencies that have led to a "hollowing of the center in return for peace."[29] Whether a system of government so conceived could also be made to work in reverse – which it would have to do to bring the two long-separated parts of Cyprus together – is an interesting speculation, but no more than that, since it has never been tested.

Fourth, in Belgium, as in all successful federal systems, while the written constitution is of undoubted importance – among other things, it defines the powers of the different levels of government and specifies procedures for constitutional interpretation and adjudication – it is not the only important thing. The way the Belgian system actually works depends largely also on its non-constitutional aspects, such as the structure of the party system, the role of interest groups and media, and the nature of the political culture (or cultures). The Belgian party system, for example, is made up of parties that are community-specific; that is, they do not compete for support across ethnic lines. But they do compete across jurisdictional lines within their own communities –

they seek to be part of governing coalitions at both the federal and regional levels.[30] Elite accommodation is thus facilitated as much by the processes of Belgian politics as by the constitution. Of course, similar processes might develop in Cyprus; but there is nothing to suggest that they would, and in a democracy it would be difficult to make them mandatory.

Finally, the Belgian model of federalism was hammered out by the Belgians themselves, in Belgium, in face-to-face negotiations. They did not have to be induced to talk to one another by the UN secretary-general; there were no "special representatives" involved; and there were no "proximity negotiations" or "confidence building measures." And, most important of all, there was no direct EU intervention. The EU was the context game within which their "game of institutional design" was firmly nested, but EU leaders did not inject themselves into the Belgian game by imposing rules or conditions for future membership or by offering incentives (although in the crucial fiscal arena, it may be argued, the EU's sheltering umbrella helped to facilitate agreement). Belgium's constitutional odyssey might have had a different outcome if the EU had intervened heavy-handedly – for example, by declaring that Flanders would remain a member regardless of the constitutional outcome, but Wallonia would not be included unless the two sides first reached a comprehensive settlement.

In the case of Cyprus, multiple external pressures and interventions are inescapable. Virtually the only certainty about any future federal arrangement for Cyprus is that the Cypriots will have to be pressured into adopting it. From all that is known about the origins and history of federations, this would not be a promising beginning.

## CONCLUSION

There is no good reason why political institutions and forms of governance that are developed in one country should not be transferred to another. But there are many good reasons why they should not be transferred without the most careful attention to the historical, social, and political contexts within which they will operate. It is precisely such factors that largely determine whether a transfer succeeds or fails. The Cyprus conflict has proved to be one of the most intractable and internationalized disputes of recent history. It has frustrated many third-party attempts to resolve it. Given this record, it is not surprising that the EU's powerful but erratic intervention has thus far failed to yield the hoped-for success.

Whatever the basis for the next round of reunification negotiations might be, whether a revised Annan Plan or some completely new document, there should be no illusions regarding the prospects of power sharing under a federal system. It must be stressed that neither federalism nor consociationalism are panaceas for deeply divided societies. Both require the presence of underlying conditions that support a political process of accommodation and compromise, and these conditions are conspicuously absent in Cyprus. It is unlikely, moreover, that the inclusion of both Cypriot communities in the EU would make any fundamental difference. In Northern Ireland, for example, common EU membership has not proved a decisive factor in efforts to promote the successful working of a power-sharing system.

At a minimum, for federalism or consociationalism to work in practice, political elites must be willing and able to bargain with one another in good faith. And they must be able to bargain with some reasonable assurance that their respective communities will support their efforts, not necessarily in every instance but over time – in recognition, in other words, that it is the overall balance of outcomes that counts in iterated games. That takes patience and at least some measure of trust. Unfortunately, as has become increasingly clear from the many examples of power-sharing failure, institutions alone cannot manufacture a willingness to cooperate where none exists. In Cyprus, a bi-communal and consociational federation brought into existence by outside pressures and inducements would be likely to fare no better than the previous power-sharing experiment in the early 1960s.

## NOTES

1 For background studies of the Cyprus question, see John Reddaway, *Burdened with Cyprus: The British Connection* (London: Widenfeld and Nicholson 1986); Oliver Richmond, *Mediating in Cyprus: The Cypriot Communities and the United Nations* (London: Frank Cass 1998); and Nathalie Tocci, *EU Accession Dynamics and Conflict Resolution: Catalysing Peace or Consolidating Partition in Cyprus* (Aldershot, U.K.: Ashgate 2004).

2 Arend Lijphart, "Power-sharing and Group Autonomy in the 1990s and the 21st Century" (paper, Constitutional Design 2000 Conference), 7.

3 Michael Emerson and Nathalie Tocci, *Cyprus as Lighthouse of the East Mediterranean: Shaping Re-unification and* EU *Accession together* (Centre for European Policy Studies, Brussels 2002), 1.

4 See Ann-Sofi Jakobsson Hatay, "'Oxi' and 'Evet': The People Deliver Their Verdict on the Annan Plan for a Re-united Cyprus," TTF *Forum* (Transitional Foundation for Peace and Future Research), 1 May 2004.

5 *Cyprus Mail*, 22 April 2004.

6 George Tsebelis, *Nested Games and Rational Choice in Comparative Politics* (Berkeley and Los Angeles: University of California Press 1990), 7.

7 Tsebelis, *Nested Games*, 98.

8 John Redmond, "From Association towards the Application for Full Membership: Cyprus' Relations with the European Union," in Heinz-Jurgen Axt and Hansjorg Brey, ed., *Cyprus and the European Union: New Chances for Solving an Old Conflict?* (Munich: Sudosteuropa-Gesellschaft 1997), 95.

9 According to Redmond, "this was intended to prevent the Turkish Cypriots from effectively having the power of veto, that is, they would be able to veto Cypriot accession to the EU simply by refusing to agree to an internal settlement with the Greek Cypriots" (Axt and Brey, ed., *Cyprus and the European Union*, 97).

10 Helsinki, European Council, *Presidency Conclusions*, 10–11 December 1999.

11 This proposal is less comparable to the Belgian or Swiss models of federalism that are often dubiously claimed to be its inspiration than to the purely hypothetical "sovereignty-association" for a future Quebec-Canada relationship that has been promoted by the nationalist Parti Québécois.

12 Article 2(1) states: "The status and relationship of the United Cyprus Republic, its federal government, and its constituent states, is modeled on the status and relationship of Switzerland, its federal government, and its cantons." Article 2 (1a) further states: "The United Cyprus Republic is an independent state in the form of an indissoluble partnership, with a federal government and two equal constituent states, the Greek Cypriot state and the Turkish Cypriot state. Cyprus is a member of the United Nations and has a single international legal personality and sovereignty. The United Cyprus Republic is organized under its Constitution in accordance with the basic principles of rule of law, democracy, representative republican government, political equality, bi-zonality, and the equal status of the constituent states." The constituent states would "sovereignly exercise all powers not vested by the Constitution in the federal government," and, as

in Belgium, "there shall be no hierarchy between federal and constituent state laws." Article 2(2) again invokes the Belgian model: "... the constituent states shall participate in the formulation and implementation of policy in external relations and the European Union affairs on matters within their sphere of competence, in accordance with Cooperation Agreements modeled on the Belgian example. The constituent states may have commercial and cultural relations with the outside world in conformity with the Constitution." (The full text of the Annan Plan is available at <www.cyprus-un-plan.org>.)

13 *Financial Times*, 9 December 2002.

14 Economist Intelligence Unit, Country Monitor, *Cyprus*, 20 January 2003.

15 "Divisions to Deepen as Peace Plan Fails," *Oxford Analytica Brief*, 12 March 2003.

16 "Umpteenth Time Unlucky," *Economist*, 12 March 2003.

17 Tsebelis, *Nested Games*, 73.

18 Emerson and Tocci, *Cyprus as Lighthouse*, 8.

19 Writing before the 2004 referenda, Emerson and Tocci describe the potential reward in glowing terms: "If successfully concluded, the re-unification of Cyprus simultaneously with accession to the EU would be a remarkable political achievement. It could come to be another example of the European method of conflict resolution, following the recent case of Northern Ireland ... and the gradual progress in transforming the multiple conflicts of the Balkans through Europeanisation of the whole region ... It might provide hope and inspiration for those only a few minutes flying time away from Cyprus, who are today locked in the deepest and bitterest of ethno-nationalist conflicts." Emerson and Tocci, *Cyprus as Lighthouse*, 8.

20 Ibid., 7.

21 *Cyprus Weekly*, "Talks Turn to Belgian Model," 4 July 2002.

22 Turkish Economic and Social Studios Foundation (TESEV), "Cyprus Update," July 2002.

23 24. Val R. Lorwin, "Belgium: Conflict and Compromise," in Kenneth McRae, ed., *Consociational Democracy: Political Accommodation in Segmented Societies* (Toronto: McClelland and Stewart 1974), 179–206.

24 Liesbet Hooghe, "Belgium: Hollowing the Center," in Nancy Bermeo and Ugo Amoretti, ed., *Federalism and Territorial Cleavages* (Baltimore: John Hopkins University Press 2004), 67.

25 Ibid., 82.

26 Stanley Kyriakides, *Cyprus: Constitutionalism and Crisis Government* (Philadelphia: University of Pennsylvania Press 1968), 83–92.

27 "The Role of the Regions in Belgium's Foreign Relations," *Federations*, 2, no.2 (February 2002): 13–14.

28 Kris Deschouwer, "The Belgian Model and the Case of Cyprus," paper presented at the conference on "The Cyprus Problem and Cyprus' Accession to the European Union," Nicosia, Cyprus, 2–6 April 2002, 6.

29 Hooghe, "Hollowing the Center," 77.

30 Deschouwer, "The Belgian Model," 6.

# 12

# Conditionality, Consociationalism, and the European Union[1]

## STEVEN I. WILKINSON

This chapter assesses the strengths and weaknesses of conditionality as a strategy to mitigate ethnic conflict. Over the past two decades, international organizations have proved increasingly willing to make membership or aid conditional on a country's willingness to subscribe to democratic norms, including norms of minority rights. Most strikingly, the European Union (EU) has over the past decade made the admission of countries in Eastern Europe and the Mediterranean conditional on reforms that make their systems more accommodating of minority rights.[2] Other regional trade and cooperation organizations explicitly treat the EU as a model, and so it does not seem unrealistic to expect similar conditionality in other parts of the world in the future. Despite the promise of conditionality as a strategy of ethnic conflict moderation, however, the answers to two questions seem unclear. First, does conditionality really work in bringing about both short-term and long-term policy change on minority rights and minority conflict resolution? Or is Joseph Stiglitz, the former chief economist of the World Bank, correct when he says that, despite the claims made for conditionality, "good policies cannot be bought."[3] Secondly, are the policy "solutions" the EU is directly and indirectly encouraging among prospective entrants, through the Organization for Security and Cooperation in Europe (OSCE) and the Council of Europe (CE) – the latter a forty-six member organization whose responsibilities include the monitoring and enforcement of human rights – really the most effective way of moderating conflict? There is after all a lively debate among political scientists over which institutions have the greatest potential to moderate conflicts in the near and long term.

The chapter is organized in two parts. In the first part I review the history of EU conditionality as it applies to policies affecting ethnic minorities. I argue that there is good evidence that EU conditionality is a highly effective way of changing the behaviour of applicant states towards minorities. In the second part of the paper I turn my attention to the specific content of the policies the EU recommends, directly as well as indirectly through the OSCE and the CE. Many of these recommended reforms reflect the norms inherent in "consociational" power sharing and emphasize ethnic proportionality, coalition governments, and cultural autonomy for minorities. I examine why the EU, the OSCE, and the CE seem to prefer these policies to other possible approaches. I also speculate on the possible effects of these policy preferences on the long-term prospects for ethnic conflict resolution in Eastern Europe and the Mediterranean.

## WHICH ORGANIZATIONS ARE IMPOSING CONDITIONS?

The ultimate prize for Eastern European, former Soviet Union, and Mediterranean states is clearly membership in the EU, because of the many financial advantages that membership would bring. Virtually every state in these areas has publicly stated that EU membership is a central foreign policy objective, and many have formally applied: for example, Poland and Hungary in 1994, and Slovakia, Romania, Bulgaria, the Czech Republic, Slovenia, the Baltic states, Cyprus, and Malta in the mid-1990s.[4] Prospective members know, however, that before joining the EU they must meet the community's "political criteria," developed at a meeting of the European Council in Copenhagen in 1993. The EU agreed in Copenhagen that, in order to obtain admission, candidate countries had first to achieve "stability of institutions guaranteeing democracy, the rule of law, human rights and respect for and protection of minorities," as well as meeting various economic criteria.[5] These political criteria were intentionally vague, reflecting the EU's desire that the admission of new states should not be a quick process. There was also a lack of consensus among EU members in 1993 over what the exact requirements for membership should be. The requirement that applicant countries should show "respect for and protection of minorities" was especially unclear, because the EU had never even mentioned the issue of ethnic minorities prior to 1993.[6] From the early 1990s, therefore, there was an acute need for some organization or individual to tell applicant states what concrete actions would allow them to conform to EU and international standards, meet with EU approval, and therefore ultimately secure admission to the EU.

The EU itself clearly lacked the capacity in the early 1990s to monitor minority rights in Eastern Europe and the Mediterranean, or to develop detailed recommendations on minority rights' policies. Senior officials also realized that developing such a capacity, and a consensus on what exactly to require, might take years of perhaps divisive debate among member states.[7] The détente-era Council on Security and Cooperation in Europe (CSCE), which was renamed the Organization for Security and Cooperation in Europe in 1995, on the other hand, was keen to establish a new and useful role for itself in the post-Cold War world, and had two main institutional advantages. First, it had already developed some norms and created some institutional capacity on the issue of ethnic minorities. In 1990, at a meeting in Copenhagen, it had sketched out a document on the "human dimension" of democratization in Eastern Europe that included a list of language, cultural, and political protections that represented good practice in dealing with ethnic minorities.[8] After the break-up of Yugoslavia in June 1992, the OSCE added some institutional capacity on minority issues by creating the office of the High Commissioner on National Minorities (HCNM), to which it appointed former Dutch Foreign Minister and UN Representative Max Van der Stoel. The second advantage the OSCE enjoyed was that the organization already included virtually all the Eastern European countries that wanted admission to the EU. This gave the organization an institutional and legal basis on which to make recommendations to its members.[9]

Since 1992, the EU has used the HCNM, and to a lesser extent the CE, as the minority-rights equivalent of financial ratings agencies like Standard and Poor's or Fitch. In part this reflects the EU's lack of capacity on minority issues, but it also reflects the personal drive, tact, and enterprise of Commissioner Van der Stoel. Although the HCNM's initial mandate seemed limited, concerned primarily with "early warning" of situations that would ultimately effect inter-state conflict, Steven R. Ratner shows how Van der Stoel "has interpreted his mandate to proactively devise and promote solutions to minority related tensions without formal permission of the Permanent Council."[10] In his first few years in office, Van der Stoel carved out a role for his office and encouraged, persuaded, and sometimes coerced countries (by credibly threatening that their non-compliance would effect their EU membership prospects) into changing policies and institutions that affect minorities, to bring them into line with his interpretation of EU requirements and international standards. The HCNM quickly established a total of twenty missions in various countries of Eastern Europe to monitor minority rights and Van der Stoel frequently visited those countries, as well as others with no formal HCNM presence, to advocate policies that he believed would reduce ethnic tensions and avert violence. Because of the drive and energy of the HCNM, and the EU's support for the HCNM, the OSCE rapidly established itself in the mid-1990s as the lead organization in charge of "translating" international norms, EU requirements, and international treaty obligations into practical suggestions on ethnic minority issues for countries in Eastern Europe, the former Soviet Union, and the Mediterranean.[11]

In assessing whether countries have made progress on minority rights issues, both the EU and the HCNM have attached considerable importance to whether countries have signed several international treaties and conventions, particularly the CE's Framework Convention on the Rights of National Minorities (1998). The EU's annual accession reports on prospective members have a checklist, for instance, showing whether countries have signed the Framework and other international human rights instruments. Those countries that sign are praised, while those that do not are urged to conform to "international standards."[12]

The authority of the HCNM and the CE to propose measures, and then to persuade countries to accept their proposals, rests largely on the fact that the EU implicitly and often explicitly supports their initiatives. The yearly reports of the European Commission on countries that have begun the membership application process all make note of the fact that these reports have been prepared in part on the basis of other reports from the OSCE, the CE, and (for the financial aspects of the application) international financial institutions. The EU also makes a clear link between applicants paying heed to the general advice of the OSCE and CE on minority rights and their progress towards admission.[13] For example, in 1999 the EU and the HCNM worked together to emphasize to the Latvian government that a language law passed by the Latvian parliament was discriminatory towards that country's large

Russian minority and would therefore effectively derail the country's chances of opening EU membership talks at the December 1999 Helsinki summit.[14] The EU has also been willing to use its power to try to force countries to accept missions from the HCNM: for instance, the EU presidency expressed its official regret at Belarus's refusal to grant a visa to a member of the OSCE monitoring group.[15]

## WHICH POLICIES? THE GROWTH OF CONSOCIATIONAL CONDITIONALITY

Many of the recommendations that the EU, the CE, and the OSCE put forward in their accession reports, statements, and letters to governments are designed to rectify overt discrimination against ethnic minorities, such as Turkey's 1980s ban on the use of the Kurdish language in private and its restrictions on the right of religious minorities to own property, the denial of citizenship to Russians in Estonia, and restrictions on the right of Russian and Hungarian speakers to stand for election in Latvia, Estonia, and Romania, respectively.[16] Interviews with several people involved with the HCMN during the 1990s make it plain that there was certainly no uniform consociational "blueprint" that the HCNM wanted to impose on all countries. One researcher in the HCNM confessed that he spent little time reading academic works and that most of his time was spent following the details of political controversies within the countries that the HCNM had on his watch list. Another individual who spent time at the HCNM in the late 1990s emphasized that, although people in the building were familiar with Lijphart's model, Van der Stoel took an "ad hoc approach," developing recommendations for countries depending on whether they seemed to be near conflict, and the attitude of each country's government and minorities, rather than according to some pre-determined model of minority rights.[17]

However, even though it would be wrong to say that the EU and HCNM were trying to push a unified "consociational model" in negotiations, it is still true that many of the policies recommended by the EU, the HCNM, and the CE are recognizably consociational. The EU, the HCNM, and the CE Framework Convention have all, for example, supported measures that increase ethnic proportionality, guarantee the inclusion of representatives of all major ethnic communities in government and parliament, create formal structures that allow for minority consultation on major policy initiatives, and secure minority communities' cultural autonomy. A content analysis of available EU accession reports and HCNM recommendations reveals a significant number of EU and HCMN requests for proportionality in politics (mentioned in 19 per cent of EU accession reports and 20 per cent of HCNM recommendations), as well as employment proportionality (19 per cent and 9 per cent). There are also a number of recommendations for increased spending on minorities, minority self-government, and greater provision of education in minority languages.[18]

The EU, the CE Framework Convention, and the HCNM all seem to regard the consociational criterion of ethnic proportionality in politics and employment as one of the primary indicators of whether discrimination against ethnic minorities exists. Although there is a wider debate among political scientists over the relative virtues of "descriptive" representation (i.e., the physical presence of a proportional number of minorities) and "substantive" representation (i.e., the representation of the vital interests of minorities),[19] the EU and the OSCE seem to take the consociational view that descriptive representation is one of the main yardsticks to use when assessing whether minorities are "represented" or not. The EU, for example, reports that the Turkish community in Bulgaria is "well integrated" into political life because the community's level of representation is politics is close to the level in the population.[20] The EU also takes the view that Slovenia – where Roma, Hungarian, and Italian minorities have the right to directly elect one representative each to parliament – offers comprehensive protections that fully meet international standards.[21] States where minority representation is much less than their proportion in the population are, correspondingly, implicitly guilty of discrimination. The CE's advisory committee on the implementation of the Framework Convention has, for instance, pressed for greater proportionality and formal minority representation in parliament – as opposed to representation through a general electorate – in its review of minority representation in Hungary.[22] The advisory committee has also "strongly welcomed" the example of states such as Romania which do constitutionally guarantee minorities representation in parliament.[23]

The HCNM has also supported ethnic proportionality in parliaments. For example, in 1994 Commissioner Van der Stoel pressed Ukraine to keep a guarantee that 10 per cent of seats in the Crimean Autonomous Republic would be reserved for members of the geographically dispersed Tatar minority (9.6 per cent of Crimea's population), on the grounds that under a plurality electoral system they "might even end up with having *no representation at all*." Dismantling the formal quota for Tatars could be justified, he argued, only if an alternative electoral system was introduced "which would give them [the Tatars] a near certainty of having a representation broadly commensurate to their percentage of the total population of Crimea."[24] The OSCE has also pressed Hungary to ensure that minority representatives were elected or appointed to parliament.[25] And it has asked Macedonia to change its electoral system to one of proportional representation (PR) and equalize the size of electoral districts in order to increase the number of Albanian representatives in parliament.[26]

The EU, the OSCE, and the CE hold to the same general principle of proportionality when considering employment.[27] So, while applauding Bulgaria for minority proportionality in parliament, for instance, the EU notes that "concerns exist as to the low level of [Turkish] representation in senior appointments in the administration or as officers in the military."[28] The CE advisory committee on the Framework Convention often points out that some ethnic groups have lower levels of representation in public employment than their population size would warrant and has urged that this be rectified.[29] And the HCNM has also made detailed recommendations to candidate countries about the need to ensure ethnic proportionality in employment.[30] In 1994, for instance, Commissioner Van der Stoel recommended that Kazakhstan introduce *de facto* quotas for ethnic groups in government employment because "it is also clearly undesirable that in state administration, or in the regional or local level of the administration, one ethnic group would be represented much more strongly, or less so, than the percentage of the population of such a group would suggest."[31] The HCNM has made similar proposals for ethnic proportionality in government employment and contracting for other groups, such as the Albanians in the Former Yugoslav Republic of Macedonia (FYROM) and the Roma/Sinti throughout Eastern Europe.[32] In the case of Macedonia, Van der Stoel recommended in 1994 that Albanian representation in the police force (5 per cent) be brought closer to the Albanian share of the population (23 per cent) through the removal of various unspecified "obstacles," and that the government should more broadly ensure proportionality by setting "specific targets for each branch of the public service for the next four years."[33]

As well as making formal requests to countries, the HCNM has tried to influence policy in Eastern Europe and elsewhere by sponsoring

groups of academics and lawyers to develop "best practice" documents
on linguistic rights, educational rights, and the rights of minorities in
administration and government (the Oslo, Hague, and Lund recommendations). While these are not official HCNM documents, they have
nevertheless been translated by the office of the HCNM into most of the
major Eastern European languages, have been circulated by his office,
and clearly carry Van der Stoel's stamp. The three sets of recommendations take care to point out that there are many types of acceptable
solutions to minority issues, but the fact that they tend to offer specific
guidance only for those consociational-style solutions that emphasize
proportionality, formal minority inclusion, and cultural autonomy
clearly points towards states adopting one set of policies rather than
another. The Lund proposals, for example, suggest that, in order to
ensure that "opportunities exist for minorities to have an effective voice
at the level of the central government," measures could include:

- special representation of national minorities, for instance, through a
  reserved number of seats in one or both chambers of parliament or
  in parliamentary committees and through other forms of guaranteed
  participation in the legislative process;
- formal or informal understandings for allocating cabinet positions,
  seats on the supreme or constitutional court or lower courts, and
  positions on nominated advisory bodies or other high-level organs
  to members of national minorities;
- mechanisms to ensure that minority interests are considered within
  relevant ministries, through, for example, personnel addressing
  minority concerns or issuance of standing directives; and
- special provision for minority participation in the civil service as well
  as the delivery of public services in the language of the national
  minority.[34]

The HCNM and the CE advisory committee have also supported
measures to bring minorities into the very centre of the policy process,
including establishing ombudsman positions to represent their interests
to the government and central government councils, with the power to
review legislation. The HCNM recommended the creation of a "national
commissioner on ethnic and language questions" in Latvia, Estonia,
and Lithuania in 1993 and has also supported similar institutions in
Romania, Slovenia, and elsewhere.[35] In some cases the clear implication

is that these individuals would themselves be members of minorities: in the case of the Baltic states, Van der Stoel recommended that several people be appointed if no individual could gain the confidence of all communities.[36] The CE's advisory committee has also supported such review organizations, for example, in Romania, where it has recommended that the Council of National Minorities "be consulted on all issues specifically affecting minorities," with the expectation that their strong opposition would be sufficient to prevent a measure.

In a few cases the HCNM has also welcomed the fact that communities have what in consociational terms would amount to a formal "minority veto." In Slovakia, for example, the commissioner backed the concept of local minority self-governing bodies for the country's ethnic minorities on the grounds that "in questions relating to local public education and culture and the use of the minority language the municipal council can only adopt bylaws if these have the consent of the local minority self-governing body."[37]

## IS CONDITIONALITY EFFECTIVE IN CHANGING POLICY TOWARDS MINORITIES?

There are obvious methodological problems in determining whether EU and HCNM conditionality is actually responsible for observed changes in countries' behaviour. There are, for example, strategic incentives for governments and politicians to pretend they are taking actions because of external pressure when in fact they are not. Governments might tell international organizations that implementing minority protections is difficult when it is not (or even when implementation might be advantageous from a political standpoint) in order to gain favour on other issues, such as the economic criteria for admission or requests for financial aid. Local politicians might overstate the power of the international community in forcing them to improve minority rights in order to give themselves political cover for actions they would have taken anyway, in the face of substantial public opposition.

The broader literature on conditionality, most of which is concerned with the efforts of international financial institutions to deny loans and aid to countries that do not carry out reforms in their economies and government administrations, has identified several general conditions under which conditionality works. First, conditionality seems to work better when a country's government (rather than an international organization) dictates the scope, sequencing, and pace of reforms. This is often referred to as "local ownership" of the reforms. Second, reforms seem to be more effective when they are implemented over a longer period, with many small steps helping to defuse opposition and build a constituency for more reforms, rather than being introduced all at once as a big reform package. Lastly, economic conditionality is more effective when large donor organizations coordinate their efforts and successfully resist countries' attempts to play one organization off against the other.[38]

Judith Kelley, in her 2001 Harvard thesis and subsequent articles, and the Hamburg University-based Centre for OSCE Research (CORE) have done the fullest assessments of the effectiveness of EU and OSCE conditionality on minority rights policy. Kelley examines policy development on several different minority rights issues in Latvia, Estonia, Slovakia, and Romania in the 1990s (a total of sixty-four cases). Crucially, she controls for domestic political alignments – the strength or weakness of parties that wanted to restrict minority language or citizenship rights – as well as the extent of international carrots and sticks, to determine whether international pressure was effective in bringing about change. The CORE project has produced studies of HCNM interventions in particular countries – Estonia, Latvia, Macedonia, Romania, and Ukraine – written by regional experts.

The Kelley and CORE studies show convincingly that, even in those cases where there was significant domestic opposition to improving minority rights, such as Latvia in the late 1990s or Romania and Ukraine in the mid-1990s, conditionality has been successful in forcing applicants or likely applicants to the EU to change their previous policies and practices on minority rights. By the end of 2001, for example, Estonia had implemented every one of the HCNM's recommendations on citizenship, representation, and language laws.[39] The HCNM was also successful in pressuring the Romanian government in 1995 to soften its language law restricting the rights of Hungarian speakers and to sign a treaty with Hungary.[40]

The reasons Kelley and the CORE studies identify as important to the success of EU and HCNM conditionality are similar to those identified in the larger literature on financial conditionality. First, the EU and the HCNM have not demanded that all their desired changes be made at once but have pushed countries to take many small steps over several years, in return for which the HCNM and the EU have provided incremental benefits prior to opening formal negotiations for membership. The EU has provided access to aid programs (especially in Eastern Europe), signed "Europe agreements" on reforms with promising candidates, and then finally entered into formal accession agreements with those countries that committed themselves to becoming fully democratic market economies.[41] The fact that the process has so many different steps has, not coincidentally, favoured exactly the type of incremental approach recommended in the conditionality literature. Kelley regards this incremental approach as good because it signals progress, and provides obtainable rewards, while still stressing the necessity to keep moving forward on implementation. As she puts it, "when institutions reward policy improvements with partial progress in the admission process, they essentially build a repeated game structure, where players can build trust and confidence in the fact that good policy will be rewarded, while still retaining leverage for future policy negotiations."[42]

Second, Kelley and the CORE studies find that persuasion works because it is backed up with a credible threat to withhold something that Eastern European countries want badly: progress towards EU admission. Kelley found that when the HCNM tried simple persuasion without the threat of sanctions, he generally failed to bring about policy change unless the domestic opposition to the reforms was already extremely weak.[43] Efforts by the HCNM to persuade the Estonian president to veto Estonian-language requirements for Russian-speaking candidates who sought election to the Estonian parliament failed, for example, because they were not backed up by the threat of real penalties. Similar efforts by the HCNM to use persuasion to change the education and citizenship laws in Latvia, and by the CE to change laws on bilingual signs in Romania, also failed to bring about speedy change because they were not backed up with credible threats of real penalties from the EU.[44] The CORE studies make many of the same points. Margit Sarv finds that there was essentially no real progress on most of the HCNM's recommendations in Estonia until 1998, when the EU became seriously involved. Sarv argues that "the fact that the EU effectively used the High Commissioner's recommendations as benchmarks for assessing whether or not the situation of the Russian-speaking population in Estonia was in accordance with EU accession criteria was crucial for the effectiveness of the High Commissioner."[45] Kulyk's study of

Ukraine similarly argues that the Ukrainian government took the HCNM's advice when it was backed by international support and the threat of credible sanctions, not otherwise.[46]

The third reason that conditionality has been highly effective in Europe is because it has often been highly coordinated, with the key European officials agreeing behind the scenes on a common response to countries that refused to make the required policy changes. According to one former staffer from the office of the HCNM, Commissioner Van der Stoel and EU Enlargement Commissioner Hans Van den Broek, for example, were in frequent communication and often coordinated their responses to governments.[47] Ratner provides additional evidence of the close cooperation between the EU and the HCNM, citing, for instance, a July 1999 letter by Van den Broek written at the request of the HCNM, in which the EU commissioner emphasised that the OSCE, the CE, and the EU were all agreed on the need to change Latvia's discriminatory language laws.[48]

## ARE THE CONDITIONALITY POLICIES THE RIGHT POLICIES?

There are two main goals in instituting or changing minority rights policies. The first is the goal of preventing conflict, especially the worst types of violent conflict between ethnic majorities and minorities. The second goal is to secure individual rights and freedoms and in some cases group rights and freedoms. In this section I will restrict myself to dealing with how EU and HCNM policies address the first goal of conflict prevention. Political scientists have developed two broad approaches to ethnic conflict prevention: the consociational power-sharing approach, best known through the work of Arend Lijphart, and the "incentives" approach, best known through the work of Donald Horowitz.[49]

There is no evidence that I know of that conclusively shows that either the consociational power-sharing or the incentives approach is clearly superior in meeting the goals of preventing or reducing violent conflict. While there have been many case studies that compare the two approaches, there has been no systematic cross-national study that would allow us to determine – when we control for a range of variables such as ethnic heterogeneity, wealth, states' previous histories of conflict, and economic and social inequalities – whether one set of institutions is more strongly associated with lower levels of ethnic violence than another. Single-country studies do not conclusively answer the question. My own empirical work on India suggests that at some times the presence of consociational indicators has been associated with higher levels of Hindu-Muslim violence, while at other times it seems to be associated with a reduction in violence.[50]

Despite the absence of systematic international comparisons, there are several good reasons for believing that "consociational" policies might be good at preventing violence in the short term, especially in sharply divided countries, while incentives policies that encourage strong competition on the part of ethnic majorities for the support of minority voters might be more sustainable and provide lower levels of violence over the long term. In the short term, it will probably be easier to allay fears and secure agreement among ethnic leaders in highly divided societies of the kind that we find in Eastern Europe through consociational policies that guarantee each group a share in power, thus minimizing their losses in the present and near future, rather than hoping that minority influence will make itself felt naturally through the electoral system, perhaps with the aid of alternative voting (AV) and single transferable voting (STV) systems. Ben Reilly and Andrew Reynolds suggest that "centripetal and consensual approaches based on AV or STV elections are likely to work best when there is a degree of fluidity to ethnic identities and lower levels of ethnic conflict, while approaches in which ethnicity was more explicitly recognized (consociationalism and explicitism) may be more appropriate for the more intense conflicts."[51]

Though appropriate for severely divided transitional societies in the short term, consociational policies are likely to be unstable in the longer term for a variety of reasons. The first and most important is that majorities dislike formal permanent agreements that seem to advantage minorities, especially when growing disparities in groups' relative population size or economic welfare seem to be making the original agreements more unfair rather than less.[52] Political leaders who continue to support such agreements are vulnerable to what Horowitz calls "outflanking" by members of their own groups, who can gain popularity by accusing the leaders of selling out. Some research on nineteenth-century local conflict resolution efforts in India suggests that efforts to bring Muslims and Hindus together through formal public agreements failed for just this reason. Public compromise weakened established leaders and encouraged those who wished to displace them politically to polarize people around divisive religious events that often led to Hindu-Muslim riots.[53]

Second, there is what we might term the "constructivist critique" of measures designed to achieve group rights rather than individual rights. It is now widely recognized that individuals have multiple ethnic and non-ethnic identities that shift over time and in response to state and economic incentives. If conditionality leads to policies that privilege only some groups and some identities, and gives these groups guaranteed representation and powers, what happens when new groups and subgroups emerge in the future, particularly when the existing groups have a minority veto over moves that threaten their privileges?[54]

Third, there is the question of what will happen to consociational agreements brought into being through conditionality once the international organization that forced their acceptance and implementation is no longer monitoring the situation or no longer willing to use its leverage to secure compliance with the agreement. The Russian government, for example, strongly protested the OSCE's closing of its missions in Estonia and Latvia in January 2002 on the grounds that the governments of those countries could not be relied upon to protect the rights of their Russian minorities. Once countries enter the EU, the prospects appear bleak for subsequent EU monitoring that has a real enforcement mechanism with sanctions. The OSCE and the CE are unlikely to provide it, since until now they have even avoided passing comments on Western European countries' policies out of fear that criticism of their role by the West could endanger their overall mandate and undoubted effectiveness in dealing with candidate countries.[55] The EU will probably not provide enforcement either. The EU cannot even persuade members to observe existing mandates over the size of state budget deficits – crucial for the European Monetary Union – and so one wonders whether there will be any serious attempt to prevent backsliding over minority rights, which are generally regarded as a less critical part of EU policy.

Fourth, consociational policies might not be good at preventing violence in the long term if, as some studies suggest, it is the level of political competition in the state as a whole – rather than the presence or absence of consociational power sharing at the national level – that explains most of the variation in anti-minority violence.[56] My analysis of state-level Hindu-Muslim riot occurrence in India from 1961 to 1995 found that there is a negative relationship between party competition and violence, even when we control for previous violence and the party in power in a particular state.[57] I argue that this is because an increase in the number of parties is the product of greater intra-Hindu competition for the Muslim vote, and that this competition gives majority-controlled governments a strong incentive to protect minorities.

## WHY ARE THE POLICIES CHOSEN?

Why do the EU, the OSCE, and the CE propose consociational policies when we have so little data in the way of systematic findings about which policies really do prevent or reduce violence, at least in the long term? This question is especially intriguing given that in some cases the consociational policies proposed for new entrants are at odds with existing practice in many EU member states.[58] Several EU member countries, for example, have refused to ratify the CE's Framework Convention on National Minorities – including France, whose constitution specifies the indivisibility of the French nation, and Belgium, where the Framework is opposed by the Flemish – yet applicant countries are being urged to sign the Framework in order to conform with "international" and "EU" standards.

The first explanation for why these policies are being proposed lies in who is proposing them. Many of the people who staff the HCNM and the CE advisory committee have either grown up in consociational democracies where proportionality and elite inter-group consensus are enshrined as values or else are from academic and intellectual circles where such policies as proportionality, grand coalitions, and minority vetoes are thought to be the natural solution to ethnic problems. Prior to 1999, Van der Stoel worked in close concert with EU Commissioner Van den Broek, his fellow Dutch politician, and both presumably drew from their long experience in the proportional system characteristic of conflict moderation in the Netherlands.[59] These two officials were in regular contact and coordinated on many important sets of policy recommendations.[60] Moreover, Van der Stoel recruited his own staff, the staff for the Foundation for Interethnic Relations (the research and operational wing of his office), and the various independent committees of experts brought in to help draft consensus "best practice" documents on minority rights in general and linguistic rights in particular (the Hague, Lund, and Oslo recommendations).

When I asked one of the participants in drafting the 1999 Lund recommendations about the form of the committee debates over the power-sharing measures recommended in the report, the participant responded, to my surprise, that essentially there was no debate: "People were all pretty much of a similar mind on issues of PR and power sharing. The team had no people who would have favoured majoritarian systems or who would have criticized consociational systems ... The answer to your question about why the views are the same is the type of people they bring in. There are 20 or so people they could call in and they are generally on the side of power sharing ... There are only two or three people who are known to put forward the other view, and they aren't usually at these meetings." In response to a question about why the views of the OSCE committees so often seemed to differ from those of some EU members, particularly the French, the interviewee responded: "I've been to lots of these things over the years, and now I come to think of it, I haven't been to one where there was a French expert there. Lots of Scandinavians, Germans, and some Spanish, but never a Frenchman or woman."[61]

The second factor in explaining why policies have been put forward that may not reflect a European consensus is that the CE, the HCNM, and the EU commissioner for enlargement have had a high degree of autonomy in devising recommendations and in their negotiations with states. The HCNM has not sought to take his recommendations to the Permanent Council of the OSCE for approval, nor has the council asked him to, because both he and the OSCE recognize that the OSCE founding principle of consensus decision making makes it highly likely that one or more countries would block the HCNM's recommendations – with potentially disastrous effects on the credibility of the HCNM when he presses for constitutional changes in Eastern Europe.[62] Many of the initial restrictions on the HCNM – for example, regulations limiting whom he could bring in as outside experts, specifying when expert teams could go to countries, and requiring that the HCNM inform the chairman-in-office of the OSCE prior to country visits – have not in practice been enforced.[63] In order to bolster the HCNM's position and secure their own objectives, the OSCE Permanent Council and the EU take every opportunity to praise his work, express their support for his initiatives, and give him a great deal of autonomy.

One of the reasons why the EU members have been content to allow the OSCE, the CE, and the European Commission to define new norms in minority rights for applicant countries that contradict their own practices is because there has been no suggestion that these norms or recommendations ought to apply, in the near term at least, to countries in Western Europe. For one thing, the initial 1992 mandate that created the position of high commissioner explicitly prevented him from dealing with minorities that used organized acts of terrorism. This clause was inserted at the insistence of Turkey and the United Kingdom, which were concerned about interference in the Kurdish and Northern Ireland issues, but it also clearly prohibits investigations into the rights of such groups as the Corsicans in France or the Basques in Spain, who have also used terrorism.[64] The 1992 mandate also specified that the HCNM should provide "early warning" of conflicts, which seems to prevent the commissioner from looking at stable Western European democracies where the risk of violent ethnic conflicts seems to be considerably less than in Eastern Europe.[65] Lastly, the HCNM has judiciously decided not to antagonize governments that have the power to undercut his authority and mandates should they wish to do so. When I asked someone who worked at the HCNM's office in the late 1990s about why the HCNM chose not to intervene in Western Europe, he replied: "The question comes up from time to time ... he [Van der Stoel] has decided that he's not going to deal with Western Europe ... He feels that would undercut his mandate. The French aren't big fans of him ... overall though he has broad-based support ... but he doesn't want to risk that by intervening in Western Europe."[66]

A third reason why consociational policies are favoured is because they allow several different constituencies – the applicant countries, the OSCE, and the EU – to demonstrate short-term progress on minority rights issues to their key constituencies. It might be true that a proportional outcome for minorities that reflects political give and take and compromise as a result of electoral competition might be more sustainable and lead to less ethnic conflict and even violence than the same outcome resulting from a set of consociational-style reforms. But it seems clear that consociational policies will provide a bigger payoff in the short term, both for applicant governments and the HCNM. Short-term action on proportionality is preferable for the governments involved because it helps them meet admission criteria for the EU immediately, and preferable for the EU and the HCNM because it allows them to demonstrate that their policies have led to measurable achievements that protect minorities.

CONCLUSION

This chapter argues that EU conditionality "works," at least in the narrow sense of forcing applicant countries to change their policies in order to become eligible for EU admission. The EU has skilfully used the HCNM and the CE as "ratings agencies" in order to certify applicant countries as meeting international standards on minority rights, and the HCNM especially has used this authority to persuade states to change many of their policies. But, in the longer term, there has to be considerable doubt as to whether these short-term policy "successes" will prevent conflict. For one thing, there is some reason to think that the policies that have been recommended – many of which are consociational – may not be the most effective at preventing long-term conflict. For another, even if these policies are highly effective in the short term, it is not clear that the EU will have the political will to police the implementation of them once the applicant countries become members, especially given the wide divergence in current practice on these issues within the community. The fourteen-country EU boycott of Austrian ministers in 2000 over the presence of the anti-immigrant right wing Freedom Party in Austria's coalition government broke down after a few months, largely because of growing rifts among the EU members over the extent to which such collective action was legitimate, and because of worries over a growing backlash in Austria and elsewhere over what was seen as EU bullying and interference. This type of problem over enforcement will surely become even more acute over the next decade as more countries join the union.


## NOTES

1 I am grateful to Judith Kelley, my colleague at Duke University, for sharing with me her expertise on the enlargement process and conditionality during several conversations. Several people who worked in the office of the HCNM during the 1990s agreed to be interviewed by me and provided valuable insights. At Duke, Sinziana Popa and Adam Brinegar provided valuable research assistance by obtaining copies of EU and OSCE documents and reviewing the literature on conditionality.

2 I am not saying that this is the prime EU objective. The EU also asks for financial and other reforms.

3 "Bank Aid Strategy Flawed Says Departing Chief Economist," *Financial Times*, 29 November 1999 (cited in Judith Kelley, "Political Conditionality: European Institutions and Ethnic Politics" [book manuscript, August 2002], 64–5.)

4 James Caporaso *The European Union: Dilemmas of Regional Integration* (Boulder, Colo.: Westview Press 2000), 107.

5 Commission of the European Communities, *2001 Regular Report on Slovenia's Progress towards Accession* (Brussels, 13 November 2001), 14.

6 Judith Kelley, "Membership, Management and Enforcement: European Institutions and Eastern Europe's Ethnic Politics" (paper, Annual Meeting of the American Political Science Association, Boston 2002), 12.

7 Kelley, "Political Conditionality."

8 Steven R. Ratner, "Does International Law Matter in Preventing Ethnic Conflict?" *N.Y.U. Journal of International Law and Politics* 32 (1999–2000): 591–698, 604–5.

9 Ratner, "Does International Law Matter?"

10 Ratner, "Does International Law Matter?" 606–7. For a sympathetic view of this process of mandate expansion, see Jonathan Cohen, "Conflict Prevention in the OSCE: An Assessment of Capacities" (Netherlands Institute of International Relations, Clingendael, October 1999). Website: <www.clingendael.nl/cru/pdf/cohen.pdf>.

11 Ratner "Does International Law Matter?" 624–5.

12 For example, the 2001 accession report on Poland notes that "in Poland, respect for and protection of minorities continues to be assured and as noted above, during the reporting period Poland ratified the Council of Europe Framework Convention for the Protection of National Minorities." EU *Regular Report on Poland's Progress towards Accession* (Brussels, 13 November 2001), 24.

13 "The EU also considers the Human Dimension to be crucial in its relations with other participating states, including in the context of the enlargement process of the EU. The EU is fully committed to supporting the OSCE institutions that are working to implement the OSCE normative 'acquis' and thus prevent conflict. The Union is a major contributor to the OSCE, its field missions and institutions." Council of the European Union, *European Union Annual Report on Human Rights* (Brussels 2001), 54–5, 65, 104–5.

14 Kelley "Political Conditionality," 118–21.

15 "EU/Belarus: Union Regrets Minsk Attitude to OSCE," *European Report*, 21 September 2002, 513.

16 Website: <www.humanrights.coe.int/Minorities/Eng/FrameworkConvention/AdvisoryCommittee/Opinions/Estonia.htm>.

17 Interviews with former HCNM/Foundation on Inter-Ethnic Relations staffers, 18 and 22 October 2002.

18 The information on which this analysis is based is incomplete since the OSCE website does not include all the letters the HCNM has written to all countries.

19 See, e.g., Jane Mansbridge, "Should Blacks Represent Blacks and Women Represent Women? A Contingent 'yes,'" *Journal of Politics*, 61, no.3 (1999): 628–57.

20 Commission of the European Communities, *2000 Regular Report from the Commission on Bulgaria's Progress towards Accession* (Brussels, 8 November 2000), 22–3.

21 Commission of the European Communities, *2001 Regular Report on Slovenia's Progress towards Accession* (Brussels, 13 November 2001), 21.

22 Advisory Committee on the Framework Convention for the Protection of National Minorities, Opinion on Hungary, 22 September 2000. Website: <www.humanrights.coe.int/Minorities/Eng/FrameworkConvention/AdvisoryCommittee/Opinions/Hungary.htm>.

23 Advisory Committee on the Framework Convention for the Protection of National Minorities, Opinion on Romania, 6 April 2001. Website: <www.humanrights.coe.int/Minorities/Eng/FrameworkConvention/AdvisoryCommittee/Opinions/Romania.htm>.

24 Max Van der Stoel, HCNM, to Hennady Udovenko, minister of foreign affairs of Ukraine, 12 October 1995. Website: <www.riga.lv/minelres/count/ukraine/941012r.htm>. Emphasis added.

25 Max Van der Stoel, HCNM, to Lázló Kovacs, minister of foreign affairs of the Republic of Hungary, 26 February 1996. Website: <www.osce.org/hcnm/documents/recommendations/hungary/1996/36hc86.html>.

26 Max Van der Stoel, HCNM, to Stevo Crvenkovski, minister of foreign affairs of the former Yugoslav Republic of Macedonia [FYROM], 16 November 1994 (OSCE web site).

27 On a few occasions the HCNM has also supported firm guidelines for ethnic proportionality in education. See, e.g., the discussion of the need to retain quotas for Albanian admission to Macedonian educational institutions in the "Statement on inter-ethnic relations in FYROM by OSCE High Commissioner on National Minorities," The Hague, 9 November 1998. Website: <www.osce.org/news/generate.php?3news_id=831>.

28 Commission of the European Communities, *2000 Regular Report on Bulgaria's Progress towards Accession* (Brussels, 8 November 2000), 22–3.

29 See, e.g., Advisory Committee on the Framework Convention for the Protection of National Minorities, Opinion on Estonia, 14 September 2001. Website: <www.humanrights.coe.int/Minorities/Eng/FrameworkConvention/

AdvisoryCommittee/Opinions/Estonia.htm>. These measures – provided for in Article 4(2) of the Framework Convention – do not conflict with the convention's prohibition against discrimination on ethnic grounds because, under Article 4(3), any measures taken to "promote, in all areas of economic, social, political and cultural life, full and effective equality between persons belonging to a national minority and those belonging to a majority ... shall not be considered to be an act of discrimination." European Treaty Series (ETS) 157 – National Minorities Convention.

30 The commissioner has highlighted the importance of merit as a criterion several times in his recommendations. However, none of his recommendations specifies how to balance the two, and all his specific recommendations focus on policies that will lead to ethnic proportionality.

31 He went on to argue that "it would then be difficult to believe that such an imbalance would not constitute a violation of article 17 of the Constitution which states: 'citizens of the Republic have equal rights to access to the state service.'" Max Van der Stoel, HCNM, to minister of foreign affairs, government of Kazakhstan, 14 June 1994. Website: <www.osce.org/hcnm/documents/recommendations/kazakhstan/1994/14c264.html>. Similar wording on the need to rectify ethnic imbalances is used in the HCNM's letter to the FYROM on the need to increase Albanian representation. Max Van der Stoel, HCNM, to Stevo Crvenkovski, minister of foreign affairs of the FYROM, 16 November 1994. Website: <www.osc.org>.

32 HCNM, *Report on the Situation of Roma and Sinti in the OSCE Area*, April 2000.

33 Max Van der Stoel, HCNM, to Stevo Crvenkovski, minister of foreign affairs of the FYROM, 16 November 1994. Website: <www.osce.org>.

34 Website: <www.osce.org/hcnm/documents/recommendations/lund/index.php3>.

35 Max Van der Stoel, HCNM, to Latvian minister of foreign affairs, 6 April 1993. Website: <www.osce.org>.

36 Recommendations by the CSCE high commissioner on national minorities upon his visits to Estonia, Latvia, and Lithuania. Website: <www.osce.org>.

37 Max Van der Stoel, HCNM, to Lázló Kovacs, minister of foreign affairs of the Republic of Hungary, 24 August 1995, 923/952. Website: <www.osce.org>.

38 Jose Leandro and Hartwig Schaefer, "Towards a More Effective Conditionality: An Operational Framework," *World Development* 27, no.2 (1999): 285–99; Randall Stone, *Lending Credibility: The IMF and the Post-Communist Transition* (Princeton, N.J.: Princeton University Press 2002); T. Killick, "Principles, Agents and the Failings of Conditionality," *Journal of International Development* 9, no.4 (1997): 497–506; P. Collier,

P. Guillaumont, S. Guillaumont, and J.W. Gunning, "Redesigning Condi-
tionality," *World Development* 25, no.9 (1997): 1399–1408; T. Killick, *The
Adaptive Economy: Adjustment Policies in Small, Low-Income Countries*
(Washington D.C.: World Bank 1993).

39 Margit Sarv, "Integration by Reframing Legislation: Implementation of the
Recommendations of the OSCE High Commissioner on National Minorities
to Estonia, 1993–2001" (University of Hamburg, CORE Working Paper
Number 7, 2002), 100.

40 Kelley, "Membership, Management," 23; István Horváth, "Facilitating
Conflict Transformation: Implementation of the Recommendations of the
OSCE High Commissioner on National Minorities to Romania, 1993–
2001" (University of Hamburg, CORE Working Paper Number 8, 2002), 19.

41 Caporaso, *European Union*, provides a good description of the process.

42 Kelley, "Political Conditionality," 5–10.

43 Kelley, "Membership, Management," 9.

44 Ibid., 27–8.

45 Sarv, "Integration by Reframing," 100.

46 Vladimir Kulyk, "Revisiting a Success Story: Implementation of the
Recommendations of the OSCE High Commissioner on National Minorities
to Ukraine, 1994–2001" (University of Hamburg, CORE Working Paper
Number 6, 2002).

47 Interview with former HCNM/Foundation on Inter-Ethnic Relations staffer,
18 October 2002.

48 Ratner, "Does International Law Matter?" 13.

49 See Lijphart, *Democracy in Plural Societies*, and Horowitz, *Ethnic Groups
in Conflict*. Both of these approaches stand in opposition to two normatively questionable models: the assimilationist model in which minorities
are coerced into membership of the dominant ethnic group, and the "control" model in which subordinate ethnic groups are suppressed to allow
the dominant group to exercise complete power over politics and the
economy. The classic historical description of the assimilationist model is
in Eugen Weber's *Peasants into Frenchmen* (Stanford, Calif.: Stanford
University Press 1976). The control model is described, though I should
point out definitely *not* advocated, by Ian Lustick in "Stability in Deeply
Divided Societies: Consociationalism versus Control," *World Politics* 31,
no.3 (1979): 325–44.

50 I find that proportionality is sometimes associated with a lower level of
conflict. See Steven Ian Wilkinson, *Votes and Violence: Electoral Competition and Ethnic Riots in India* (Cambridge, U.K.: Cambridge University

Press 2004). Compare Steven I. Wilkinson, "India, Consociational Theory and Ethnic Violence," *Asian Survey* 40, no.5 (2000): 767–91.

51 Ben Reilly and Andrew Reynolds. *Electoral Systems and Conflict in Divided Societies* (Washington, D.C.: National Academy Press 1994), 48.

52 As Horowitz puts it, "formal guarantees are virtually always resented by the group on which they are imposed in the same measure as they are insisted upon by the group seeking to benefit from them." Donald L. Horowitz, *A Democratic South Africa: Constitutional Engineering in a Divided Society* (Berkeley: University of California Press 1991), 44.

53 Katherine Prior, "Making History: The State's Intervention in Urban Religious Disputes in the North-Western Provinces in the Early Nineteenth Century," *Modern Asian Studies* 27, no.1 (1993): 179–203.

54 Lijphart has recognized the worth of the constructivist critique of his original model of consociationalism. See Arend Lijphart, "Self-Determination versus Pre-Determination of Ethnic Minorities in Power-Sharing Systems," in Will Kymlicka, ed., *The Rights of Minority Cultures* (Oxford, U.K.: Oxford University Press 1995), 275–87. However, his solution – the regular self-definition of ethnic or non-ethnic groups through PR elections – does not fix the key problem of what to do when the new groups defined by these PR elections demand substantial changes to the existing consociational system and the original groups respond by exercising their minority veto to prevent reforms.

55 Kelley, "Political Conditionality."

56 Wilkinson, *Electoral Competition.*

57 This analysis was of Hindu-Muslim riot data that I collected collaboratively in 1994–96 with Ashutosh Varshney, now of the University of Michigan.

58 Frank Schimmelfennig, Stefan Engert, and Heiko Knobel, "The Conditions of Conditionality: The Impact of the EU on Democracy and Human Rights in European Non-Member States" (working paper, European University Institute, Florence, March 2002), 10, citing work by Antoaneta Dimitrova and Heather Grabbe.

59 While the Netherlands is no longer the classic "pillarized" consociational democracy, a recent review article by Ruud Koole and Hans Daalder shows that, despite the decline of religious ideology as a force in the Netherlands, as well as the decline of the Christian Democrats as a party, several key aspects of consociational practice – in particular, elite accommodation and proportionality – are still alive and well. Ruud Koole and Hans Daalder, "The Consociational Democracy Model and the Netherlands: Ambivalent Allies?" *Acta Politica: International Journal of Political Science* 37 (Special

Issue on "Consociationalism and Corporatism in Western Europe," 2002): 23–43.

60 Interview with a former member of the HCNM/Foundation on Inter-Ethnic Relations staff, 18 October 2002.

61 Interview with a participant in the Lund meetings, 7 October 2002.

62 The Lund, Copenhagen, and Hague proposals on minority rights have not been formally adopted by the OSCE's Permanent Council precisely because of opposition to some of their proposals by a few countries. In pushing the proposals, their supporters argue that the proposals nonetheless have clout because they have been discussed in the Permanent Council.

63 Cohen, "Conflict Prevention in the OSCE," 55, 80.

64 CSCE Helsinki Document 1992: The Challenges of Change, Section II, "CSCE High Commissioner on National Minorities," Clause 5b, 6, 7–13. Website: <http://www.osce.org/docs/english/1990–1999/summits/hels92e.pdf>.

65 Hans-Joachim Heintze, "Minority Issues in Western Europe and the OSCE High Commissioner on National Minorities," *International Journal on Minority and Group Rights* 7 (2000): 381–92.

66 Interview, 22 October 2002.

# 13

# Federation as a Method of Ethnic Conflict Regulation

JOHN McGARRY AND BRENDAN O'LEARY

Federations are distinct political systems.[1] In a genuinely democratic federation there is a compound sovereign state in which at least two governmental units, the federal and the regional, enjoy constitutionally separate competencies – although they may also have concurrent powers. Both the federal and the regional governments are empowered to deal directly with their citizens, and the relevant citizens directly elect at least some components of the federal and regional governments. In a federation, the federal government usually cannot unilaterally alter the horizontal division of powers: constitutional change affecting competencies requires the consent of both levels of government. Therefore, federation automatically implies a codified and written constitution and normally is accompanied at the federal level by a supreme court, charged with umpiring differences between the governmental tiers, and by a bicameral legislature in which the federal – as opposed to the popular – chamber may disproportionately represent the smaller regions. Daniel Elazar emphasises the "covenantal" character of federations; that is, the authority of each government is derived from a constitution and convention rather than from another government.[2]

Federations vary in the extent to which they are majoritarian in character but most constrain the power of federation-wide majorities; in particular, they constrain the federal *demos*, though there is extensive variation in this respect.[3] The United States, Australia, and Brazil allow equal representation to each of their regions in the federal chamber, which means massive over-representation for the smaller ones. Other federations also over-represent less populous units, but not to this extent. Federations differ additionally in the competencies granted to the upper house or federal chamber. Some chambers, such as the United States Senate, are extremely powerful, and arguably more powerful than the House of Representatives because of its special powers over nominations to public office and in treaty making. Others, including those in Canada, India, and Belgium, are weak.[4] In some instances, a single state, province, or region can block constitutional change, but normally a veto requires a coalition of two or more such entities. Negatively defined, a federation is majoritarian to the extent that it lacks consociational practices of executive power sharing, proportionality principles of representation and allocation, cultural autonomy, and veto rights. Further, it is majoritarian to the extent that it lacks consensual institutions or practices – such as the separation of powers, bills of rights, and courts and monetary institutions insulated from immediate governing majorities. A majoritarian federation concentrates power and resources at the federal level and facilitates executive and legislative dominance either by a popularly endorsed executive president or by a single-party premier and cabinet.

The federal principle of separate competencies says nothing about how much power each level enjoys. Regions in some federations may enjoy less *de facto* power than those in decentralized unitary states. The constitutional division of powers (even as interpreted by the courts) is not always an accurate guide to the policy-making autonomy and discretion enjoyed by different tiers. Some powers may have fallen into abeyance, or the superior financial and political resources of one level (usually the federal) may allow it to interfere in the other's jurisdiction. A better indicator of the degree of autonomy enjoyed by regions may be the proportion of public spending that is directly under their control.

A key distinction for our purposes is that federations can be multinational/multi-ethnic or mono-national in character. In the former, the boundaries of the internal units are usually drawn in such a way that national or ethnic minorities control at least some of them. In addition, more than one nationality may be explicitly recognized as co-founders and co-owners of the federation. The first such federation was Switzerland, established in its current from in 1848, and the second was Canada, established in 1867. The Indian subcontinent was divided after decolonization into the two multi-ethnic federations of India and Pakistan. Africa has two federations, Nigeria and Ethiopia, while South Africa appears federal in all but name. The communist Soviet Union, Yugoslavia, and Czechoslovakia were organized as multinational federations, and the Russian Republic, one of the constituent units of the Soviet Union, was itself organized along federal lines. These communist federations, which did not bestow genuine democratic self-government on their minorities, fell apart in the early 1990s (although Yugoslavia continued as a dyadic federation incorporating Serbia and Montenegro until 2003, when it was transformed into a confederation).[5] Bosnia-Herzegovina became a multinational federation under the internationally enforced Dayton Accord of 1995, with one of its units itself being a bi-national federation of Bosniacs and Croats. Belgium has recently evolved into a federation, and both Euro-optimists and pessimists think that the European Union (EU) is moving in the same direction. Multinational federations have been proposed for a significant number of other divided societies, including Afghanistan, Burma, China, Cyprus, Georgia, Iraq, and Indonesia.

National federations may be nationally or ethnically homogeneous (or predominantly so), or they may be organized, often consciously, so as not to recognize more than one official nationality. This often happens in such a way that the state's national and ethnic minorities are also minorities in each of the constituent units. The intention behind national federalism is nation building and the elimination of internal national (and perhaps also ethnic) differences. The founding and paradigmatic example of a national federation is the United States. The Latin American federations of Mexico, Argentina, Brazil, and Venezuela adopted its model. Germany, Austria, Australia, and the United Arab Emirates are also national federations. American and American-educated intellectuals often propose national federations as a way to deal with ethnic heterogeneity in post-colonial and post-communist societies.

This chapter is primarily concerned with multinational and multi-ethnic federations. We shall first discuss the debate on the value and feasibility of federations as management devices for ethnic and national differences. Then, we will turn to the track record of multinational federations in mitigating conflict, concluding with an analysis of the factors that contribute to their success and failure.

THE DEBATE: NATIONALISM AND FEDERALISM
IN PRACTICAL POLITICAL DESIGN
AND ARGUMENT

There are four important positions on the value of federalism and
federation as a method of accommodating national and ethnic minorities. All have been articulated by intellectuals, constitutional lawyers,
and political scientists, and all have had an effect on the design of
particular states.

## 1. Jacobin Unitarism: Federalism as State Destroying

In the French revolutionary tradition, associated with the Jacobins,
federalism was part of the counter-revolution, hostile to the necessity
of linguistic homogenization, a roadblock in the path of authentic,
indivisible, monistic popular sovereignty. Rather than accommodating
minorities through self-government, the Jacobins sought cultural assimilation; they were determined to make peasants into Frenchmen; and
therefore they were deeply hostile to all forms of accommodation that
inhibited this goal, including federalism. The Jacobin response to diversity was a strong unitary state and one French nation. This tradition
survives in contemporary France, where it is central to the myth of the
French Republic.[6] Those in the Jacobin tradition see federalism, with
its multiple governments, as incompatible with equal citizenship and a
sovereign people. This is not just a concern about regional governments
creating uneven ("patchwork quilt") public policy. Latter-day Jacobins
cannot accept the federal principle that allows citizens in regions with
small populations to be over-represented at the expense of those in
more populous regions, and they have difficulty with the federal idea
of a judicial umpire who can overrule the people's elected representatives.[7]

Modern Jacobins think that the accommodation of minorities and
ethnocentrism go together. If minorities do not want to promote ethnocentrism, the argument goes, why do they seek self-government?
They think that political recognition of multiple nations or ethnic
communities leads to regressive government and discrimination against
minorities dominated by local or regional majorities, and institutional-
izes and reinforces divisions, endangering national/state unity. These
views are shared on the left and right. French communists, for example,
claim that Paris's proposals to give self-government to Corsica will

undermine "solidarity between Corsican and French workers, who can only defend their interests by working together" and will lead to discriminatory measures against those on the island who are not of Corsican descent.[8] In 2001 the then French interior minister, Pierre Chevenement, resigned over the proposals, protesting that they would lead to an "island ruled by an underworld that spends three-quarters of its energy settling accounts and internal battles."[9] While the proposals for Corsica fall short of federation, both Chevenement and French President Jacques Chirac attacked them as leading in that direction: Brittany, Alsace, and Savoy, as well as French Basques and Catalans, they alleged, would follow Corsica's lead.[10] Ultimately, in this view, federation promotes state break-up, with the attendant risks of ethnic cleansing and Matrioschka-doll secessions emerging as ethnic nationalism takes hold.

The Jacobin view that unitarism is needed for unity – if not always other Jacobin views, such as support for civic equality and popular sovereignty – is replicated throughout the world. It was the dominant view in Great Britain until recently, particularly among Conservatives. Most ex-colonies in Africa, Asia, and the Caribbean have shunned federalism as an obstacle to economic development, political stability, and state unity. Post-colonial state builders' antipathy to federalism is now matched among the intellectuals and governing elites of Eastern Europe, who regard it as a recipe for disaster, given the Czechoslovakian, Yugoslavian, and Soviet experiences. Federalism is their "f" word. The recent emergent principle of international law, stemming from the report of the Badinter Commission on the former Yugoslavia, which permits the disintegration of federations along the lines of their existing regional units, may strengthen the belief that federation should not be considered a desirable form of multinational or multi-ethnic accommodation.[11] Several Eastern European states have moved in the opposite direction in recent years, replacing multinational federations with what Rogers Brubaker calls "nationalizing" states, that is, states that are tightly centralized and controlled by their dominant national community.

Ironically, "hardline" nationalists trapped inside states controlled by other nations share the Jacobin argument that federalism is incompatible with nation building. They concur that nation and state should be congruent, although they disagree on the appropriate boundaries. This has been the position of Quebec's Parti Québécois, particularly the faction around the ex-premier Jacques Parizeau, and of the Basque nationalist party, Batasuna. It is also the view of the Chechens and, until recently, the Turkish Cypriots and the Liberation Tigers of Tamil Eelam. Such hardliners seek independence as unitary, sovereign, and indivisible nation-states, although some are prepared to consider confederation.[12]

## 2. Federalism as Nation Building

Unlike the Jacobins, who see state nationalism and federalism as inconsistent, some exponents of federalism think that state nationalism and federalism go together. The earliest federalists in the German-speaking Swiss lands, and in what became the Netherlands, the United States, and Germany, were "national federalists" – i.e., they saw the prime function of federalism as being "to unite people living in different political units, who nevertheless shared a common language and culture."[13] They maintained that only an autonomous federal government could perform certain necessary functions that confederations or alliances found difficult to perform, especially a unified defence and external relations policy.[14] They advocated federation as a tool for nation building and sometimes saw it as a stepping-stone towards a more centralized unitary state.

American national federalists have little difficulty with what Jacobins consider the "*demos*-constraining" features of federalism: radical autonomy for regions or states (non-centralization), the over-representation of small states in upper chambers, electoral colleges, and constitutional amending formulas. Alfred Stepan has argued that the United States competes with Brazil for the title of the world's most *demos*-constraining federation.[15] The attractiveness of demos-constraining institutions reflects the historic stress of some Americans on liberty rather than equality. The American founding myth is of colonies that won independence from empire. Many Americans reject the strong state favoured by French republicans and praise federalism precisely because it diffuses power to multiple points. American exponents of federalism, such as William H. Riker, have argued that the *demos*-constraining features of American federalism are liberal because they protect individuals from populist majorities.[16] Americans insisted on a federation for post-war Germany because they were convinced that it would make a resurgence of fascism less likely. The view that federalism is essential to liberty is central to American discourse, in spite of the abysmal track record of federalism in all of the Latin American federations, as well as in Pakistan, Nigeria, and the Soviet Union.

But America's makers and their celebrants have taken the position that federalism is antithetical to nation building if it is multinational, multi-ethnic, or "ethno-federal." As the United States expanded southwestward from its original largely homogeneous (except for African slaves) thirteen colonies, it was decided that no territory would receive statehood unless white Anglo-Saxon Protestants (WASPs) outnumbered minorities.[17] Sometimes, the technique employed was to gerrymander state boundaries to ensure that Indians or Hispanics were outnumbered, as in Florida. At other times, as in Hawaii and the southwest, statehood was delayed until the region's long-standing residents could be swamped with enough WASP settlers. American authorities were even sceptical of immigrant groups concentrating in particular locations lest this lead to ethnically based demands for self-government, and grants of public land were denied to ethnic groups in order to promote their dispersal. William Penn, for example, dissuaded Welsh immigrants from setting up their own self-governing barony in Pennsylvania.[18] In consequence, the U.S. federation shows "little coincidence between ethnic groups and state boundaries."[19] National federalism was part and parcel of American nation building, aiding the homogenization of white settlers and immigrants in the famous melting pot of anglo-conformity.[20] Celebration of the homogeneity of the founding people is evident in *The Federalist Papers*.[21]

America's experience with federalism has informed an interesting argument over how federalism can be used to manage divisions in contemporary ethnically heterogeneous societies. Donald Horowitz[22] and Daniel Elazar,[23] building on earlier work by S.M. Lipset[24] (and, indeed, on an important American tradition that goes back to James Madison), suggest that federations can be partly designed to prevent ethnic minorities from becoming local provincial majorities. The strategic thinking here is to weaken potentially competing ethno-nationalisms: federalism's territorial merits are said to lie in the fact that it can be used as an instrument to prevent local majoritarianism, with its attendant risks of local tyrannies of the majority, or of secessionist incentives. The borders of the federated units, in this argument, should be designed according to "balance of power" principles, i.e., proliferating points of power and directing them away from one focal centre, encouraging intra-ethnic conflict, and offering incentives for inter-ethnic cooperation (for example, by creating provinces without majorities) and alignments based on non-ethnic interests. This logic is interesting, but empirical support for it seems so far confined to the rather uninspiring case of post-bellum Nigeria.[25] In most existing federations, to redraw regional borders deliberately to achieve these results would probably require the services of military dictators or one-party states.[26] Historically, mobilized ethno-national groups have not taken kindly to efforts to redraw internal political boundaries.

American (small "r") republicans have shared with Jacobins the view that minority nationalists are backward, representing a "revolt against modernity,"[27] or people who "tend to subordinate all free government to [their] uncompromising position."[28] Republicans think that it is both counterproductive and unnecessary to accommodate minority nationalists. This view may have been strengthened by America's own experience in the Deep South, where southern whites used their control of state governments to oppress blacks. America's disastrous civil war over secession attuned its intellectuals to the centrifugal potential of federalism, particularly when distinct cultural communities control regions. Eric Nordlinger, one of the first contemporary American political scientists to take an interest in ethnic conflict regulation, rejected the use of federalism as an instrument for accommodating minorities, since he feared that it would lead to state break-up and the abuse of power by ethnocentric minorities.[29]

Reflecting these sentiments, a number of American academics have argued that the break-up of the former communist federations and the accompanying chaos can be traced squarely to "ethno-federal" structures. Rogers Brubaker, for example, maintains that the Soviet regime went to "remarkable lengths, long before glasnost and perestroika, to institutionalize both territorial nationhood and ethnocultural nationality as basic cognitive and social categories." Once political space began to expand under Mikhail Gorbachev, these categories quickly came to "structure political perception, inform political rhetoric, and organize political action."[30] The implication is that at least some of these divisive identities did not exist before the Soviet Union federated and would not have come into play had it not federated. In Jack Snyder's view, "ethnically based federalisms ... create political organizations and media markets that are centered on ethnic differences." According to him, the decision to establish ethno-federations in the Soviet Union, Czechoslovakia, and Yugoslavia was unnecessary: "Arguably, ethnofederalism was a

strategy of rule actively chosen by its Communist founders, not a necessity forced upon them by the irresistible demands of ethnic groups."[31]
The results of ethno-federalism, Snyder claims, were straightforward:
only the communist federations broke up and "nationalist violence
happened only where ... ethnofederal institutions channelled political
activity along ethnic lines (USSR and Yugoslavia)."[32]

### 3. Cosmopolitans: Federalism as a Stage in Nation-transcendence

A third perspective holds that federalism is capable of dissolving all
national allegiances, including minority and majority nationalisms. This
perspective comes in two different variants. The first is represented by
several nineteenth-century anarchist and liberal federalists, notably
Joseph Proudhon and Carlo Cattaneo, who were resolutely hostile to
nation-state nationalism.[33] Many twentieth-century liberal federalists,
notably those within the European federalist movement, represent the
second.[34] Such federalists have been, and are, resolutely anti-nationalist,
associating both state and minority nationalisms with ethnic exclusive-
ness, chauvinism, racism, and parochially particularistic sentiments. For
them, federalism belongs to an entirely different cooperative philosophy
– one that offers a non-nationalist logic of legitimacy and is an antidote
to nationalism, rather than a close relative of it. This viewpoint was
most clearly articulated by Pierre Trudeau – before he became Canadian
prime minister.[35] Thinkers like Trudeau regard federalism as both the
denial of and the solution to nationalism, though occasionally they
adopt the view that federalism must be built upon the success of
nationalism, which it then transcends in Hegelian fashion.[36]

The Austro-Marxists Karl Renner and Otto Bauer, during the last
days of the Habsburg Empire, articulated a different perspective.[37] For
them, nationalism had to be accommodated en route to a global
socialist and communist order; and the way to do this, they argued,
was to combine national autonomy with federal and consociational
formats. Lenin and Stalin adapted their argument and pressed it into
service in the Soviet Union. For them, federalism was to be used to
offer a limited accommodation to minority nationalism, but solely
towards the end of building a socialist society. Minorities were to be
offered the fiction, but not the fact, of national self-government.[38]
While this policy was superficially similar to that of multinational
federalists (to be discussed below), Marxist-Leninists were formal

cosmopolitans, committed to a post-nationalist global political order. However, pending the world revolution, they maintained that federal arrangements – "national in form, socialist in content" – were the optimal institutional path to global communism.

### 4. Multinational Federalists: Multinational Maintenance Engineers

Multinational or multi-ethnic federalists, by contrast, advocate federation "to unite people who seek the advantages of membership of a common political unit, but differ markedly in descent, language and culture."[39] They seek to express, institutionalize, and protect at least two national or ethnic cultures, on a durable and often on a permanent basis. Any greater union or homogenization, if envisaged at all, is postponed for the future. They explicitly reject the strongly integrationist and/or assimilationist objectives of national and or post-national federalists, and see these as nation destroying rather than nation building. They believe that dual or multiple national loyalties are possible, and indeed desirable. Multinational federalists represent a third branch of liberalism, distinct from the Jacobin (federalism breaches civic equality) and American (national federalism promotes individual liberty) varieties. For multinational federalists, a proper understanding of liberal individual rights requires respect for the culture of individuals, and this means allowing minorities the power to protect and promote their culture.[40] Unlike unitarists and national federalists, multinational federalists reject the view that minority-controlled governments are more backward or illiberal in their treatment of *their* minorities than majority-controlled central or federal governments. Minority nationalisms are as likely to be of the civic variety as dominant nationalisms, according to these liberals; indeed, Michael Keating argues that contemporary minority nationalisms are strongly modernist, responding to the shift in power from the state to the global marketplace.[41]

Multinational federalism has considerable, albeit critical, support among contemporary academics.[42] Some supporters make quite remarkable claims for federalism. Klaus Von Beyme, referring to Western democracies, in 1985 claimed that "Canada is the only country in which federalism did not prove capable of solving ... ethnic conflict."[43] Others are more modest: Will Kymlicka supports multinational federalism normatively, while acknowledging it faces considerable difficulties in practice.[44] Multinational federalists have been influential in the development of federations in the former British Empire, notably in Canada, the Caribbean, Nigeria, South Africa, India, Pakistan, and Malaysia. Austro-Marxists and Marxist-Leninists, while committed socialists first, espoused multinational federalist principles and have had an enduring impact in the post-communist development of the Russian Federation, Ethiopia, and the rump Yugoslavia. While unitarism has been in the ascendancy in Eastern Europe, multinational federalism has become more popular in Western Europe, as is attested by the decision to create a federation in Belgium and perhaps also by the creation of new decentralized, devolutionary, regional – and potentially federal – institutions in Spain, the United Kingdom, France, and Italy.

Multinational federalists are often "soft" minority nationalists, such as state elites who oppose separation but believe that accommodating national minorities is the key to stability and unity. They include the Quebec Liberal Party, the Basque Nationalist Party (PNV), and the Catalan Convergencia I Unio. The most ambitious multinational federalists of our day are those who wish to develop the European Union from its currently largely confederal form into an explicit federation, a "Europe of the nation-states and a Europe of the citizens," as the German foreign minister recently urged.[45]

Multinational federalists reject the view that every minority must inevitably seek its nation-state, and maintain that even those that do may settle for their own region instead.[46] They argue that, if the borders of the components of the federation match the boundaries of the relevant national, ethnic, religious, or linguistic communities – i.e., if there is a "federal society" that is congruent with the federal institutions – then federation may be an effective harmonizing device. That is precisely because it makes an ethnically heterogeneous political society less heterogeneous through the creation of more homogeneous sub-units. Multinational federalism thus involves an explicit rejection of the unitarist and national federalist argument that self-rule for minorities necessarily conflicts with the territorial integrity of existing states.[47]

National minorities within a multinational federation often argue that they should have powers beyond those enjoyed by the federal units dominated by the national majority: they support asymmetrical federalism, insisting that their distinct status be officially recognized and institutionalized. They may seek to share in powers that are normally the prerogative of the centre or federal government: some minorities, for example, seek a role in federal foreign policy, or to be directly represented in international organizations. This may not mean the same as supporting confederation, because the minorities may be content for most purposes to remain part of a federation, but they are clearly stretching the limits of traditional federations and moving in the direction of confederation.[48]

Multinational federations may originate from the union of previously self-governing ethnic communities, as happened in the case of Switzerland. However, in other cases, multinational federalists may engage in deliberate democratic engineering to match certain ascriptive criteria with internal political borders. This occurred at founding of the Canadian federation in 1867, when the united province of Canada (1841–67) was divided largely along linguistic lines into the separate provinces of Ontario and Quebec. It also happened in post-independence India, where internal state borders were reorganized along linguistic lines.[49] Nigeria has reorganized its internal boundaries on several occasions, to the advantage of certain minorities. Whereas Ibo, Hausa, and Yoruba groups dominated its original tri-partite federation, its current thirty-six-state structure includes fourteen states that are dominated by other groups.[50] Switzerland carved a new canton of Jura (largely French and Catholic) out of the mostly German-speaking canton of Berne in 1979.

## WEIGHING THE EVIDENCE

There is considerable evidence for the French and American republican argument that multinational federalism has, as Snyder puts it, "a terrible track record."[51] Multinational or multi-ethnic federations have either broken down, or have failed to remain democratic, throughout the communist and post-colonial worlds. The federations of the Soviet Union, Yugoslavia, and Czechoslovakia disintegrated during or immediately after their respective democratizations. Indeed, of all the states in the former communist bloc of Eastern Europe, it was only federations that irretrievably broke apart, and all of them did.[52] Moreover, of all these states, it was the federations that experienced the most violent transitions. In the post-colonial world, multinational or multi-ethnic federations failed, or failed to be successfully established, in the Caribbean, a notable example being the West Indies Federation. Even the miniature federation of St Kitts-Nevis recently faced the prospect of break-up.[53] Multinational or multi-ethnic federations have failed in sub-Saharan Africa, in francophone West and Equatorial Africa, in

British East Africa (Kenya, Uganda, and Tanganyika), and in British Central Africa (Northern and Southern Rhodesia and Nyasaland); or have failed to remain durably democratic (Nigeria and Tanzania). The break-up of the Nigerian federation between 1966 and 1969 was prevented only after a secessionist conflict that caused approximately a million deaths. In the Arab world, only the United Arab Emirates has survived, but it is a national federation and hardly democratic. The Mali and the Ethiopian federations in independent Africa broke up, too, while the Cameroons experienced forced unitarism after a federal beginning. In Asia there have been federative failures in Indochina, in Burma, in Pakistan (the secession of Bangladesh), and in the union of Malaya (the secession of Singapore). In short, new multinational federations appear not to work as conflict-regulating devices – even where they allow a degree of minority self-government. They have broken down, or failed to be durably democratic, throughout Asia, Africa, and the Caribbean. India stands out as the major exception in Asia.

It also seems clear that multinational federations make it easier for groups to secede should they want to do so. Federalism provides the minority with political and bureaucratic resources that it can use to launch a bid for independence. Giving a minority its own unit makes it possible for it to hold referendums on secession, which can be useful for gaining recognition. Multinational federations implicitly suggest the principle that the accommodated minorities represent "peoples" who might then be entitled to rights of self-determination under international law. It is far more likely, as the Badinter Commission on the former Yugoslavia confirmed, that the international community would recognize a bid for independence from a federal unit than from a group that lacks such a unit. This is why all of the full constituent units of the Soviet Union, Yugoslavia, and Czechoslovakia that broke away are now seen as independent states, whereas breakaway regions that were not constituent units, such as Abkhazia, Trans-Dniestria, the Turkish Republic of Northern Cyprus, and Kosovo, are not recognized. To this extent, unitarists and national federalists have a point – although it is a point that multinational federalists have little difficulty conceding.[54]

However, this assessment of the track record of multinational federations has to be qualified in five important ways. First, the major communist federal failures – the Soviet Union, Yugoslavia, Czechoslovakia – were, to a significant extent, sham or pseudo-federations. In several cases, they were forced together. The constitutional division of powers and the rule of law were often ignored in practice and they were not authentically representative (i.e., democratic). There was, therefore, no possibility of genuine dialogue, never mind cooperation, among the different national communities involved. In sum, these states had weak or no overarching identities to begin with, and no democratic mechanism for developing them. While the United States can be seen as the paradigmatic example of national federalism, the Soviet Union is the most prominent case of pseudo-federalism. Territorially, it consisted of those remnants of the Tsarist Empire that the Red Army was able to subjugate after the October Revolution, plus those countries (Estonia, Latvia, Lithuania, and Moldova) it conquered as a result of the Ribbentrop-Molotov pact and its victory in the Second World War. While its state structure was federated from the beginning, real power lay in the tightly centralized Communist Party (the CPSU), which operated according to the principle of "democratic centralism."[55] The Soviet Union's republics were therefore not autonomous in any meaningful way. Moreover, their legislatures (the Soviets), although in theory elected by local populations, were in fact rubber-stamp bodies nominated by the CPSU. Key institutions, including the army and police, were controlled by Moscow. No effective judicial review existed to decide on the division of rights and functional spheres between the centre and the republics. Yugoslavia was more decentralized than the Soviet Union or Czechoslovakia, at least after reforms in the late 1960s, but it was no less undemocratic, and was held together by the League of Communists.

Second, the failed colonial federations arose out of colonies that had been arbitrarily consolidated. In some cases, even the decision to federate at independence was made by the departing imperial power rather than the colony's indigenous elites. For example, Nigeria's original three-unit federation, which collapsed in the mid-1960s, was "bequeathed" by the vacating British.[56] The Cameroons federation was a construct of British and French colonialists (particularly the latter), who wanted to preserve the dual personality they thought they had created.[57] The Cameroons were converted into a unitary state by military strongmen soon after independence, while Nigeria has been ruled by centralizing military dictators for more than two-thirds of its post-independence history – and its presidential contenders in recent times have all been ex-generals. Even under democratic conditions, Nigeria is so centralized that it has been described as a "hollow federation" and "a unitary state in federal guise."[58] Corruption and abuse of power are so pervasive that the rule of law can hardly be said to exist.[59]

Third, both communist and post-colonial federations were additionally burdened by economic systems that were incapable of providing a reasonable or growing standard of living for their citizens. In each case this caused resentment, not least among minorities in relatively enterprising regions of the state who saw their inclusion in the federation as a drag on their enterprise. It was therefore hardly surprising that, when the communist planning system became discredited and collapsed in the late 1980s, it produced a legitimacy crisis.

Fourth, the case against multinational federalism would be stronger if it could be shown, as critics claim, that it was unnecessary to accommodate national minorities, and that there were democratic civic-nationalist (unitarist or national-federalist) alternatives that would have worked better, if not much better. Once this claim is probed, however, the critics' position looks less credible. The decision to create both the Soviet and Yugoslav federations was taken in the midst of bitter civil wars and external invasions, when parts of both states had seceded.[60] The decision was regarded as essential for restoring unity and luring breakaway regions back into the state, and it was taken in both cases by socialist internationalists, Lenin and Tito, neither of whom was ideologically committed to multinational federalism. Before he assumed power, Lenin had expressed his vehement opposition to federalism and his clear preference for unitary structures.[61] Tito, before taking power, appeared to be a conventional Leninist. If federalism was unnecessary, we must conclude that both Lenin and Tito were extraordinarily incompetent from their own perspectives. The thesis that communist multinational federalism created divisions cannot explain easily why strong ethnic identities exist among groups that were not accommodated through federal institutions, such as the Chechens or Crimean Tatars.[62] Similarly, while some have argued that Nigeria's divisions at the time of independence reflected British divide-and-rule strategies, few think that the state could have been (or could be) held together without some form of decentralized or federal structure.[63] When an Ibo leader, General Aquiyi Ironsi, tried to convert Nigeria into a centralist state in 1966 it led to his downfall. Even though the Nigerian federation witnessed a failed and bloody bid for secession in Biafra (1967–70), the victors were careful to retain ethno-federal structures, albeit reformed, with new internal boundaries.

Fifth, civic nationalism of the French or American variety has not been particularly successful when it has been applied as an alternative to multinational federation in multinational states, even under seemingly propitious circumstances. Turkey still faces a large dissident Kurdish minority despite eight decades of "Kemalist" civic nationalism. British civic nationalism, within a tightly centralized union at the centre of a global empire, could not prevent the breaking away of Ireland in 1921.[64] Irish nationalists mobilized successfully without the advantages of their own self-governing institutions. They were able to establish democratic legitimacy without the need of a referendum, by winning the overwhelming majority of Ireland's seats in every election between 1885 and 1918. Britain's civic and unitary state proved incapable of preventing a nationalist rebellion in Northern Ireland from the late 1960s, or of preventing the resurgence of Scottish and Welsh nationalism. Even France, the home of Jacobinism, has been unable to erode Corsican nationalism in the late twentieth century. The failure of unitarist or national-federalist forms of civic nationalism may explain why all Western multinational democracies, including the United Kingdom, Spain, Belgium, France, and Denmark, are now more disposed towards decentralized autonomy regimes, if not full-blown multinational federalism.

If one accepts that federalism was necessary in the failed federations, the focus of blame for the violence accompanying their break-up can be shifted from multinational federation per se. To some extent, one can argue that secession – and violence – followed from attempts by certain groups to centralize these federations, i.e., to move away from the spirit of multinational federalism. Yugoslavia's break-up, including the *de facto* breaking away of Kosovo, followed successive Serbian-dominated moves against the autonomy of Yugoslavia's republics.[65] The Soviet Union broke up after an abortive right-wing coup aimed at repudiating Gorbachev's decentralizing initiatives. Violence was also caused by the centre's unwillingness to permit secession; that is, one can argue that federal constitutions with procedural and negotiable secession rules might have helped to avoid violence.[66] There was no violence in Czechoslovakia because mutual secession was agreed on. In the territory of the former Soviet Union, the worst violence has been in Chechnya, a region that did not enjoy the status of a republic within the Soviet Union. Had it done so, it would likely have seceded with the other republics, and with as little violence as most of them.

In many cases, one might argue that post-communist violence resulted from the *absence* of ethno-federalism, i.e., from the lack of congruency between constituent unit and ethnic boundaries. In the case of Yugoslavia, Slovenia's secession was relatively peaceful because Slovenia was homogeneous. The "velvet divorce" in Czechoslovakia was facilitated because there were few Czechs in Slovakia and few Slovaks in the Czech lands.[67] War started in Croatia in 1991 largely because Croatia had a significant Serb population that wanted to stay united with Yugoslavia, and spread to Bosnia because it had Croats and Serbs who also wanted to stay linked to their respective ethnic kin. These groups were aided and abetted by Serbia and Croatia, respectively. Bosnia, the most multi-ethnic republic, was perhaps destined to be the most violent.[68] In 2001 violent conflict broke out in Macedonia, whose significant Albanian minority resented the dominance of Slavs. War between Armenia and Azerbaijan was largely fought over the inclusion of an Armenian ethnic enclave (Nagorno-Karabakh) in the latter. In Georgia, two conflicts broke out, between Georgians and South Ossetians who were cut off by Georgia's secession from their kin in North Ossetia (within Russia), and between Georgians and Abkhazians who baulked at being included in what they saw as a Georgian state. The only other violence was in the Trans-Dniestrian region of Moldova, where Ukrainians and Russians resented their inclusion in Moldova. Just as communist federal break-up was fuelled by centralizing measures, the same could be said of the violence that arose in the newly independent, still heterogeneous, but unitary republics. The wars in Croatia, Macedonia, and the South Ossetian and Abkhazian regions of Georgia and Trans-Dniestria were all influenced by the majoritarian policies of the states' dominant groups. In Croatia, a minority rebellion broke out after the newly independent Croatia adopted a flag that resembled that of the wartime Croatian Ustashe regime that had committed genocide against the Serbs, and after it moved to disarm its Serbian policemen.[69] Seen in this way, these conflicts were similar to those in the Kurdish regions of Turkey and Iraq, or the Basque region of Spain under Franco; that is, they were reactions to centralization. It seems unreasonable simply to attribute them to multinational federation per se.

While it is true that only federations broke apart in communist Eastern Europe, this glosses over the more basic fact that the states that broke apart were also the most nationally diverse states – which explains why they were federations.[70] In the case of the Soviet Union, Russians had a bare majority of the total population (51 per cent), while in Czechoslovakia and Yugoslavia the largest groups had 63 and 39 per cent respectively. In none of the communist unitary states did the total minority population constitute more than 17 per cent. The largest single minority group were the Turks of Bulgaria, with roughly 8 per cent of the population. It is thus reasonable to argue that the instability of the communist federations resulted as much from their ethno-national diversity as from their ethno-federal structures. In other research, Brendan O'Leary has shown that national federations that are durably democratic and majoritarian have a *staatsvolk*, a dominant people.[71] While lacking a *staatsvolk* does not guarantee political instability in a federation, it makes it more likely. The United States, built around a historically dominant nationality of WASPs, proved more stable than Nigeria – which lacks a clearly dominant people. The same comparison helps suggest why the Russian Federation is more stable and secession-proof, thus far, than the Soviet Union. Russians are a majority of 81.5 per cent in the Russian Federation; they had accounted for only 51 per cent of the population in the USSR. The unitary states of Eastern Europe may have held together, in other words, not because they were not federations, but because each of them has dominant communities that were able to hold their states together if they wanted to. Conversely, it is not at all certain that Yugoslavia would have stayed together if it had been a unitary state when it democratized. Ireland was able to secede from the much less diverse but unitary United Kingdom after the first elections under universal male suffrage were held in 1918.

It is simply wrong to claim, as Jack Snyder and others do, that ethno-federalism is unworkable. Two of the world's oldest states, Switzerland and Canada, are ethno-federations. They have lasted since 1848 and 1867 respectively, and both demonstrate that the accommodation of ethnic minorities through ethno-federalism is consistent with prosperity and the promotion of basic individual rights. The world's largest democracy, India, is also an ethno-federal state, and the most successful large-scale post-colonial democracy.[72] The Belgian federation, while of more recent vintage, has adopted successful ethno-federalist structures, while Russia, if Chechnya is left aside, may be on its way towards establishing itself as a democratic ethno-federation. Within each of these states, there is plenty of evidence, including polling data and the positions of their political parties, that minorities are content with less than a sovereign state. Together, these qualifications question the assumption that multinational federalism is bound to fail. Our next task is to inquire into the conditions that make success more or less likely.

## EXPLAINING SUCCESS AND FAILURE

The five conditions that facilitate, but do not guarantee, successful multinational federations are implicit in the preceding discussion. Here we spell them out.

### 1. The Presence of a Staatsvolk

National federations are more stable than multinational federations. The latter are more likely to fail or break up. The reason is straight-forward: national federations are generally nationally homogeneous, or virtually so. However, the relative stability of multinational federations is also related to the demographic preponderance of their largest national communities – i.e., to whether or not these constitute a *staatsvolk*. A *staatsvolk* can feel secure in a multinational federation, and live with the concessions it must make under such a structure, because, *ceteris paribus*, it has the demographic strength and resources to resist secessionism by minority nationalities. Multi-national federations without a *staatsvolk* are more likely to be unstable, and to face secessionism or break-up, because minorities are more likely to think they can prevail.[73] Thus, Russia's future cannot be extrapolated from the experience of the Soviet Union, because Russians are far more dominant within the former than they were within the latter. The same argument implies that Nigeria and a future European federation will, *ceteris paribus*, be relatively unstable, since neither possesses a *staatsvolk*. What must be considered in our *ceteris paribus* clause? We hypothesize as follows:

- Multinational federations without a *staatsvolk*, if they are to survive as democratic entities, must develop consociational practices that protect the interests of all the encompassed national and ethnic communities with the capacity to break away.
- The existence of a *staatsvolk*, or the existence of consociational practices, will not themselves assure the stabilization of a multinational

democratic federation, though they will separately or conjointly increase its survival prospects.

- Other external and internal political, economic, and social relationships may decide the fate of a multinational federation. The character of multinational power sharing, whether a national minority has backing from a powerful neighbouring state and whether its region is on the border of the federation, will assuredly matter, as will the democratic and legal character of the federation, its mode of formation, and its prosperity.

### 2. The Federation's National Communities Should Not Only Have Self-government, There Should Also Be Consociational Government at the Centre.

When federalism is defended as a method of conflict regulation, the emphasis is usually on how it can provide minorities with guaranteed powers of territorial self-government. Sometimes it is also argued that a virtue of federalism is that it avoids the "winner takes all" outcomes associated with Westminster-type regimes: a group that is excluded at the centre may be able to console itself with regional power.[74] However, federalism is about "shared rule" as well as "self-rule," and national minorities are likely to want a federal government that represents them, that is inclusive, and indeed, we would say, consociational. National and ethnic minorities excluded from the federal government will have a reduced stake in the federation and the federal government will be less inclined to promote their interests. It is not surprising, then, that all of the durable democratic multinational federations have practised consociational forms of democracy within the federal government. Such arrangements involve four features: cross-community executive power sharing, proportional representation of groups throughout the state sector (including the police and judiciary), ethnic autonomy in culture (especially in religion or language), and formal or informal minority-veto rights.[75] Consocational practices within the federal government are relatively undisputed in the cases of Canada, Switzerland, and Belgium,[76] and Arend Lijphart has recently claimed that India had effective consociational traits during its most stable period under Jawaharlal Nehru.[77] Since the Congress Party's decline, India has been governed by a broad multi-party coalition representing its diversity. Even if one does not count India as consociational in respect of having cross-community executive power sharing in New Delhi, it has usually had diverse representation of religious, ethnic, and linguistic groups in the cabinet and civil service.

We can see the salience of consociational organization in the federal government in the case of many of the failed federations, where unrepresentative federal governments often exacerbated centrifugal pressures. In Pakistan, before the secession of Bangladesh, the army, a crucial federal agency, was dominated by West Pakistan.[78] In Yugoslavia, the army was dominated by Serb officers – many of them from Serbian minorities who shared Slobodan Milosevic's vision of a recentralized state. The Yugoslav Federal Council, the most important political institution, and one based on (non-democratic) consociational principles, was subject from the late 1980s to an undisguised takeover by Serbian politicians. After having suspended the autonomy of Kosovo and Voivodina, the Serbian-Montenegrin alliance was able to dominate the Council, plunging the federation into crisis. The Soviet Union broke up after an abortive takeover of the central government by conservatives opposed to decentralization. This episode undermined Gorbachev's attempt to reorganize the federation in ways that would have given the republics more self-government and better representation in Moscow. The breakdown of the Nigerian federation in 1966–67, which included anti-Ibo violence in the northern Hausa region and the bloody Biafran war of secession, arose after a coup, which led to the centre being dominated by Ibo officers, and a counter-coup in which these officers were overthrown.[79] Much of Nigeria's post-1970 conflict, including sectarian warfare between Muslims and Christians and the rise of violent separatism in the oil-rich Delta area, has also been traced to the lack of inclusiveness at the centre.[80] Similarly, the breakdown of the West Indies Federation was linked to Jamaicans' lack of representation and influence at the centre, and, in the case of the federation of Nyasaland, Northern, and Southern Rhodesia, it was black Africans who were under-represented.[81]

This suggests that it will not be sufficient for the Nigerian, Ethiopian, and Pakistani federations, or any prospective Iraqi federation, to practise democracy. Past evidence suggests that they will need to adopt and maintain consociational governance at the federal centre.[82] It also suggests that calls to have a fully fledged European federation, with the classic bicameral arrangements of the United States, to address the so-called democratic deficit in the European Union will fail unless such calls are accompanied by strong commitments to consociational devices. Consociational governance would imply strong mechanisms to ensure the inclusive and effective representation of all the nationalities of the European Union in its core executive institutions, proportionate representation of its nationalities in its public bureaucracies and legal institutions, national autonomy in all cultural matters deemed of profound cultural significance (e.g., language, religion, education), and, last but not least, national vetoes to protect national communities from being out-voted through majoritarian rules. In short, many of the current consociational and confederal features of the EU – which some federalists want to weaken or temper in their pursuit of formal federation – are in fact required to ensure the EU's prospects as a multinational democratic federation. The EU's greatest current danger stems from its ardent majoritarian federalists.

This argument about the importance of accommodation through consociational devices is different from that put forward by Juan Linz and Alfred Stepan.[83] They put their faith in the ability of federation-wide political parties to win support from all groups, to balance majority and minority concerns, and to build what Linz elsewhere calls *bundestreue* – an overarching loyalty to the state.[84] In their view, the key reason for the disintegration of the Yugoslav and Soviet federations was that the first democratic elections were held in the republics rather than the state (whereas in post-Franco Spain it was the other way around). In Yugoslavia, this sequencing gave divisive republican elites the resources and space to promote break-up and obstructed the organization of federation-wide parties with an interest in holding the state together. Had federal elections been held first, federation-wide parties would have been able to act as unifying forces.

This reasoning is, however, questionable. State-wide parties may well be likely to do better in state-wide elections than in regional elections, but there is no guarantee, or even likelihood, that they will do well at any level in societies with noticeable national divisions. In the United Kingdom's first democratic elections, in the mid-1880s, Irish nationalist parties won the overwhelming majority of Irish seats.[85] The fact that they were elected in state-wide elections, as opposed to regional elections, does not appear to have coloured their view of the United Kingdom, or their ability to secede from it, and they won despite the presence of competitors from state-wide parties. Czechoslovakia's first democratic elections, which involved concurrent federal and regional elections, produced no state-wide parties at the federal level other than the discredited Communist Party, which won 23 of the country's 150 seats. And even this party subsequently divided into Czech and Slovak factions. All of the other parties that won seats were based on the Czech, Slovak, or Hungarian populations.

Perhaps this fragmentation into ethno-national voting blocs in Czechoslovakia was due, as Leff claims, to the simultaneity of elections at both levels (i.e., to the fact that the federal election was not held in advance).[86] But how, then, are we to explain the first democratic election returns in the unitary states of Eastern Europe, where there were no regional elections? In these cases, party support still broke down almost exactly along ethno-national lines, with little evidence of integrative vote-pooling activities by either party elites or voters.[87] These results are difficult to square with Linz and Stepan's assumption that Yugoslav state-wide elections would have produced strong Yugoslav state-wide parties, unless one is to assume that Yugoslavia was a good deal less divided than its neighbours. Given that it was the only state in Eastern Europe whose major communities included persons who had butchered each other within living memory (1941–45), this assumption is implausible. The comparative evidence suggests that state-wide elections in Yugoslavia would have resulted in elections that reflected its national divisions. Hoping for state-wide parties to hold Yugoslavia together was probably wishful thinking. Stability would have required successful bargaining among the different minority-nationalist parties on a new consociational and confederal constitution. Such bargaining as there was on this agenda did not succeed.

### 3. Authentic (Democratic) Multinational Federations Are More Likely to Be Successful than Pseudo (Undemocratic) Federations.

An authentic multinational federation is democratic. It allows the representatives of its respective national communities to engage in dialogue and open bargaining about their interests, grievances, and aspirations. Such democratic dialogue is a prerequisite for the development of cooperative practices. Democratic multinational federalism may help to preclude the systematic transgression of individual and group rights. It can prevent minority (secessionist) elites from exaggerating support for their preferences.[88] An authentic multinational federation is also based on the rule of law, law that recognizes national, ethnic, or communal rights, a constitutional division of powers, and a judiciary whose powers approach those of impartial umpires. There is not yet an example of an established democratic multinational federation failing (admittedly, the number of cases is small), although there are, as we have seen, numerous examples of democratizing federations that have not worked. The evidence, limited as it is, suggests that we should not automatically assume that Canada, Switzerland, Spain, India, or Belgium will go the way of the flawed communist or post-colonial federations.

### 4. "Voluntary" or "Holding Together" Multinational Federations Are More Likely to Endure under Democratic Conditions than Those That Are Coercively Constructed after Modern Social Mobilizations.

Stepan distinguishes between the following three types of multinational federations: (1) those that voluntarily come together from distinct polities/colonies, like the Swiss and Canadian federations; (2) those that are created from unitary states in an attempt to hold the polity together, such as Belgium and, one might argue, India; and (3) those that are forced together (or put together) by a dominant group, such as the Soviet Union.[89]

Federations that are consensually established as a result of elite bargaining, whether of the voluntary or "holding" variety, are more likely to be considered legitimate by their citizens and more likely to survive than those that result from coercion. A foundational act of cooperation is also more likely than one of coercion to promote traditions of accommodation. The Canadian federation's success is owed in part to the fact that it originated in 1867 from a compact between anglophone and francophone elites led by John A. Macdonald and George-Étienne Cartier. The Swiss federation was also the result of different groups agreeing to federate. While the Spanish and Belgian federations emerged from unitary states, they too were based on agreement between representative elites. India, which stands out as one of the few post-colonial federal success stories, is also one of the few where indigenous elites took the decision to federate by themselves – albeit reluctantly, and albeit after prior British tutelage. Most of the failed federations, on the other hand, were put together without the consent of minority leaders.[90] This does not augur well for Bosnia-Herzegovina, which exists as a federation because of the internationally imposed Dayton Accord.

## 5. *Prosperous Multinational Federations (or States) Are More Likely to Endure than Those That Are Not.*

Walker Connor has correctly counselled against exaggerating the importance of materialism when questions of national identity are at stake. Prosperity should not be considered a sufficient or even a necessary condition (as the example of India shows) for holding a multinational federation together.[91] Nonetheless, prosperity – and distributive fairness – may matter. The plight of the communist federations and post-colonial federations was plainly exacerbated by their inability to provide materially for their citizens and by the discrediting of communist central planning. In the Ukraine and the Baltic republics, even Russians voted for the break-up of the USSR. In both Yugoslavia and the Soviet Union, the catalyst for break-up was necessary economic reforms, and the charge was led in both cases by those republics (Slovenia and Croatia in the case of Yugoslavia, the Baltic republics in the case of the Soviet Union) that had the most to gain materially from going it alone.

## CONCLUSION

We have attempted to offer a more balanced and nuanced assessment of the value and durability of multinational federations than that put forward by critics of ethno-federalism, without falling victim to the blandishments of the most ardent federalists. Democratic federalism did not cause the break-up of the communist states, since these were not authentically democratic (or economically efficient) federations. Not all multinational federations have failed. There are also a small number of remarkable success stories. We have tried to identify conditions that are conducive to the success of multinational federations. It is important that they be democratic and respect the rule of law. It helps if they are prosperous. It helps if they came together voluntarily. If federations develop from a unitary state, our arguments suggest that early and generous responses to expressed demands for minority self-government will work better than delayed and grudging responses. The demographic composition of the federation matters: a federation that has a dominant ethno-national community is likely to be more stable than one that does not. Lastly, federalism is usually not enough: consociational practices, particularly at the level of the federal government, are highly important to the success of multinational federalism.

NOTES

1 Ronald L. Watts, "Federalism, Federal Political Systems, and Federations," *Annual Review of Political Science* 1(1998): 117–37.

2 Daniel J. Elazar, *Exploring Federalism* (Tuscaloosa: University of Alabama Press 1987), 4–5, 33.

3 Alfred Stepan, *Arguing Comparative Politics* (Oxford, U.K.: Oxford University Press 2001), 340–57; Alfred Stepan, "Federalism and Democracy: Beyond the U.S. Model," *Journal of Democracy* 10, no.4 (1999): 19–34.

4 Ronald L. Watts, *Comparing Federal Systems* (Kingston, Ont.: Institute of Intergovernmental Relations, Queen's University 1999), 93–4.

5 This confederation, named Serbia and Montenegro, looks likely to dissolve into two independent states.

6 Article 2 of the French constitution declares, "France is an indivisible, secular, democratic, and social Republic."

7 Both facts explain the reported French astonishment at George W. Bush being elected U.S. president in 2000 with fewer popular votes than his opponent and the disputed outcome being effectively decided by the federal Supreme Court.

8 "Partial autonomy for Corsica splits French government," *World Socialist Web Site*, 5 September 2000. Website: <www.wsw.org/articles/2000/sep2000/corss05.shtml>.

9 "Corsica: The perils of devolution," *Economist*, 7 July 2001, 49.

10 Chevenement claimed that self-government for Corsica would be as contagious as the "I love you" computer virus. "Partial autonomy for Corsica splits French government," *World Socialist Web Site*, 5 September 2000.

11 Donald L. Horowitz, "Self-Determination: Politics, Philosophy and Law," in Margaret Moore, ed., *National Self-Determination and Secession* (Oxford, U.K.: Oxford University Press 1998), 181–214; M. Weller, "The International Response to the Dissolution of the Socialist Federal Republic of Yugoslavia," *American Journal of International Law* 86 (1992): 569–607.

12 Confusingly, hardline minority nationalists sometimes say that they support federation when they mean confederation, as in the case of the Turkish Cypriot leader, Rauf Denktash. The Parti Québécois does not commonly use the term confederation but offers as a synonym "sovereignty-association."

13 M. Forsyth, ed., *Federalism and Nationalism* (Leicester, U.K.: Leicester University Press 1989), 4.

14 William H. Riker, *Federalism: Origin, Operation, Significance* (Boston: Little, Brown 1964).

15 Stepan, *Arguing Comparative Politics*, 334.

16 Riker, *Federalism*.

17 N. Glazer "Federalism and Ethnicity: The American Solution," in N. Glazer, ed., *Ethnic Dilemmas, 1964–82* (Cambridge, Mass: Harvard University Press 1983), 274–92.

18 M. Gordon, *Assimilation in American Life* (New York: Oxford University Press 1964).

19 Glazer, "Federalism and Ethnicity," 276.

20 Gordon, *Assimilation*, 274.

21 "Providence has been pleased to give this one connected country to one united people – a people descended from the same ancestors, speaking the same language, professing the same religion, attached to the same principles of government, very similar in their manners and their customs, and who, by their joint counsels, arms and efforts, fighting side by side throughout a long and bloody war, have nobly established liberty and independence." Publius [John Jay], in James Madison et al., *The Federalist Papers* [1788], ed. Isaac Kramnick (Harmondsworth, U.K.: Penguin 1987), paper II, 91.

22 Donald L. Horowitz, *Ethnic Groups in Conflict* (Berkeley: University of California Press 1985), chapters 14, 15.

23 Daniel J. Elazar, *Federalism and the Way to Peace* (Kingston, Ont.: Queen's Institute of Intergovernmental Relations 1994), 168.

24 Lipset argues that the main benefit of federalism for divided societies is that it creates cross-cutting cleavages, but it can only do this if internal federal boundaries and ethnic boundaries intersect. Federalism "increases the opportunity for multiple sources of cleavage by adding regional interests and values to the others which crosscut the social structure." S.M. Lipset, *Political Man: The Social Bases of Politics* (Garden City, N.Y.: Doubleday 1960), 91–2.

25 Rotimi N. Suberu, *Federalism and Ethnic Conflict in Nigeria* (Washington D.C.: United States Institute of Peace 2001), 4–6.

26 Belgium may, however, become an interesting exception: the Brussels region, created in the new federation, is neither Flemish nor Walloon.

27 S.M. Lipset, "The Revolt against Modernity," in Lipset, ed., *Consensus and Conflict: Essays in Political Sociology* (New Brunswick, N.J.: Transaction 1985), 253–93.

28 Elazar, *Federalism and the Way to Peace*, 128–9, 163–4.

29 Eric Nordlinger, *Conflict Regulation in Divided Societies* (Cambridge, Mass.: Harvard University Center for International Affairs 1972), 32–3.

See also C. Tarlton, "Symmetry and Asymmetry as Elements of Federalism: A Theoretical Speculation," *Journal of Politics* 27, no.4 (1965): 861–74.

30 R. Brubaker, *Nationalism Reframed* (Cambridge, U.K.: Cambridge University Press 1996), 9. See also V. Bunce, *Subversive Institutions: The Design and the Destruction of Socialism and the State* (Cambridge, U.K.: Cambridge University Press 1999). C.S. Leff, *The Czech and Slovak Republics: Nation versus State* (Boulder, Colo.: Westview Press 1998); P. Roeder, "Soviet Federalism and Ethnic Mobilization," *World Politics* 43 (1991): 196–232.

31 Jack Snyder, *From Voting to Violence: Democratization and Nationalist Conflict* (New York: Norton 2000), 327 (our emphasis).

32 Snyder, *Voting*, 252 (our emphasis).

33 L.V. Majocchi, "Nationalism and Federalism in 19th Century Europe," in A. Bosco, ed., *The Federal Idea: The History of Federalism from Enlightenment to 1945* (London: Lothian Press 1991) 155–65.

34 See, e.g., Bosco, *Federal Idea*, Part 3.

35 Pierre Elliott Trudeau, *Federalism and the French Canadians* (Toronto: Macmillan 1968), 182–203.

36 Majocchi, "Nationalism," 161. In effect, they echo Einstein's reported remark that nationalism is the measles of mankind.

37 See, e.g., O. Bauer, *The Question of Nationalities and Social Democracy* (Minneapolis: University of Minnesota Press 2000); T. Hanf, "Reducing Conflict through Cultural Autonomy: Karl Renner's Contribution," in U. Ra'anan et al., ed., *State and Nation in Multi-Ethnic Societies: The Breakup of Multi-National States* (Manchester, U.K.: Manchester University Press 1991), 33–52; A. Pfabigan, "The Political Feasibility of the Austro-Marxist proposal for the Solution of the Nationality Problem of the Danubian Monarchy," in U. Ra'anan et al., ed., *State and Nation*, 53–63.

38 In the authoritative words of Walker Connor, Lenin's second commandment on the management of nationalism was strategically machiavellian: "Following the assumption of power, terminate the fact – if not necessarily the fiction – of a right to secession, and begin the lengthy process of assimilation via the dialectical route of territorial autonomy for all compact national groups." Walker Connor, *The National Question in Marxist-Leninist Theory and Strategy* (Princeton, N.J.: Princeton University Press 1984), 38.

39 Forsyth, *Federalism*, 4.

40 Stepan, *Arguing Comparative Politics*, 31–2; Will Kymlicka, *Multicultural Citizenship* (Oxford, U.K.: Oxford University Press 1995).

41 Michael Keating, *Plurinational Democracy: Stateless Nations in a Post-Sovereignty Era* (Oxford, U.K.: Oxford University Press 2001); see also Kymlicka, *Multicultural Citizenship*.

42 Michael Hechter, *Containing Nationalism* (Oxford, U.K.: Oxford University Press 2000); Juan Linz, "Democracy, Multinationalsm and Federalism," working paper (1997); Keating, *Plurinational Democracy*; Kymlicka, *Multicultural Citizenship*; Margaret Moore, *The Ethics of Nationalism* (Oxford, U.K.: Oxford University Press 2001); Stepan, *Arguing Comparative Politics*; Watts, *Comparing Federal Systems*; Brendan O'Leary, "An Iron Law of Nationalism and Federation? A (Neo-Diceyian) Theory of the Necessity of a Federal Staatsvolk, and of Consociational Rescue," *Nations and Nationalism* 7, no.3 (2001): 273–96.

43 Klaus Von Beyme, *Political Parties in Western Democracies* (Aldershot, U.K.: Gower 1985), 121. The more usual claim is that Canada is the only country, or Canada and Switzerland are the only countries, where federalism has been successful in preventing conflict.

44 Will Kymlicka, *Politics in the Verna*cular (Oxford, U.K.: Oxford University Press 2001).

45 J. Fischer, "Apologies to the UK, but 'Federal' is the Only Way," *The Independent* (16 May 2000), 4. This model of federalism appears to be limited to the accommodation of the European Union's current member states, and it says nothing about minorities within these states. Contrast this with Michael Keating's version of Euro-federalism, which anticipates complex and overlapping levels of governance that include regions (including minority regions), states, and the European Union (Keating, *Plurinational Democracy*, 4).

46 Plainly, the multinationalists' defence of federation as a way of managing nations – to each nation let a province be given – is not able to accommodate minorities that are so small in number, or so dispersed, that they cannot control federal units or provinces. These include Canadian francophones who live outside Quebec, Flemish-speakers in Wallonia, francophones in Flanders, and small and scattered indigenous peoples in Australia, India, and the Americas.

47 It is also a prima facie challenge to the tacit Gellnerian notion that in modern times the equilibrium condition is one sovereign state, one culture (or nation). If we treat broadly the "political unit," in Gellner's definition, to encompass regional or provincial units in a federation, then his theory can accommodate such arrangements, but at the significant concession of

recognizing that federal systems are compatible with dual and possibly multiple nationalities. See Ernest Gellner, *Nations and Nationalism* (Ithaca, N.Y.: Cornell University Press 1983).

48 For an account that is sympathetic to the claims of national minorities for asymmetrical federation and for an international role, see Keating, *Plurinational Democracy*. Keating supports multinational federalism but rejects as too simplistic the view that minorities can be accommodated within traditional sovereign states. Instead, he argues, particularly within the European Union, new post-sovereigntist institutional arrangements are taking shape in which national minorities seek to play within several different forums – the state, the (trans-border) region, the European Union, and the world – simultaneously.

49 B. Arora and D.V. Verney, *Multiple Identities in a Single State: Indian Federalism in Comparative Perspective* (New Delhi: Konark Publishers PVT 1995); P. Brass, *The Politics of India since Independence* (New Delhi: Cambridge University Press 1990). Paradoxically, the redrawing of new boundaries to accommodate minorities is easier if the federal centre has more power. In India the central government has been able to create new boundaries without the approval of the state governments concerned. In Canada, by contrast, the federal government is unable to alter boundaries without the consent of the affected provinces. It cannot even create a new province out of federal territories without the consent of existing provinces, which is one reason why the new region of Nunavut is a federal territory rather than a province.

50 Suberu, *Federalism and Ethnic Conflict*, 5.

51 Snyder, *Voting*, 327.

52 The latest victim may well be Yugoslavia (i.e., the rump Yugoslav federation of Serbia and Montenegro). In 2003 it was restructured into a looser union to be called Serbia and Montenegro. There is provision for Montenegrins to hold a referendum in three years on whether or not they want to stay part of this union.

53 Ralph Premdas, *Secession and Self-Determination in the Caribbean: Nevis and Tobago* (St Augustine, Trinidad: University of the West Indies 1998).

54 Stepan, who supports multinational federalism and argues that the U.S. (national) federal model has little relevance for multinational societies, concedes that the "greatest risk" posed by federalism is that it can "offer opportunities for ethnic nationalists to mobilize their resources." See Stepan, *Arguing Comparative Politics*, 19.

55 Dominic Lieven and John McGarry, "Ethnic Conflict in the Soviet Union and Its Successor States," in John McGarry and Brendan O'Leary, ed., *The Politics of Ethnic Conflict Regulation* (London: Routledge 1993), 62–83.

56 Suberu, *Federalism and Ethnic Conflict*, 4.

57 Elazar, *Exploring Federalism*, 240.

58 Nigeria's hyper centralism is a function of Abuja's control of oil revenues, but it also has a basis in the 1979 and 1999 constitutions. According to Michael Joye and Kingsley Igweike, under the new constitution (which largely copies the old one), there "are few, if any ... areas in which state governments can act independently of the Federal Government." Cited in Rotimi N. Suberu and Larry Diamond, "Institutional Design, Ethnic Conflict Management, and Democracy in Nigeria," in Andrew Reynolds, ed., *The Architecture of Democracy: Institutional Design, Conflict Management and Democracy* (Oxford, U.K.: Oxford University Press 2002), 15. The existence of such separate competencies, as we have pointed out, is an essential hallmark of federalism.

59 Unitarists often claim that decentralization leads to corruption and inefficiency, but contemporary Nigeria demonstrates that corruption and centralization can go hand in hand. Supporters of anti-corruption reforms in Nigeria argue that this requires "power and resources [to be] shifted downward, to levels of authority that are closer to the people and more visible." Larry Diamond, "Foreword," in Suberu, *Federalism and Ethnic Conflict*, xviii.

60 Connor, *The National Question*, 198; Susan Woodward, *Balkan Tragedy* (New York: Brookings Institution 1995), 30.

61 In 1913, before he had responsibility for governing the Soviet Union, Lenin made clear his contempt for federalism and his preference for unitarism: "We are in principle against federation. It weakens the economic connection and is inappropriate for a unified state. Do you want to separate? we say. Then go to the devil and cut yourself off altogether ... You don't want to separate? Then, please, don't decide *for me*, don't believe you have the 'right' to federation" (Connor, *The National Question*, 217; italics and grammatical errors in original). As Connor notes, Lenin dropped his opposition to federalism upon assuming power in order to reassure those nations that had seceded that "reunion would not result in political subservience" (218).

62 There is an explanation for this implicit in the arguments of critics of multinationalism federalism. It is that the decision to accommodate some national groups led those excluded to mobilize. We endorse this argument,

but we think that the way to deal with it would have been to accommodate the excluded identity groups, not to refuse to accommodate any of them.

63 "As the rivalries among these three groups (Yoruba, Ibo, Hausa) crystallized into bitter political struggles during the late colonial period ... it became increasingly clear to all interested observers that only by some form of highly decentralized political arrangements could the main groups be accommodated within a single country." Suberu, *Federalism and Ethnic Conflict*, 20.

64 Supporters of civic nationalism might respond that British (or other forms of) civic nationalism were not neutral between the United Kingdom's diverse peoples, and that a more genuinely inclusive version of civic nationalism might have worked. This is indeed part of the weakness of civic nationalism. It often reflects the values and interests of the state's dominant national community.

65 The Kosovo rebellion of 1997 was a response, albeit delayed, to the Milosevic regime's removal of Kosovo's autonomy in 1989. Hechter, *Containing Nationalism.*

66 They might also have avoided secession.

67 Interestingly, Czechoslovakia is absent from Snyder's account of the relationship between ethno-federalism and violence.

68 It is useful to remember this when considering the Horowitz/American argument that cross-cutting republican and ethnic boundaries have conflict-reducing effects.

69 R. Hayden, "Constitutional Nationalism in the formerly Yugoslav Republics," *Slavic Review* 51 (1992): 654–73.

70 As Watts claims: "It is not so much because they are federations that countries have been difficult to govern but that it is because they were difficult to govern in the first place that they adopted federation as a form of government." Watts, *Comparing Federal Systems*, 110.

71 O'Leary, "Iron Law."

72 India's success is explained away by Snyder as a result of the unwillingness of its civic central authorities to recognize ethnicity (*Voting*, 287–96). It is odd that a federation, the internal boundaries of which are constructed along ethno-linguistic lines, can be seen in this way. Where there is some truth is that Indian governments have refused to recognize religiosity as the basis of provincial formation.

73 O'Leary, "Iron Law."

74 "Federalism reduces conflict by allowing those political forces excluded from power at the top the opportunity to exercise regional power" (Hanf, "Reducing Conflict," 43).

75 Arend Lijphart, *Democracy in Plural Societies: A Comparative Exploration* (New Haven, Conn., London: Yale University Press 1977).

76 S.J.R. Noel, "Canadian Responses to Ethnic Conflict: Consociationalism, Federalism and Control," in McGarry and O'Leary, ed., *The Politics of Ethnic Conflict Regulation*, 41–61; Jurg Steiner, "Power-Sharing: Another Swiss Export Product?" in J. Montville, ed., *Conflict and Peacemaking in Multi-ethnic Societies* (Lexington, Mass.: Lexington Books 1989), 107–14; Liesbet Hooghe, "Belgium: From Regionalism to Federalism," in J. Coakley, ed., *The Territorial Management of Ethnic Conflict* (London: Frank Cass 1993), 44–68.

77 Arend Lijphart, "The Puzzle of Indian Democracy: A Consociational Interpretation," *American Political Science Review* 65 (1996): 682–93.

78 V. Nasr, "The Negotiable State: Borders and Power-Struggles in Pakistan," in Brendan O'Leary, Ian S. Lustick, and T. Callaghy, ed., *Right-Sizing the State: The Politics of Moving Borders* (Oxford, U.K.: Oxford University Press 2001), 168–200.

79 The Ibo coup led by Major-General Aguiyi-Ironsi in January 1966 was followed by a "Unification Decree" that moved Nigeria towards a unitary state. See Suberu, *Federalism and Ethnic Conflict*, 31.

80 In a country that is equally divided between Muslim and Christian and between north and south, northern Muslims headed all four military governments in the 1984–99 era. See Suberu and Diamond, "Institutional Design."

81 Watts, *Comparing Federal Systems*, 111.

82 This is particularly important where, as in Nigeria, the lion's share of power is allocated to the centre. Since federal regions are also usually ethnically heterogeneous, it is helpful to have consociational practices at the intra-regional level as well. This not only addresses the criticism that giving self-government to national minorities will lead to an abuse of their powers against local minorities, it also promotes good inter-regional and regional-centre relations.

83 Juan Linz and Alfred Stepan, "Political Identities and Electoral Sequences: Spain, The Soviet Union, and Yugoslavia," *Daedalus* 121, no.2, (1992): 123–39.

84 Linz, "Democracy, Multinationalism and Federalism."

85 From 1885, elections in the United Kingdom were based on a universal male franchise and, from 1918, a universal franchise.

86 Leff, *Czech and Slovak Republics*, 98.

87 See Project on Political Transformation and the Electoral Process in Post-Communist Europe, University of Essex. Website: <www.essex.ac.uk/elections/>.

88 Linz, "Democracy, Multinationalism and Federalism."

89 The Canadian federation's birth was a hybrid of "coming together" and "holding together" processes: on the one hand, it involved the joining together of a number of previously separate British North American colonies; on the other hand, it involved the division of the (nominally) unitary colony of the United Canadas into the separate provinces of Ontario and Quebec.

90 The importance of voluntary origins for the legitimacy and stability of states, whether federal or unitary, is often recognized in the rival historiographies of federalists/unionists and separatists, with the former arguing that the federation/union arose voluntarily while the latter argue it was imposed. Thus, in Canada, Quebec separatists point to the British conquest of 1759 as Canada's starting point, and/or argue that the confederation agreement of 1867 was not "really" voluntary since francophone elites did not have a serious alternative of separating. Federalists, on the other hand, point to the key role that francophone elites had in shaping the federal agreement. Similar debates take place between unionists in Britain and Scottish separatists.

91 Walker Connor, *Ethnonationalism: The Quest for Understanding* (Princeton N.J.: Princeton University Press 1994), 145–64.

# Contributors

TOZUN BAHCHELI is professor of political science at King's University College at the University of Western Ontario, London, Ontario, Canada.

FLORIAN BIEBER is senior non-resident research fellow, Belgrade, of the European Centre for Minority Issues, Flensburg, Germany, and recurrent visiting professor in the Nationalism Studies Program at the Central European University in Budapest, Hungary.

MATTHIJS BOGAARDS is assistant professor of political science at the International University Bremen, Germany.

REETA CHOWDHARI TREMBLAY is professor and chair of the Department of Political Science at Concordia University in Montreal, Quebec, Canada.

LANDON E. HANCOCK is an adjunct faculty member of the Institute for Conflict Analysis and Resolution at George Mason University, Virginia, United States.

KRISTIN HENRARD is associate professor of human rights in the Faculty of Law at the University of Groningen, Netherlands.

JOHN MCGARRY is professor of political studies and Canada Research Chair in Nationalism and Democracy at Queen's University, Kingston, Ontario, Canada.

SID NOEL is senior fellow of King's University College and co-director of the Nationalism and Ethnic Conflict Research Group at the University of Western Ontario, London, Ontario, Canada.

PATRICK J. O'HALLORAN is a major in the Canadian Armed Forces and assistant to the director general, international security, Canadian Defence Headquarters, Ottawa, Canada. He has served with Canadian forces in Bosnia and Afghanistan. He also holds a PHD in political science from York University, Toronto.

BRENDAN O'LEARY is Lauder Professor of Political Science and director of the Solomon Asch Center for the Study of Ethnopolitical Conflict at the University of Pennsylvania, Philadelphia, Pennsylvania, United States.

GORDON PEAKE is a research officer at the International Police Academy in New York City, U.S. He holds a D.Phil. from Oxford University and has worked on United Nations police-reform projects in Bosnia, Macedonia, and Albania.

IAN S. SPEARS is assistant professor of political science at the University of Guelph, Ontario, Canada.

STEVEN I. WILKINSON is assistant professor of political science at Duke University, Durham, N.C., United States.

STEFAN WOLFF is professor of political science in the department of European studies at the University of Bath, United Kingdom.

# Index